Exp͟o   the
Cri   ica

The University of North Carolina Press

Chapel Hill and London

Export Agriculture and the Crisis in Central America

by Robert G. Williams

© 1986 The University of North Carolina Press

92 91 90 89 88   5 4 3

Manufactured in the United States of America

Library of Congress Cataloging-in-Publication Data

Williams, Robert G. (Robert Gregory), 1948–
Export agriculture and the crisis in Central America

Bibliography: p.
Includes index.
1. Cotton trade—Central America. 2. Beef
industry—Central America. 3. Cattle trade—Central
America. 4. Central America—Politics and government—
1979– . 5. Central America—Foreign relations—
United States. 6. United States—Foreign relations—
Central America. I. Title.
HD9884.C352W55   1986   382′.41′09728   85-20978
ISBN 0-8078-1693-0
ISBN 0-8078-4154-4 (pbk.)

Woodcuts by Homer Yost

For the people of my own Southland,
whose history runs parallel to Central America's

Contents

Figures, Charts, and Tables

Figures

Charts

Tables

Acknowledgments

Most of the research for this book was carried out during the academic year 1982–83, when I took a leave-without-pay from Guilford College. At first I thought the venture was foolhardy, considering that my zero income was not bolstered with a major cash grant. In retrospect, however, the lack of major grant money was a blessing, because it made me the recipient of many smaller gifts from people with more modest resources than those of the large foundations. Each of these gifts of time, expertise, office space, shelter, and transportation encouraged me more in the work I was doing than a large lump sum from a philanthropic trust. Without these gifts there would be no book.

For early encouragement to pursue the project, I thank Henry Atkins, Lewis Bateman, Gil Joseph, and Franklin Parker. For assistance throughout the project, and for the assurance that my homeplace would not fall into ruin in my absence, I thank Ed Burrows. For the computer that allowed me to finish the project, I thank my mother.

The five Central American countries examined here have differences that make studying the region as a whole difficult. I am indebted to the scholars who shared their insights of the countries where they did fieldwork, and I thank them for releasing their personal libraries for my use. This list should be much longer, but special thanks are due to Carol Smith for help with Guatemala, William Durham for El Salvador, Jefferson Boyer for Honduras, Joseph Collins for Nicaragua, and Marc Edelman for Costa Rica. I express deep appreciation to Allan Hruska who assisted me in fieldwork in Central America during the autumn of 1982.

Office space and access to research materials were made possible through the generosity of a number of persons and institutions. Particular thanks are due to Kathy Durham and John Wirth at the Stanford-Berkeley Center for Latin American Studies, Jim Breedlove, curator of the Latin America collection at the Stanford University Library, José Luís Vega Carballo and Rafael Bolaños at the Instituto de Investigaciones Sociales in Costa Rica, and Ivan García at MIDINRA in Nicaragua. A more general word of thanks is extended to the many librarians who assisted me in Central America, and to the workers and managers of ranches, packing houses, plantations, and cotton gins who shared the knowledge of their work with me.

During the year of research, people invited me to stay in their homes, offered the use of their automobiles, or assisted me in finding inexpensive lodging. Without this help my meager financial resources would have been depleted in a few months. I am grateful to the country people of Central America who invited me to stay in their homes. I thank Harlan Halsey for resurrecting his 1956 Volkswagen for my personal use in California, Muriel Bell for finding housesitting jobs, Doug and Susan Kincaid for a room in their home in Costa Rica, John and Elizabeth Gaman for their generous hospitality in Portola Valley, and my wife, Charlotte Rosenthal, for financial, intellectual, and spiritual support during the writing phase of the project.

Many people have criticized earlier drafts of the manuscript. Those whose labors deserve special recognition are: Lewis Bateman, Philippe Bourgois, Marc Edelman, Elizabeth Gaman, Sally Gladstone, Allan Hruska, Tom Huey, Doug Kincaid, Turner McGehee, William Meade, and Carol Smith. All remaining logical errors, historical inaccuracies, and stylistic confusions are faults of my own making.

R. G. W.
Kernersville, North Carolina

List of Abbreviations

AID. United States Agency for International Development
BID. Banco Interamericano de Desarrollo (Inter-American Development
Bank)
CEPAL. Comisión Económica Para América Latina
CIA. Central Intelligence Agency
CIERA. Centro de Investigaciones y Estudios Para la Reforma Agraria
CONAL. Comisión Nacional de Algodón
CONOCIT. Consejo Nacional de Investigaciones Científicas y Tecnológicas
CSUCA. Consejo Superior Universitario Centroamericano
DGECCR. Dirección General de Estadística y Censos de Costa Rica
DGECH. Dirección General de Estadística y Censos de Honduras
DGECN. Dirección General de Estadística y Censos de Nicaragua
DGECS. Dirección General de Estadística y Censos de El Salvador
DGEG. Dirección General de Estadística de Guatemala
EDUCA. Editorial Universitaria Centroamericana
EPICA. Ecumenical Program for Interamerican Communication and Action
FAO. United Nations Food and Agriculture Organization
IADB. Inter-American Development Bank
IBRD. International Bank for Reconstruction and Development
ICAITI. Instituto Centroamericano de Investigación y Tecnología Industrial
IMF. International Monetary Fund
INIES. Instituto de Investigaciones Económicos y Sociales
INTAL. Instituto Para la Integración de América Latina
MIDINRA. Ministerio de Desarrollo Agropecuario y Reforma Agraria
MRN. Ministry of Natural Resources
NACLA. North American Congress on Latin America
OAS. Organization of American States
OIT. Organización Internacional del Trabajo
OTS. Organization for Tropical Studies
SEPSA. Secretaría Ejecutiva de Planificación Sectorial Agropecuaria y de
Recursos Naturales Renovables de Costa Rica
SIECA. Secretaría Permanente del Tratado General de Integración
Económica Centroamericana

STICA. Interamerican Technical Service for Agricultural Cooperation
UCA. Universidad Centroamericana José Simeón Cañas
USDA. United States Department of Agriculture

Introduction

For nearly three decades, U.S. policy makers have seen rapid growth of the private sector as the economic cure for political instability in Central America.[1] Whenever U.S. security interests have perceived a threat in the region, large doses of economic aid have been administered to stimulate private-sector growth, and military aid, combined with social reforms, has been administered to create a safe environment for private investment. A host of policies aimed at rapid economic growth have been tried, but the one that has been most favored—and the one that has proven most successful over the years—has been to expand and diversify the region's exports.

For a number of reasons, Washington has encouraged the development of nontraditional exports from Central America. Policy makers have understood that without a steady stream of export earnings, international banks are less likely to lend money for development, multinational corporations are less likely to invest, and local investors have greater difficulty importing modern technology and capital equipment. Coffee and bananas have traditionally generated large inflows of foreign exchange, but heavy reliance on these two crops has made export earnings extremely volatile. Also, coffee and bananas have very definite geographic limits beyond which they cannot be grown on a profitable basis, so U.S. policy has promoted alternative crops that can be grown in areas not yet developed for export production. Finally, promotion of nontraditional exports has been seen as a way to broaden elite structures by creating investment opportunities for others besides the large fruit companies and wealthy coffee growers.

Before World War II, U.S. policy in Central America focused narrowly on defending U.S. strategic interests and U.S. corporations that already had investments in the region. After World War II, only when revolutionary crises threatened stability did official U.S. policy shift to promoting economic growth and export diversification. The first time the policy was attempted was in Guatemala in 1954. Ten years of reformist government had encouraged the political participation of Guatemala's poor majority, and by the early 1950s the traditional oligarchy and the large U.S. corporations operating in Guatemala felt threatened by land reform and the growth of labor unions. When idle lands of the fruit company were expropriated by the agrarian reform, the U.S.

government began portraying developments in Guatemala as part of the global spread of Soviet communism. In 1954 a CIA (Central Intelligence Agency) force similar to that of today's "contras" invaded Guatemala and ousted the democratically elected Arbenz government.[2] In addition to giving large amounts of military and security assistance to the new regime, the U.S. government began to implement a program of economic and social development that closely resembled earlier programs of the World Bank.[3] The program included incentives for foreign investment, centrally controlled reform measures, and schemes to stimulate the diversification of Guatemala's exports.[4]

Only after the Castro regime came to power in Cuba (1959) did pressure mount for a new foreign policy for Latin America and the Caribbean. Using the threat of more Cubas as a justification, the Kennedy administration pushed through a $20 billion, ten-year program for the hemisphere that closely resembled the Guatemala experiment. For Central America and elsewhere in Latin America, the Alliance for Progress brought large increases in military and security assistance, centrally controlled social reforms, and programs to stimulate growth of the private sector. The economic development programs contained incentives for foreign investors and measures to promote new exports. It was believed that only through economic diversification and growth could the conditions for long-run political stability be met.

Measured by macroeconomic indicators, the economic development program applied during the 1960s was a success. During the decade of the Alliance for Progress, the average annual growth rate of the Central American economy approximated 6 percent, and real incomes per person grew by more than 2 percent a year, making Central America's economy one of the healthiest in Latin America at that time.

The rapid economic growth of the 1960s was fueled by export earnings that grew 10 percent a year on the average, providing foreign exchange for the importation of new technology and creating a healthy monetary environment for foreign investment.[5] Between the early 1960s, when the Alliance for Progress began, and 1973, when the first wave of crisis hit, coffee and banana exports doubled in volume, but the most remarkable growth occurred in the export of nontraditional products. Between 1961 and 1973 sugar exports quadrupled in volume, cotton exports expanded fivefold, beef exports went up seven times, and a host of previously insignificant commodities like frozen shrimp, tobacco, cacao, lumber, and flowers, began to be exported. Export diversification lowered Central America's dependence on coffee and bananas from 60 percent of export earnings in 1961 to 40 percent in 1973. New exports brought modern agricultural technologies, direct investment by multinational corporations, and vigorous investment by local farmers and businessmen.

But when the world economic crisis hit in the 1970s, Central America experienced its most profound social upheaval since the Great Depression. Like those in the 1930s, the more recent waves of unrest and repression have followed natural disasters or severe economic shocks from the world system.

When earthquakes or hurricanes assaulted Central America in the 1970s, they were followed by fierce strikes, peasant land invasions, and military repression in the areas affected by the disasters. For example, after the Managua earthquake in December 1972, the conflict between Somoza's national guard and organizations of the poor noticeably escalated; studies of the Nicaraguan Revolution point to the earthquake as a benchmark date for the popular struggle there.[6] Similarly, when Hurricane Fifi hit the northern coast of Honduras in September 1974, peasant land occupations increased dramatically, especially in areas where hurricane damage was most severe. And immediately following the Guatemalan earthquake in February of 1976, the Guatemalan military and the associated death squads began a systematic attack on leaders of peasant leagues, labor unions, slum-dweller organizations, and cooperatives. The zones of Guatemala where repression was greatest were the areas most disrupted by the earthquake.[7]

Natural disasters struck the Central American landscape in an uneven fashion, but shocks from the world economy, first from 1973 to 1975 and then from late 1977 to the present (1985), sent spasms of unrest through the entire region. Both periods began with runs on the dollar and oil price hikes followed by soaring interest rates and worldwide contractions of a severity not witnessed since the 1930s. The escalating costs of imported oil, fertilizer, pesticides, tractors, and intermediate products sent bursts of inflation through the domestic economies. Shortly thereafter, worldwide recessions dampened the prices for Central American exports, forcing the region deeper into debt at a time when interest rates were at record levels. Like earthquakes and hurricanes, world system shocks triggered labor strife, peasant land occupations, and public protests.

In the past when shocks of unusual strength occurred, elites counted on quick applications of terror to halt peasant land occupations and to suppress the demands of wage workers. When these traditional policies were applied in the 1970s, however, they no longer seemed to work. Instead of splitting up the opposition into hundreds of ineffective units, official terror produced grand coalitions of groups that had never worked together before. Instead of isolating the armed opposition from the rest of the population, government repression in the 1970s produced closer links between guerrilla factions and grassroots groups.

The first wave of unrest (1973–75) left several thousand people dead. The second wave, which began in late 1977, has already claimed the lives of more than a hundred thousand. The first wave of official terror forced thousands to flee their homes. The second wave has already displaced several million people from their homes, and more than a million have sought refuge in other countries. The first wave of crisis forced Central American governments to spend more on reform and repression. The second wave toppled the forty year-old dictatorship of Somoza in Nicaragua and placed the governments of El Salvador and Guatemala under siege.

Ever since the overthrow of Somoza in July 1979, U.S. military aid to Central America has escalated, and more U.S. troops have been committed to the area. By 1981 the CIA had assembled an invasion force to harass the Sandinista government of Nicaragua, a team of U.S. military advisers had been sent to El Salvador, and preparations were being made for U.S. training bases in Honduras. By 1985 the U.S. government was spending half a billion dollars a year on military aid to Central America, "temporary" military advisers in El Salvador had become a permanent fixture, and between two and five thousand U.S. troops were in Honduras taking part in "maneuvers."

It was understood that military aid alone would not produce conditions for stability in the area. To halt the spread of revolution, a comprehensive development program combined with military aid was called for. By the middle of 1981 President Reagan first announced the need for a Marshall Plan for Central America, and by February 1982 the Caribbean Basin Initiative was unveiled. It included export-promotion schemes and incentives for foreign investors, but the $350 million requested in this initial program was too small an amount to have much impact on a regional economy suffering from acute capital flight, burdensome international debts, soft markets for exports, and growing social unrest. To begin to address the crisis, thirty to forty times the initial request was thought to be needed.

To persuade Congress to come up with the funding at a time when domestic programs were being cut, President Reagan appointed Dr. Henry Kissinger to select a bipartisan panel whose task would be to study the Central American crisis and to make policy recommendations on the basis of the study. The blue-ribbon panel, composed of harsh critics of the administration along with staunch supporters, published its recommendations in January of 1984. The report predicted that for 1980 levels of per capita income to be reached by 1990, some $24 billion would be required from outside sources. The U.S.

government was expected to pay $10–$12 billion over that seven-year period, multilateral lending institutions were to provide $6–$8 billion, and the private sector would be expected to produce the remaining $6 billion.[8] Since 1984 the Kissinger Report has been used to facilitate the drafting and passage of military and economic aid bills in Congress.

The perspective of the Kissinger Report—and the one held by many in Congress from both political parties—is that the Alliance for Progress was successful in promoting conditions of stability in the region, but the world economic shocks reversed the gains made in the 1960s. The solution for the region today is to repeat the performance of the 1960s. In the words of the Kissinger Commission, "The most successful growth efforts of the post-war period—including Central America's own sustained expansion during the 1960s and 1970s—were led by the private sector. In these cases governments provided appropriate incentives and eliminated roadblocks, rather than trying to make themselves the engines of growth. This must be done again."[9]

Almost line for line, the Kissinger Report recommends policies that were applied during the 1960s. Military aid is to be greatly expanded, and some of the programs that were suspended because of human rights abuses are to be funded once again. Centrally controlled social reforms are to be reinstated, and some of the agencies responsible for those reforms in the 1960s are to be resurrected. Incentives for foreign investors are to be strengthened, infrastructure to serve the private sector is to be constructed, and the U.S. market is to be further opened to exports from Central America. The Kissinger Commission even recommended expanding the region's sugar and beef quotas, specific exports that that were promoted in the 1960s.

There has been great controversy in Congress—and there was controversy within the Kissinger Commission—over the proper mix of military aid and social reforms. But one article of faith held by most members of Congress (and one of the views held by all members of the Kissinger Commission) is that export expansion and diversification, foreign investment incentives, and other measures intended to promote rapid private-sector growth will also promote social stability.

But what if this assumption of policy makers is incorrect? What if the rapid economic growth of the 1960s, instead of creating conditions for social stability, did the opposite? After all, the social unrest of the 1970s followed closely on the most remarkable growth period the region had experienced in this century.

The experience of Nicaragua also suggests that the question is worth considering. Of the five Central American countries, Nicaragua was the most successful in expanding and diversifying its export base during the 1960s. From 1960 to 1970 Nicaragua's export earnings grew an average of 11 percent a year, the fastest in the region, and several new exports surpassed coffee as earners of foreign exchange. The export boom generated overall economic growth rates of more than 7 percent a year, and per capita income of Nicaraguans grew faster than 4 percent a year, nearly twice the regional average.[10] Yet when the world crisis struck in the 1970s, Nicaragua was the first to break out in revolution.

This book questions the widely held view that the economic cure for instability in Central America is another program of export expansion and diversification. The approach is to examine critically the two most successful cases of export expansion and diversification in Central America's recent past: cotton and beef. From negligible levels in the 1950s, by the mid-1960s cotton had become the region's second-most-important export after coffee, and beef ranked fourth after bananas. More so than the other new exports, cotton and beef attracted the attention of foreign and local investors and stimulated the introduction of modern technology. Because the cotton boom preceded beef, Part One focuses on cotton and Part Two on beef.

Each export drive is subjected to the same series of questions. First, the major causes of the export boom in question are explored, and several questions are addressed: To what extent was export success due to favorable market conditions and unusually low costs of production in Central America, and to what extent was it the result of favorable government policies? What role did the U.S. government, the World Bank, and other institutions play in promoting the export, and in what ways did modern agricultural technologies permit its development?

Second, the beneficiaries of each export boom are discussed. Who became cotton growers and cattle ranchers? Which companies supplied the growers and ranchers with inputs? Who came to own the cotton gins and beef-export houses? What other investment opportunities were generated by cotton and beef? Were elite structures broadened by the expansion of beef and cotton? If so, who were the new investors?

Third, the ways in which each boom affected material life for the average person are examined. How did people use the land before it was turned into cottonfields and cattle ranches? How did each export drive influence opportunities for making a living? How did it affect the environment? How did it affect the relations between large landowners and the rural poor? Is there any evidence of social tension in the areas where cotton and cattle were introduced?

Part Three examines the relation between export-led growth and the crisis. What contributions did cotton and cattle make to the economic and social vulnerability of the region? How did the natural and economic disasters of the 1970s and 1980s tear through the altered social fabric? How did the five governments respond to the heightened social stress? How did the U.S. government respond? Is another ambitious economic development program—like the one being promoted today—the answer for Central America's future?

Part One: Cotton

1. The Cotton Boom and Its Primary Causes

A chain of volcanoes flanks the Pacific side of Central America, beginning in the state of Chiapas in southern Mexico and running through Guatemala, El Salvador, Honduras, Nicaragua, and Costa Rica. For thousands of years bursts of subterranean pressure have spewed ash into the air. Prevailing winds have carried the fine ash to the south and west, dumping much of it on the Pacific slope and on the coastal plain below. Pounding rains have washed the ash from the steeper grades, leaving alluvial deposits along the banks of rivers and streams. The cycle of fire, wind, and water has blessed Central America with some of the finest cropland to be found anywhere on earth. The rich volcanic soils of the cooler elevations, claimed by coffee farms during the latter half of the nineteenth century, thereafter provided Central America with its most important source of foreign exchange. The fertile soils of the hot lowlands, however, lay virtually untapped by the export trade until almost a century later, when this area was opened up for the cultivation of cotton.

Central America's Pacific coastal plain is an ideal spot for growing cotton. The strip is only ten to twenty miles wide, but along the plain are found pockets of deep, loose soil, rich in volcanic ash and organic matter, perfectly suited for cotton. Furthermore, the land is flat, so that it is suitable for mechanization. A rainy season permits the healthy growth of young plants without the need for irrigation, and the dry season that follows permits the bolls to ripen without the risk of rain damage. A glutted labor market holds wages far below those of cotton-growing regions of the United States. Not only have low wages lowered the costs of chopping by hand early in the season, but they have permitted the crop to continue to be picked by hand; this process yields a cleaner product that fetches a premium on world markets. But despite cheap labor, superb soil, and favorable weather conditions, the Pacific coastal plain was not developed for cotton exports until after World War II.

During the 1940s the five countries of Central America together produced only about 25,000 bales a year—most of it for the fledgling textile mills of the region, not for the world market. In the late 1940s several growers on the coastal plain of El Salvador demonstrated the profitability of raising the crop on large holdings with new technologies. The news of their success quickly spread southward into Nicaragua and northward into Guatemala. By 1950

Nicaragua and El Salvador together produced 50,000 bales (see Chart 1-1 for production figures), and by 1952 Central American production exceeded 100,000 bales. By 1955 300,000 bales were produced, and in Nicaragua cotton surpassed coffee as the most important earner of foreign exchange for the year. By 1962 production had doubled again and exceeded 600,000 bales. At that time the region ranked tenth in the world as a producer of cotton, and cotton replaced bananas as the second-most-important export from the region. Favorable conditions pushed production to more than a million bales in the mid-1960s. In the late 1960s unfavorable production conditions forced cotton into decline, but in the 1970s production and exports surged once more, and in 1977 the crop exceeded the peak levels of the mid-1960s. By the late 1970s the narrow Pacific coastal strip of Central America ranked third, behind the United States and Egypt, in sales of cotton on the world market.

What caused this remarkable export boom?

Demand for Cotton by Central American Manufacturing

Before 1950 Central American cotton found its way into the world market only during periods of extreme shortages, when world prices were unusually high. For example, around the time of the U.S. Civil War, worldwide shortages briefly encouraged hacienda owners in Guatemala and El Salvador to grow cotton for sale in New York. But after the war cotton prices fell and Central American producers could no longer compete in the market. During the early years of World War II Germany and Japan purchased Nicaraguan cotton, but immediately following the war most of Nicaragua's cotton was sold once again within the region, not on the world market.

The small quantities of cotton that were raised in Central America were more likely to be spun and woven by mills in Guatemala City or San Salvador than to end up in Lancashire or New Bedford. From the time when the first modern textile mills were built in the 1870s until 1950, Central American cotton production was an appendage of Central American textile manufacturing. The bulk of the yard goods produced by the mills was made into coarse work clothes for agricultural laborers or rough cotton bagging for the coffee-export houses.

In the 1950s the mills of the region continued to process approximately thirty thousand bales a year, and in the 1960s textile manufacturers, especially those in Guatemala and El Salvador, received an extra boost from the Central American Common Market. By 1968 Central American mills were processing

Chart 1-1
Central American Cotton Production 1950–1979
Bales
(thousands)

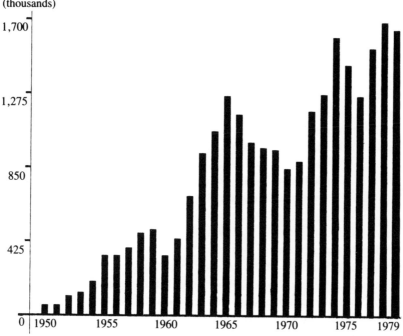

Sources: U.S. Department of Agriculture (USDA) and Secretaría Permanente del Tratado General de Integración Económica Centroamericana (SIECA). For more detail on sources and individual country data for 1941 through 1979 see Table A-1 in the Appendix.

a hundred thousand bales a year.[1] In addition to domestic uses of cotton lint, during the 1950s and 1960s an industry for processing cotton by-products arose; especially important was the growth of cotton seed oil as a substitute for lard in Central American kitchens, and to a lesser extent cottonseed meal was turned into a cake to feed animals. Despite the expanding demand for cotton by Central American industry, after 1950 the world market became a more important buyer of the region's cotton, and from 1955 on, 90 percent of the region's cotton was exported to larger, more modern mills far away.

World Demand for Cotton after World War II

World War II devastated Europe and Asia. Following the war, reconstruction efforts generated jobs throughout the world market economy, and wage earners began spending more on food, housing, transportation, and clothes.

Textile mills in the Carolinas immediately responded to the increased demand for cloth, and in a few years the spindles and looms of war-torn Europe and Japan had been replaced. By 1950 Japan had regained her prewar supremacy in the world cloth trade, and the mills of West Germany, France, Belgium, the Netherlands, Britain, and Italy were humming once again.

The favored raw material in this burst of activity was cotton. By the late 1940s it appeared that the cotton market had permanently recovered from the low prices of the Great Depression. Planters in the southern United States quickly responded to the market incentives, and soon irrigated cotton became an important crop in California and much of the West. American growers produced enough cotton not only to supply the booming U.S. textile business but also to provide about half of Western Europe's and Japan's cotton needs.

Manufacturers in Europe and Japan bought cotton from traditional suppliers: India, Pakistan, South Korea, and Egypt, but they also combed the world for new areas where cotton might be raised. During a period of shortage in the early 1950s, they discovered the Pacific coastal strip of Central America.

While the Korean War was in progress, expectations of shortages and intense speculation placed heavy stress on the world cotton market. A flurry of orders from Western Europe and Japan offered record prices to Central American growers, and in El Salvador and Nicaragua some growers became millionaires from a single year's crop.

When prices declined after their peak during the Korean War, something unusual happened. Instead of being forced out of the international market, as had happened before in such situations, cotton growers in Central America continued to expand their acreage, successfully competing with producers elsewhere for the European and Japanese market. Despite a drop in price from $276 a bale during the Korean War to $105 a bale in 1959,[2] growers expanded their exports of cotton more than tenfold, from 50,000 bales to more than 660,000 bales over the same period.

What accounts for this unusual turn of events?

The Insecticide Revolution

The climate along the Pacific coastal strip is nearly perfect for growing cotton, but the humidity and heat combine to favor cotton's worst enemy: insects. There is no hard freeze in the winter to keep the insect population in check, and the arsenic and copper compounds, sulfur poisons, and nicotine concoctions of the nineteenth and early twentieth centuries are quickly washed off by the hard-driving tropical rains.

Early experiments with cotton as a commercial crop in Central America quickly proved how delicious the plant was to tropical insects. In the 1870s some enterprising Guatemalan landowners attempted to raise cotton on a large scale to supply Guatemala's first modern cotton mill. According to the reports, "The efforts of these progressive farmers . . . were dashed by a plague of insects commonly called the 'picudo,' against which they had no means of combat."[3] The main reason why Central American cotton continued to fail as an export crop was the low yield resulting from insect damage, and only exceptionally high cotton prices would finance the costly applications of insecticides known at that time.

The insecticide revolution changed the situation. DDT was discovered in 1939, and it was soon found to be more potent than any of the insecticides then known. Minute traces of the substance were shown to be deadly to a wide variety of insects. Unlike most insecticides, DDT not only could kill chewing insects through ingestion, but also could kill sucking insects on contact. During World War II the U.S. Army proved the miracle killer's effectiveness in combating lice, fleas, and mosquitoes. After the war DDT was made available to the public in a variety of forms. One of its great advantages for agriculture was its durability. It was practically insoluble in water, unweakened by bright sunlight, and very slow to oxidize, so that it was particularly suitable to the tropics. For cotton, DDT spelled death to bollworms, pink bollworms, fleahoppers, thrips, and stinkbugs. For Central Americans, it temporarily reduced malaria infestations, making the Pacific strip more inhabitable for cotton workers. For the chemical companies, DDT spelled profits and a grand incentive to synthesize related compounds.

By the late 1940s aerial sprayings of new insecticides had been proved effective against cotton pests in El Salvador, and a new era for Central American cotton was opened. By the mid-1950s crop dusters were a commonplace along the coastal plain in Guatemala, El Salvador, and Nicaragua, and shortly thereafter they were seen in Honduras and Costa Rica. DDT was not particularly effective against boll weevils, red spider mites, aphids, or leafworms; for those pests doses of toxaphene (a compound closely related to DDT), ethyl

parathion, and methyl parathion became popular. Even with the greater durability of the new insecticides, the heavy rains during the growing season
required frequent applications for insect control. A USDA publication of the
early 1960s reported that sometimes as many as thirty-five to forty applications
were administered per season in El Salvador. Throughout the region insect
control became the largest single component of production costs.[4]

Despite the heavy applications required and their high costs, the miracle
insecticides removed the most important obstacle that had held Central American cotton production in check for centuries.

Chemical Fertilizers

Along with the insecticide revolution came a revolution in the use of fertilizers. The first few years of cotton cultivation on the rich soils of the Pacific
coastal plain required little or no fertilizer to achieve high yields. In fact,
sometimes growers complained that the earth was too rich, producing plants
ten feet tall and higher, with thick, tangled branches and excessive foliage.
This abnormal plant growth not only raised the costs of picking but also tended
to lower the fiber strength of the lint harvested.[5]

The problem of excessive soil fertility was short-lived, and Central American planters learned what planters in the southern United States had known for
more than a century: cotton is a hungry plant. After four or five years of
consecutive cultivation, as well as exposure to heavy rains and windstorms,
the light soils of the coastal plain began to leach and to lose their natural
fertility. Fertilizer had to be applied to maintain yields. The USDA studies of
the 1960s reported substantial use of chemical fertilizers by cotton planters in
the region, and agricultural statistics indicate that of all the crops that came to
use chemical fertilizers, cotton remained the most demanding.[6]

Tractors

Along with insecticides and fertilizers came tractors with special attachments
to apply the chemicals. Unlike the more mountainous areas where coffee is
grown, the land suitable for cotton is flat and lends itself to cultivation by
tractor. Furthermore, much of the cotton land is light and porous; tractor
cultivation is possible within days after heavy rainfall without the risk of
machinery getting stuck or the soil becoming compacted.

In the 1960s other crops came to be cultivated with tractors, but even by the late 1960s and early 1970s most of the tractors in Central America were still in the cotton belt. According to the 1971 agricultural census of El Salvador, the three major cotton departments (out of a total of fourteen departments altogether) had half the tractors in the entire country.[7] According to a Nicaraguan agricultural survey of the late 1960s, tractors were "mainly associated with cotton." In 1968 the three major cotton departments of Nicaragua (out of sixteen altogether), where nine-tenths of the country's cotton was raised, had nine-tenths of the country's tractors.[8] In fact, wherever cotton came to be grown, tractors became a familiar sight.

Modern Technology and Cotton Yields

The application of fertilizers, insecticides, herbicides, and mechanization produced sharply higher cotton yields throughout the world following World War II, but the gains made in Central American cotton outstripped those of most other cotton-producing areas (see Chart 1-2). In the 1940s, before the modern technologies were introduced, yields of lint per acre in Central America were substantially lower than in the Delta region of the southern United States. By the 1950s, however, average yields in Guatemala and El Salvador had surpassed those of the Delta, and by the 1960s average yields in Guatemala, El Salvador, and Nicaragua exceeded those of the Delta by 20 to 25 percent. By the early 1970s Guatemala had achieved the second-highest average cotton yield in the world. El Salvador ranked fourth, Nicaragua sixth, and Honduras tenth out of fifty-two major cotton-producing countries. The achievement is all the more remarkable considering that Central American cotton does not require irrigation, unlike that grown in most of the other high-yielding areas.[9]

The insecticide revolution, combined with tractors and fertilizer, made it possible for Central America to continue to sell cotton in the world market even when prices declined after the Korean War. But the Central American cotton boom was not merely the work of pure market forces linking expanding demand in one location with low-cost sources of supply elsewhere. State institutions at a number of levels were busily promoting the link between the rich soils of the Pacific strip and the textile mills of Europe and Asia.

Chart 1-2
Cotton Yields

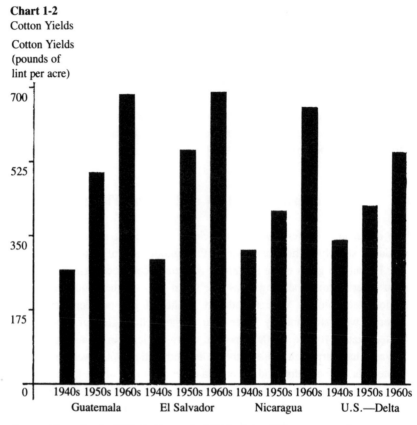

Cotton Yields
(pounds of
lint per acre)

700

525

350

175

0

| 1940s 1950s 1960s | 1940s 1950s 1960s | 1940s 1950s 1960s | 1940s 1950s 1960s |
| Guatemala | El Salvador | Nicaragua | U.S.—Delta |

Sources: Figures for the 1940s for Guatemala, El Salvador, and Nicaragua come from Stevenson, *Cotton Production*, pp. 44, 46, 48. Figures for the 1950s for Guatemala, El Salvador, and Nicaragua come from Harness and Pugh, *Cotton*, pp. 3, 11, 18. Figures for the 1960s and for the U.S.—Delta come from Economics Research Service, *Statistics on Cotton*, p. 9.
Note: "U.S.—Delta" is an average for the cotton areas of Mississippi, Louisiana, Arkansas, Tennessee, Missouri, Illinois, and Kentucky.

Government Road-building Programs

Before the cotton boom, most of the transportation infrastructure of Central America consisted of railroads built to serve coffee zones and banana plantations. Certain stretches of railroad crossed the Pacific coastal strip on their way from coffee farms or banana plantations to ports on the Pacific. When cotton production began in earnest in the late 1940s and early 1950s, owners of gins most often took advantage of this already developed infrastructure and located their facilities along the rail lines that passed through cotton districts. Even by the early 1960s much of the baled cotton was still shipped to port by rail.

The major transport blockage was not in getting the bales to port but in getting trucks, tractors, and other equipment into and out of the fields. Without all-weather roads, access to cotton inputs could be blocked at any number of critical points in the crop cycle, thereby increasing the risk of losing the crop because of bad timing.

Cotton requires frequent inspections to determine when to plant, when to thin, when to weed, when to apply insecticides, and when to harvest. Without good all-weather roads, inspections are made difficult, especially during the crucial rainy season. Tractors do better than trucks on muddy roads, but tractors require daily servicing and frequently break down. Parts, gasoline, and oil, as well as fertilizers, seeds, and insecticides, must be brought in from outside. At harvest time a large number of wage laborers must be attracted from afar to pick the crop, and fields remote from major transportation arteries have a difficult time securing a labor force during picking season, when competition for day labor is keen. Finally, oxcarts are extremely slow in getting the raw cotton from the fields to the gin; with good roads large wagons capable of holding several bales worth of loose cotton can be brought to the fields.

For these reasons, the development of cotton was contingent upon building roads through the sections of the Pacific coastal plain suitable for cotton cultivation. Before the cotton boom, the Pacific strip had been relatively neglected by government road-building programs. The best roads before the 1940s tended to connect the major population centers of the highlands, and when the Inter-American Highway system was begun during World War II (primarily for U.S. strategic purposes), it followed the path of these earlier roads through the highlands. In certain spots along this first major highway project, the road crossed fertile valleys or dipped into the Pacific strip, thereby stimulating cotton development as a by-product. The big effort to develop the Pacific coastal plain for commercial agriculture did not come about until the early 1950s, when the World Bank began pushing for a coastal highway. By 1960 the Pacific highway in El Salvador and Nicaragua was virtually complete, and sections had been built in Guatemala. During the 1960s the World Bank was joined by the Inter-American Development Bank (IADB) and the United States Agency for International Development (AID) in promoting the Pacific highway. By 1970 the road was complete all the way from the Mexican border to La Barranca, Costa Rica, with a single unfinished stretch on the Honduran/Nicaraguan border (see Figure 1-1).

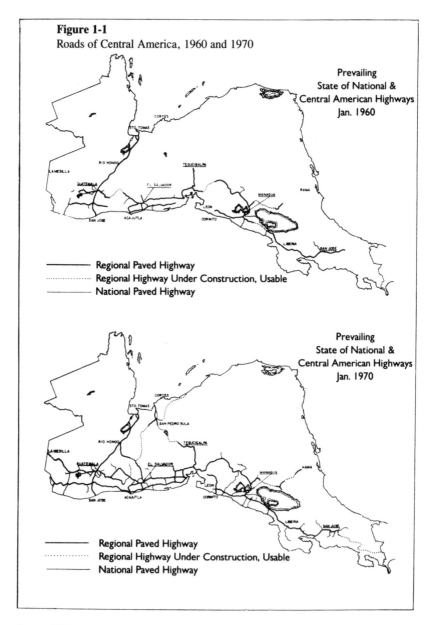

Figure 1-1
Roads of Central America, 1960 and 1970

Prevailing
State of National &
Central American Highways
Jan. 1960

—————— Regional Paved Highway
·············· Regional Highway Under Construction, Usable
—————— National Paved Highway

Prevailing
State of National &
Central American Highways
Jan. 1970

—————— Regional Paved Highway
·············· Regional Highway Under Construction, Usable
—————— National Paved Highway

Source: SIECA, El desarrollo integrado, 6:16.

In 1945 the government of El Salvador, without outside assistance, completed a fifty-mile stretch of road, thirty miles of it paved, into one of the pockets of rich soil along the coastal plain, and by 1950 more than half of all the cotton acreage in the country was located in the twelve counties (*municipios*) through which this fifty-mile strip of road traveled.[10]

In 1954 the government of El Salvador and the World Bank initiated an ambitious program to extend the pavement eastward to the port of La Union and then westward to the Guatemalan border. Between 1955 and 1963, 80 percent of the country's highway budget was spent on the Pacific highway and its network of feeder roads. The foreign exchange required to build the road was provided by $16.1 million in loans from the World Bank ($11.3 million for the main highway and $4.8 million for access roads), and another $20.9 million came out of the general budget of the government of El Salvador.[11] As sections of the highway were completed, land adjacent to the highway was soon put into cotton production. By 1962 the entire length of the littoral highway of El Salvador had been paved, and the program of feeder roads was begun in earnest in 1963. By 1971 88 percent of El Salvador's cotton was being raised in twenty-five *municipios* through which the Pacific highway ran, and another 7 percent was being cultivated in seven more *municipios* that were connected to the highway by good feeder roads.

Nicaragua followed El Salvador's lead in building a paved road through the Pacific coastal plain; and again, cotton acreage closely paralleled the paving of the highway. By the time of the 1963 census, four-fifths of Nicaragua's cotton acreage was in fifteen *municipios* through which the Pacific highway ran. [12]

Guatemala lagged behind Nicaragua and El Salvador in cotton production until the 1960s, when the government finally began a road-building program along the Pacific coastal plain with help from the World Bank. A Brookings Institution report argued that the Guatemalan government's slowness in shifting attention to road-building in this area "prevented a full and early participation in the cotton boom. Thus, higher foreign exchange earnings and possibly overall economic growth as well were retarded five or six years as a result."[13]

For the three major producers, cotton was as much a cause of the road-building programs as a consequence. In Nicaragua, for example, one of the reasons the World Bank mission gave for its recommendation to fund the Pacific highway was that the cotton boom had already placed a severe strain on the existing railroad, which could not handle the traffic to the port of Corinto at harvest time. The mission felt that instead of an expanded railroad system, the region would be better served by a road network, which would carry the added advantage of replacing the high-cost oxcarts with lower-cost trucks and wagons for transporting cotton from the fields to the gins, a task the railroad could not achieve.[14] Furthermore, as economic and political groups began to cluster around expanding cotton profits, they pressured governments to build roads into zones suitable for cotton cultivation. One reason El Salvador's Pacific highway was begun so early was the creation of the Cotton Cooperative (Cooperativa Algodonera) in 1940. Controlled from the beginning by the largest cotton growers in El Salvador, the Cotton Cooperative expanded its economic and political power as private fortunes in cotton began to be made, making sure that government policy, including the highway budget, favored the further growth of those fortunes. In Guatemala the cotton growers' associations began forming later than in El Salvador, but according to one analysis of interest groups in Guatemala, "by the early 1960s, the [cotton] growers were making demands parallel to those of other interest sectors, and the government's role had become that of reactor."[15] The shift of the Guatemalan highway program to the Pacific strip resulted from the ability of growers' associations to influence government policy. As in all of the other cases, cotton acreage in Guatemala expanded prior to the building of highways, and once the highways were built, it exploded.

Cotton and Credit

Cotton is a cash hog. To gain access to prime cotton land, many growers must pay a money rent in advance to the owner of the land. The rains begin in April or May, and the grower must pay a team to plow the soil earlier, so that when the lull comes in late June, July, or August, the soil needs little preparation before the seed is planted. At that time a team must be hired to do the planting, and seed and fertilizer must also be purchased. After the plants are up, the grower must pay for thinning the young plants to prevent crowding, and the rows must be chopped or an herbicide applied to choke off the incipient jungle of tropical weeds. On lands that have been planted in cotton for a number of years, a side dressing of fertilizer is needed. At about the same time large expenditures begin in an effort to control the insects. If a crop is to be made, the fields must be doused twenty-five times or more with expensive insecticides, and the grower must pay for the services of a crop duster or a team of workers with hand spraying equipment. If all goes well, when the dry season comes the bolls will begin to open, and the fields will become white from the abundance of lint. But at this time the grower is faced with a cash outlay that will equal or exceed what has already been spent on insecticides: harvest wages. In order to get the lint out of the fields, a grower must have access to huge piles of small bills to pay the pickers. After the fields have been picked, the costs of transport of the raw cotton to the gin and a ginning fee per bale must be paid. The timing may vary depending on how sales are transacted, but generally a grower is faced with eight months of heavy expenditures before an inflow of cash brings relief after the harvest.

Judging from reports in the early 1960s, it was not uncommon for a planter with a thousand acres in cotton to face outlays of $130,000 to $170,000 (including rental of land) before the sale of the cotton at the end of the season.[16] By 1969–70, increasing insecticide, fertilizer, and other costs had pushed cash outlays for a similar operation up to the $180,000 to $260,000 range.[17] By 1979–80, after two bursts of worldwide inflation, a similar operation faced outlays of $350,000 to $650,000.[18] Some of the seed, fertilizer, and insecticide costs were reportedly purchased on credit from the agribusinesses that sold these inputs, and occasionally cotton-export houses would advance funds to growers for harvesting the crop, but overwhelmingly expenditures were financed by short-term bank loans. Studies from the 1960s show that 80 to 90 percent of a typical grower's out-of-pocket expenses was borrowed.[19]

Of all the agricultural crops raised in Central America, cotton requires the most credit. In 1955, when cotton (39 percent of export earnings) surpassed coffee (35 percent) as Nicaragua's biggest export earner, it did so by absorbing 68 percent of all the agricultural credit lent by the banking system that year. Even though cotton had declined in relative importance over the period from 1969 to 1978, it remained the largest single consumer of agricultural credit for Guatemala, El Salvador, and Nicaragua.[20]

Government Promotion of Cotton Finance

Lending to cotton growers was not merely the result of private banks' recognizing a high-growth sector. By the early 1950s every Central American country had a central bank and at least one government development bank able to influence the direction of private lending. In Guatemala, El Salvador, and Nicaragua, these government financial institutions promoted cotton.

In Guatemala the newly established National Development Bank (INFOP) lent 11 cotton growers a total of $150,000 in 1949–50. By 1954–55, the number of loans had expanded to 104, for a total of more than $1.3 million. During the last crop year before the CIA overthrow of the Arbenz government,[21] 68 percent of INFOP's agricultural credits were pumped into cotton.[22] In addition to subsidized loans, INFOP promoted cotton through a price-stabilization program and a cotton experiment station. Following the overthrow of Arbenz, support prices were halted, but promotional loans were expanded and shifted from INFOP to the Bank of Guatemala. In addition to direct lending, the Bank of Guatemala began to stimulate private banks in their lending to cotton by rediscounting private bank loans to cotton growers at a favorable rate. It is estimated that by 1964 the Bank of Guatemala was giving 40 percent of all its rediscounts for cotton loans, and the rediscounting was being done at the preferential rate of 3 percent, 2 percent below the cost of funds from commercial bank deposits.[23]

In El Salvador the Central Reserve Bank promoted cotton in a similar way. The policy consisted of lending to private-sector banks and the Cotton Cooperative at a subsidized rate for cotton loans. Instead of leaving it up to competition to pass off some of the subsidy to growers, the bank placed a low ceiling rate on cotton loans. In 1969–70, for example, the Central Reserve Bank is reported to have given private commercial banks and the Cotton Cooperative loans at the preferential rate of 3 percent, while an official ceiling rate of 6 percent was set on the loans they made to growers. According to one study, this policy provided Salvadoran growers with the cheapest cotton credit anywhere in Central America.[24]

In Nicaragua the National Bank adopted a policy of promoting cotton by directly lending to growers. At the beginning of the cotton boom in Nicaragua in the early 1950s, the National Bank of Nicaragua provided all of the bank credit that went into cotton, directly financing more than three-fourths of the area planted. After 1955–56 some private-sector banks began making cotton loans, but throughout the 1960s the National Bank directly provided 85 percent of the bank financing for cotton, the highest government support for the crop in all of Central America.[25]

The importance of government-subsidized credit in promoting cotton is suggested by a brief look at government financial policies in Honduras and Costa Rica, which have differed from those of the three big cotton countries. The National Development Bank of Honduras (BANAFOM) is said to have provided about 80 percent of all the cotton credit in the early 1960s, when cotton was expanding into the south coast.[26] Later in the decade BANAFOM began promoting sugar, and in the 1970s it pushed basic grains and coffee instead of cotton, further reducing cotton's attractiveness as a cash crop in Honduras.[27] In Costa Rica the government banks in charge of agricultural lending never promoted cotton. A USDA study reported that a major deterrent to cotton expansion in Costa Rica was the system of financing and marketing, which left the cotton planter with the financing costs for the entire time until the cotton was used in a domestic mill or sold abroad.[28] Between 1969 and 1977 less than 1 percent of the agricultural credit of the national banking system of Costa Rica was destined for cotton.[29]

Government credit subsidies were important not just for the direct loans they generated but for the indirect way in which they lowered risk for private-sector banks lending to cotton. When government banks inject liquidity into a particular activity, it is easier for private banks to get paid back because the activity is flush with cash. In the three countries where governments took an active role in removing the financial constraint to cotton development, private banks soon rushed in and provided financing as well. As we shall see in the next chapter, some of the private banks that discovered the opportunities of cotton were foreign.

Summary

Cheap labor, rich soil, and a favorable climate gave Central America great potential for becoming a producer of cotton; but without modern insecticides, yields were too low to make the crop commercially viable. With the discovery of DDT and related compounds, the most important barrier to Central American cotton production was removed. After World War II the growing demand for cotton in the world market and the availability of fertilizers, herbicides, and modern agricultural equipment were some of the other factors that boosted Central America's potential as a cotton producer. Private market conditions were favorable for Central American cotton, but government intervention was crucial in turning a possibility into a reality. With the guidance and financial support of the World Bank, governments built paved roads through the middle of the zones where the potential for growing cotton was greatest, and governments subsidized cotton by providing cheap credit to growers. After several years of promotional efforts, the wish of the World Bank, government officials, landowners, and businessmen came true. The Pacific coastal plain of Central America had been converted into an export zone.

2. The Cotton Boom and Its Primary Beneficiaries

Buoyant markets, new technologies, improved roads, and state finance all promoted cotton, and the boom began. Cotton changed the Pacific coastal plain from a lazy, provincial backwater into a bustling commercial zone.

Cotton sales roughly indicate the magnitude of business opportunities directly generated by the boom. The sales of cotton lint in the world market (Chart 2-1) increased from approximately $13 million a year in the early 1950s to $50 million later in the decade, peaking in the mid-1960s at almost $150 million. A six year decline in cotton export revenues was followed in the 1970s by a resumption of the cotton boom, and once more the Pacific strip was flush with cash from cotton-export sales; some years the revenues exceeded $250 million. In 1978 sales of cotton lint on the world market passed $400 million.

Not so dramatic in its upward surge, but more stable, was the revenue generated by sales of lint to the domestic textile industry (Chart 2-2). From a $4.5 million market in the 1950s, the Central American textile mills had more than doubled the value of their cotton purchases by the mid-1960s, and for some of the unusual years in the 1970s sales of cotton lint to domestic textile producers exceeded $50 million.

In the 1960s a regional market developed in cooking oil and margarine, and cottonseed became a raw material for this growing industry. In the 1950s cottonseed was primarily exported, and revenues seldom exceeded a few million dollars a year. By 1970, however, Central American vegetable-oil factories were buying 95 percent of the cottonseed produced, providing the cotton sector with $22 million in revenues, and by 1978 revenues from domestic cottonseed sales exceeded $60 million.[1]

The total revenues to the cotton sector, including export and domestic sales of cotton lint and cottonseed, rose from $20 million a year in the early 1950s to more than $160 million by the mid-1960s. A decline in revenues in the late 1960s was followed by a resurgence of cotton in the 1970s, and by 1978 total revenues had reached the half billion dollar mark.

The voluminous cash flow from cotton created fresh opportunities for a whole spectrum of business activities. In addition to the direct profits earned by the growers from cotton cultivation, merchants were able to earn profits at various phases of the crop cycle, and demand for a host of services sprang up

Chart 2-1
Value of Central American Cotton Exports, 1951–1978
U.S. $ (Millions)

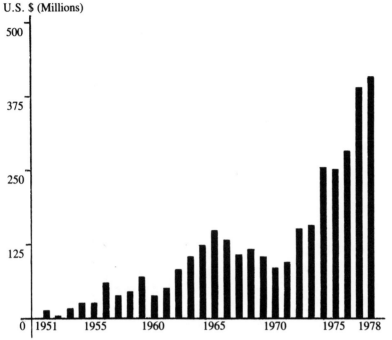

Sources: Comisión Nacional de Algodón (CONAL) and SIECA. For more detail on sources and individual country data see Table A-2 in the Appendix.

as well. Because of cotton's heavy reliance on credit, banks and financiers tapped part of the cotton wealth in the form of interest payments. Because of cotton's need for deep, rich earth and flat terrain, the holders of title to prime cotton land collected part of the cotton wealth in the form of rental payments from growers.

The relative shares of the cotton bounty during good years, and the relative burden of losses during bad years, shifted among these various claimants from year to year and from country to country depending on market conditions and government policies. But the basis of all of the claims, the ultimate source of wealth for all of the activities, was found in the growing of cotton itself. For the whole network of marketing, finance, and services to survive in the long run, Central American cotton production had to maintain a competitive edge over production elsewhere in the world system. Only with a competitive edge in production could the cotton economy survive the periodic decline of prices in the world market.

Chart 2-2
Central American Cotton Consumption, 1951–1978

U.S. $ (Millions)

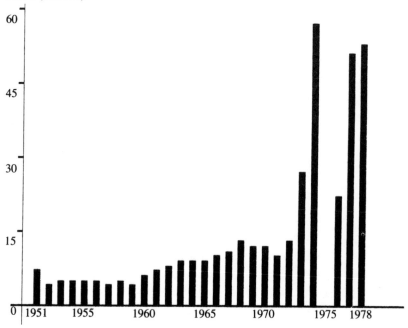

Sources: USDA, SIECA, and CONAL. For more detail on sources and individual country data see Table A-3 in the Appendix.

Several factors have allowed Central American production an absolute cost advantage over production elsewhere in the world: soil, climate, and an abundant supply of landless labor. The special climate and soil conditions along the Pacific coastal plain have permitted some of the highest cotton yields in the world, without the expenses of irrigation and heavy fertilizer use. Migratory laborers, because of their willingness to work hard for a few dollars a day, have enabled profits to be realized even when world cotton prices have dropped or when other production costs have risen. Furthermore, inexpensive harvest labor has permitted Central American growers to avoid the high fixed costs of mechanical pickers and has guaranteed Central American producers a special marketing advantage in Europe and Japan, where textile mills place a premium on clean, hand-picked cotton.

The Cotton Growers

Cotton growers have directly tapped the wealth from cotton, but their earnings have proved more volatile than those of landlords, bankers, merchants, and other beneficiaries of the cotton boom. Cotton grower profits have risen to unbelievable heights during years of good weather, few insects, and favorable prices, only to fall to abysmal lows during years of flood, drought, insect invasion, high interest rates, high insecticide prices, and low cotton prices.

Who have been the participants in this crucial and risky phase of the cotton economy?

Information from censuses and cotton-licensing boards gives a first impression that Central America's cotton boom spawned a large number of middle-sized growers. By the late 1950s more than two thousand farms, mostly located on the Pacific coastal plain, were cultivating cotton (Table A-4). By the peak in cotton cultivation in the mid-1960s, six thousand more farm units had been pulled into cultivation. A little more than a decade later the number of farms growing cotton reached ten thousand. Despite annual fluctuations in the average size of farms, the average cotton plot in Central America over the postwar period has been around one hundred acres. Only in Guatemala do the figures reveal large acreages per tract on the average, and for Honduras, Nicaragua, and El Salvador the average size has been smaller than a hundred acres, at least during the last two decades.

A closer look at census reports forces a modification of the first impression that cotton has been an activity dominated by middle-sized growers. At the lower end of the spectrum we find a sizable cluster of very small farms, with insufficient access to land to support a family year round. For farmers in this category, cotton has provided an opportunity to raise some much-needed cash to pay rent to their landlords and to serve as a hoard for family survival during the months when stores of corn and beans have been depleted. Cotton has also offered a way to avoid spending months away from home in a desperate search for wage income.

From the evidence available, the class of very small growers did not emerge in Guatemala or Costa Rica, but in El Salvador, Honduras, and Nicaragua these small growers became numerous during periods of favorable markets. In the early 1960s small growers made up one-fourth of all the growers in Nicaragua, cultivating an average of 5 acres of cotton on farms smaller than 17 acres.[2] Half of the growers in Honduras planted only 2 acres of cotton on farms smaller than 25 acres.[3] Similarly, in El Salvador in the early 1960s some 58 percent of the growers were small farmers planting an average of 5 acres of cotton on farms smaller than 25 acres.[4] Many of these small growers, especially those with access to very small plots or poor land, have had to supplement their earnings by picking cotton for the large cotton plantations nearby.[5]

Middle-sized farmers constitute the second-largest group of cotton growers in Central America. In Guatemala the cotton growers from middle-sized farms have remained few, whereas in Nicaragua cotton growers planting an average of 14 acres of cotton on farms of between 17 and 86 acres have made up by far the largest group, representing some 40 percent of the growers in the early 1960s.[6] In Honduras and El Salvador growers planting cotton on farms of between 25 and 125 acres have been the second-largest group. During the early 1960s in El Salvador one-fourth to one-fifth of the cotton growers planted an average of 30 acres of cotton on medium-sized farms.[7]

The number of small and medium-sized farms participating in the cotton boom may have been large, but if we consider the total cotton acreage planted, these farms were peripheral. In Guatemala farms with fewer than 112 acres accounted for less than 2 percent of the area planted in cotton in the early 1960s.[8] In El Salvador farms under 125 acres represented 82 percent of the growers, but they accounted for only 17 percent of the cotton under cultivation.[9] In Nicaragua in 1963, 68 percent of the growers were on farms smaller than 87 acres, but they planted only 11 percent of the cotton.[10] In Costa Rica in 1963, 34 percent of the cotton growers were on farms smaller than 121 acres, but they harvested less than 2 percent of the cotton area.[11]

The cotton boom, then, may have attracted the attention of small and medium-sized farmers, but the bulk of Central American cotton was grown on large estates. In Guatemala in 1964 farms larger than 1,100 acres cultivated 62 percent of the cotton.[12] In 1961, 125 farms with 500 or more acres of land cultivated 60 percent of El Salvador's cotton.[13] In Nicaragua in 1963 farms larger than 364 acres accounted for 60 percent of the cotton area harvested,[14] and in Costa Rica the same year farms with 500 acres or more harvested 86 percent of the cotton.[15]

The figures do not begin to show the degree of concentration of grower profits, because large growers frequently cultivate cotton on more than one farm. Reports from El Salvador reveal that the very largest growers began cotton operations on one of the family haciendas. Once the operation proved successful on the family estate, the grower proceeded to extend his cotton acreage by renting land close by, sometimes from a relative. The three largest grower families in El Salvador, the Wrights, the Dueñas, and the Krietes, all had at the center of the family cotton business a family hacienda on the Pacific strip where cotton got its start.[16] In 1972–73 one-fourth of the Salvadoran cotton crop was controlled by eighteen families, many of whom rented land in addition to owning some themselves.[17]

Field reports from other countries confirm a similar pattern. A USDA study in the early 1960s reported that in Guatemala "large cotton-cattle operations . . . are common. An estimated 20 percent of cotton acreage is rented."[18] Another study of Guatemala in the early 1960s reported that most of the cotton plots smaller than 86 acres were being rented by large landowners as a way to extend their cotton holdings.[19]

In Nicaragua before the cotton boom, the Pacific coastal plain was the most important cattle zone in the country. A look at the list of Nicaraguan growers with more than 346 acres of cotton planted shows an amazing number of listings under persons with the same family name, and many of these names are those of old families with haciendas before the cotton boom. The family name Arguello, for example, appears eighteen times on the list and is attached to 19,644 acres of cotton, representing more than 10 percent of the large holdings listed in León and Chinandega that year. Orlando Nuñez points out that relatives' names were used on the list of prominent growers to obscure the size of a single grower's operations; it may well be, however, that the grower paid rent to sisters, mothers, aunts, and cousins who actually held title to lands broken up by inheritance or land-reform evasion. Almost as prominent on the list as Arguello are the names Deshón, Gurdián, Lacayo, Montealegre, and several others.[20]

Between the center of the cotton economy, with its basis in large blocks of inherited property, and the fragmented fringes of small peasant cultivators, there emerged a space for a new class of grower, one with little prior experience in agriculture but with other advantages particularly relevant for cotton. Leon Hirsch attributes the dynamism of the cotton economy of El Salvador not to the large landowners but to a group of absentee investors he calls:

"agricultural entrepreneurs," professional or business people most of whom live in San Salvador, who rent land from the large owners . . . recognizing the profit potential from cotton. Many of them are members of the growing middle class who supplement their incomes through investment of their relatively moderate savings. They have been described as sophisticated and willing to take risks and to spend some time managing their investments. Investments in cotton growing proved to be an ideal outlet for them, especially after the highway was completed . . . permitting easy access to the land. Part time farm management became practical on a large scale for nonresidents only when people could drive in a few hours from San Salvador to the areas of production.[21]

Ridgway Satterthwaite reported that during his fieldwork in 1968 he observed a high frequency of late-model cars parked by the cottonfields alongside the

Pacific highway of El Salvador; from a number of interviews, he concluded that most of these belonged to absentee renters inspecting their crops. On the cotton-authorization lists he found the names of a number of well-known medical doctors, and from an interview with a loan supervisor for the Zacatecoluca branch of the most important cotton lending bank (Banco Hipotecario), he found that all of the branch's cotton loans went to renters of parcels larger than 50 acres, most of them larger than 250 acres, and that all of the renters on the list lived in San Salvador.[22]

The pattern of doctors, lawyers, engineers, and businessmen from the capital cities and the commercial centers of the Pacific coastal plain participating directly in the profits (and losses) from cotton growing is not just a phenomenon of El Salvador but is noted to various degrees up and down the coastal plain. Jaime Biderman suggests that the large initial spurt of cotton growing in the department of Managua in the early 1950s (before the good road was built through Chinandega and León) was due to "the involvement of a large number of new, urban-based producers from the capital city."[23] In a mid-1960s study of the Pacific highway of Nicaragua, George Wilson emphasizes the importance of the road in allowing for the frequent inspections so important for cotton, especially considering that "many of the growers live in the cities at some distance from the fields."[24] Other researchers stress the dynamic entrepreneurial thrust of the cotton planters, resulting in part from the merchant and professional origins of many of them. Pedro Belli compares Nicaraguan coffee planters with the new breed of cotton growers: "It may be said that whereas coffee breeds gentlemen of leisure, cotton forges old-fashioned entrepreneurs."[25]

The disadvantage that many of these new growers faced, with little previous experience in agriculture, was counterbalanced by a number of advantages. It was easy for this group to pool a certain portion of investment capital from its own professional and business sources, and the rest of the expenses could be met by borrowing with a lien on the crop from government or private-sector banks, with whom the growers had connections. Richard Adams suggests that some of the early cotton investors of Guatemala moved into that status by virtue of their connections with the "revolutionary" government and its new development bank, INFOP. Adams singles out Jacobo Arbenz, president of the republic until the CIA coup in 1954, as one example of this new breed of cotton grower.[26]

Cotton's heavy reliance on credit favored this group of urban professionals over the small peasants, who find it difficult to deal with creditors. The new breed of farmer could invest in cotton because many of the problems associated with this crop could be dealt with by purchases of commodities or services instead of by reliance on accumulated knowledge of the land. Agricultural extension stations and information from insecticide and fertilizer distributors were readily available for those who could read and had a basic education in modern science, and on many sections of the coastal plain the services of plowing, weeding, spraying, and harvesting could be purchased directly from corporations specializing in those tasks. Investment in cotton became popular among urban professionals because of its short crop cycle. Whereas coffee requires four or five years for trees to mature, a cotton investment can be turned over in less than a year; short-term cash rentals of land and equipment therefore did not make it necessary to freeze large blocks of capital. For many of these new growers, an investment in cotton was not greatly different from more familiar investments in urban real estate, retailing, banking, or manufacturing, and compared to these other investments, cotton was often more liquid.

The fortunes of growers fluctuated widely. In the early 1960s cotton became an investment fad of the urban professionals, and several years of good weather and favorable markets attracted droves of small cotton producers as well. During these favorable years cotton spread onto marginal lands, including upland river valleys where yields per acre were considerably lower than on the rich deposits of the Pacific coastal plain. When the whitefly struck in the mid-1960s and world prices soured, many small and medium-sized growers went bankrupt, and the banks became reluctant to lend money for investment in cotton except to the very largest growers, who controlled the best lands. Only in the 1970s did cotton profits improve sufficiently to attract enough capital to reach the peak production levels of the mid-1960s; then, once again, small and medium-sized growers swarmed into cotton, only to be driven out yet again in the bust years of the early 1980s.

The Cotton Landlords

Before cotton, cash rental was not even a possibility for most large landholders along the Pacific strip, but with the infusion of cash and credit that cotton brought, cash rentals became widespread. As early as 1952 the Honduran census registered that half of the cotton land harvested in the country had been rented for cash, and the Nicaraguan census of 1963 shows that 56 percent of the land rented for cash in all of Nicaragua was located in Chinandega and León, the two major cotton-producing departments.[27] The Guatemalan and Salvadoran censuses also reveal the phenomenon of cash rentals on large plots of land, an unusual phenomenon found only in the zones where cotton was raised. In Guatemala, for example, cash rentals are rare in rest of the country for farms exceeding 112 acres, but the 1964 census indicates that half the land area rented in Escuintla and two-thirds of the land area rented in Retalhuleu, the two most important cotton departments where almost 90 percent of the cotton was being grown, were on farms larger than 112 acres.[28] The 1971 Salvadoran census shows that one-third of the land area planted in cotton that year was rented for cash. Four-fifths of the rental land was on farms larger than 123 acres, and half of it appeared on thirty-three farms each larger than 494 acres.[29]

The opportunity for landowners to rent large blocks of cropland for cash spread with the building of the Pacific coastal highway. The Salvadoran peasants interviewed by Satterthwaite claimed that their landlords began to demand cash payments, as opposed to the traditional payments in corn, as sections of the littoral highway were completed. With parts of the highway finished, Satterthwaite reports that Salvadoran landlords along it could roughly double their earnings per acre by renting for cash to cotton growers, and those blessed with inheritance of prime land stood the chance of tripling their earnings, without even taking the initiative of becoming growers themselves.[30]

The spread of cash rentals did not stop with national boundaries. The Honduran section of the Pan American Highway runs through the middle of the Pacific coastal plain of Honduras. Before the mid-1960s few Honduran landowners actually engaged in cotton growing. Instead, they rented (or sold) their lands to aggressive Salvadoran growers who extended their operations into Honduras. Salvadoran growers used the highway in transporting their equipment and their labor force into Honduras, and at harvest time the highway was used once more in transporting the crop back to the Salvadoran Cotton Cooperative for ginning. To a lesser degree the same process was taking place on the portion of the strip bordering Nicaragua, as cotton growers from neighboring Chinandega began renting or buying land over the border in Honduras. For Honduran landowners, cotton meant a rapid increase in rental income. Robert White estimates that the cash value of rentals per acre more than doubled with the advent of cotton in coastal Honduras, and for landlords with prime land these values quadrupled.[31]

The landlord's take in the cotton bonanza was a more steady source of income than the grower's profits, because the grower had to pay cash in advance for the right to plant. In this way, all the risk was shifted to the growers and their creditors. As the cotton boom spread and the demand for cotton land increased, rental rates were bid up. Joseph Stevenson reports that cotton acreage in El Salvador, which rented for $20 to $30 an acre in 1954–55, increased in value to $25 and $35 an acre by 1963–64, and Honduran cotton rents were driven up from $12 an acre in 1960–61 to $20 an acre in 1963–64. In the latter half of the 1960s growers' profits were hit by unprecedented insect invasions, declining soil fertility, bad weather, and softening world cotton prices. Many growers went bankrupt, cotton acreage dropped, and the landlords that still rented to growers had to lower their rates. In Nicaragua landlords rented forty thousand fewer acres to cotton growers in 1969–70 than in 1966–67, and the entire structure of rental rates declined.[32] When growers' profits climbed once more in the early 1970s, so too did landlords'.[33] The inflation of the middle 1970s and the resumption of the cotton boom once again bid up rents for cotton land all along the Pacific coastal plain.[34]

Cotton Gins

For cotton to be sold on the world market it must first be cleaned of seeds and trash and packed into bales of standard size for shipment. Through investment in ginning equipment, profits can be made in several ways. An industrial profit can be earned on the wage labor hired to operate the gin, but ginning companies also have the opportunity, by virtue of their middle role between growers and export houses, to earn merchant and finance profits. Many of the ginning companies purchase cotton in advance from growers, paying a low price compared to the futures price they can in turn obtain from the export houses. In Nicaragua during the 1960s one-third to one-half of the crop was purchased from growers in advance, especially from the smaller growers, who had a more difficult time obtaining production loans from the banking system.[35]

The industrial profits from ginning of cotton were much more reliable than those from growing it. By charging the grower a flat ginning fee per bale, the ginning company removed itself from risks associated with fluctuations in the world price or input-cost fluctuations.[36] The risk in ginning depended primarily on fluctuations in the volume of cotton harvested.[37] Typically, if a gin could operate at a rate of ten thousand bales or more in a season, the large fixed costs of plant and equipment could be spread over enough output to lower the unit costs to a profit-earning level. The number of cotton gins and their locations closely followed the expansion or contraction of the cotton harvested. By 1962–63 there were sixty gins processing cotton along the Pacific strip, more than triple the number operating a decade earlier.[38] During the late 1960s, as cotton production dropped, gins located in marginal cotton-growing areas had to dismantle and move to the prime cotton zones or shut down completely. Six gins were forced out of business in Nicaragua between 1966–67 and the early 1970s, and the gins located in Matagalpa and Rivas, two marginal cotton zones, went out of business at that time.[39]

Despite the risks of a precipitous decline in the cotton harvest, handsome profits could be earned in the ginning business. Very early on, large growers throughout Central America recognized the profit potential in the ginning phase and either grouped together in cooperatives to lower their ginning costs or invested in private ginning companies to tap a share of those profits directly. After 1940 all of El Salvador's ginning was done through the Cotton Cooperative, a group dominated from the start by El Salvador's largest cotton growers. The cooperative has been successful in offering growers the lowest ginning fees in Central America, thereby passing on some of the industrial profits to the growers. In Guatemala the first cotton-growers' association was established in 1953 so that members could "free themselves from excessive ginning costs."[40] By 1962–63 there were three cotton cooperatives controlling eleven gins in Guatemala; ten gins were privately owned, with large portions of their stock owned by the six largest growers in the country. In Honduras all cotton was sent to the Salvadoran Cotton Cooperative to be ginned until 1957, when the first gin was set up in Tegucigalpa by the government development bank;[41] today all of Honduran cotton is ginned by the Cotton Cooperative in San Lorenzo on the Pacific strip. In Nicaragua ginning was primarily the business of privately owned ginning companies, whose stock was held either directly by large growers or by the bank owned by the large growers, Banco Nicaraguense (BANIC).[42]

Investment in ginning companies was a way for large growers to diversify their earnings from the risky activity of growing. It also enabled them to earn merchant and financial profits from the small growers who sold them cotton at a reduced rate in return for advances on the crop. Alternatively, cooperative ginning companies provided a way for participating growers to prevent some of the customary drainage of wealth by privately owned gins.

The Cotton-Export Houses

Much of the world's cotton trade is channeled through large-volume cotton merchant houses, many of them operating out of centers of cotton commerce in the United States. As the cotton trade grew in Central America, local agencies representing these larger houses began to operate out of the cotton ports and commercial centers of the Pacific strip. Stevenson reported that in the early 1960s in Guatemala, most of the export trade was handled by local cotton merchants, "many of whom represent U.S. firms." The largest six growers in Guatemala (responsible for 30 percent of the crop in 1962–63) sold their crop directly to these merchant houses; 60 percent of the crop was sold to the merchant houses by the three grower cooperatives, and the remaining 10 percent was sold directly to the merchants by other independent growers.[43] During the early stages of the cotton boom in El Salvador, similar merchant houses began operating, but the relative volume of their business declined as the Cotton Cooperative increasingly by-passed the merchants, selling the cotton directly to import houses in Japan and Western Europe and thereby preventing a drainage of grower profits into the hands of the export merchants.[44] At first all of Honduras's cotton exports were marketed through the El Salvador Cotton Cooperative, but by 1961–62 a single, private export house located in Honduras was buying all of the cotton from the Honduran Cotton Cooperative.[45]

Nine-tenths of the cotton exported from Nicaragua in the early 1960s was handled by a dozen or so privately owned merchant houses.[46] A look at a list of the sixteen principal export houses of Nicaragua in 1972–73 reveals that half of them were agent representatives of U.S. firms (three from Dallas, two from Memphis, one from Montgomery, one from San Francisco, and one without a city designated). Two were connected to Japanese import houses (Mitsui and Toyoshima), one was affiliated with a German import house (F. A. Kumpers), one was a representative of a Mexico City cotton merchant house, and one represented a cotton merchant house incorporated in Panama. Only three of Nicaragua's sixteen export houses were not affiliated with larger multinational trading companies.[47]

The world marketing channels that linked cotton-growing regions with the textile mills of Europe and Asia were not easily broken into by newcomers because large buyers preferred not to have production runs disrupted by temporary shortfalls. Large merchant operations with affiliates in growing zones around the world could be relied on to supply the regular needs of the large buyers; small, independent houses were therefore at a commercial disadvantage. Likewise, affiliates of large houses with numerous sales outlets could better guarantee growers a market during years when the world market became glutted with cotton. In Central America a portion of the cotton wealth was accordingly siphoned off each year to the corporations that dominated these marketing channels. Large growers and local merchants could sometimes recoup a portion of this wealth by buying stock in the local affiliate of the international marketing corporation. Only in El Salvador, however, were the growers able to prevent the drainage by having the Cotton Cooperative directly market the country's cotton exports.

The Suppliers of the Cotton Boom

As cotton acreage expanded, so too did the sales of modern agribusiness. Tractor dealerships, seed companies, fertilizer distributors, airplane spraying companies, gasoline/diesel stations, parts-supply houses, and insecticide companies sprang up along the highways of the Pacific coastal plain to service the growing cotton economy. Of all the products and services that cotton cultivation demanded, the greatest business opportunities were generated for the insecticide companies and the fertilizer distributors.

The demand for insecticides and fertilizers grew at a faster rate than the expansion of cotton acreage. After years of heavy insecticide applications, almost every major cotton pest had developed populations resistant to DDT, toxaphene, and related compounds, and new pests appeared yearly. The response of cotton growers was simple: either increase the dosage per acre or try out the latest product recommended by the insecticide company. Similarly, after five years of growing cotton on the same land, yields declined. The response of growers was predictable: pump in more chemical fertilizer. So, with time, the fortunes of the insecticide and fertilizer companies grew.

A cost survey by the National Bank of Nicaragua found that in 1964–65 growers spent 40 percent more on insecticides and 50 percent more on fertilizers for each acre of cotton cultivated than they had in 1962–63. The heavier applications occurred at a time when insecticide and fertilizer prices were both declining.[48] Nonetheless, heavier applications per acre and larger areas cultivated far outweighed the impact of price reductions. In two years insecticide businesses doubled their sales to Nicaraguan growers, from around $5.5 million in 1962–63 to $11 million in 1964–65, and fertilizer businesses increased their sales from $1.9 million to $4.2 million over the same period. When cotton acreage collapsed in the late 1960s, so did the sales of the fertilizer and pesticide companies, but by the early 1970s these businesses had recovered nearly to the peak levels of the mid-1960s.[49] The same boom-and-bust trend in sales coincided with the expansion, contraction, and recovery of cotton acreage in El Salvador and Guatemala, but all indications point to even heavier applications per acre in these two other major cotton countries.

In the 1970s, when oil prices exploded and the cotton boom resumed, insecticide and fertilizer expenditures did so as well. In 1972–73 the big three cotton producers were spending around $38 million on insecticides. A year later the bill approached $60 million, and by 1974–75 sales of insecticides to cotton growers topped $107 million. Additional oil-price increases and expansion of cotton acreage in the late 1970s boosted Central American insecticide sales to $145 million, and fertilizer sales rose almost as dramatically.[50]

The market for insecticides and fertilizers was controlled by a handful of multinational corporations. At first, the business was conducted as an ordinary merchandising operation. The prepackaged insecticides or fertilizers were imported and sold to growers. But during the 1950s investors in Central America became more successful in pressuring their governments to adopt protective tariffs. Insecticide and fertilizer companies began to enjoy the benefits of tariff protection on the final product without having to pay any tariff on intermediate inputs or imported raw materials. Therefore, an outlet of Monsanto could import the ingredients and packaging materials duty free from the plant in Saint Louis, have workers in León, Nicaragua, mix and package the ingredients, and then sell the final product at an inflated price, protected from world competition by the tariff on premixed insecticides.

With increasingly effective protection, companies did indeed move toward mixing and packaging in Central America.[51] In 1952 insecticide distributors in Nicaragua mixed only 25 percent of the insecticide sold that year to growers. By 1955, 40 percent was being mixed locally, and by 1959 the proportion mixed locally was 98 percent.[52] The move toward mixing and packaging in Central America continued in the 1960s with the formation of the Central American Common Market. Effective tariff protection was extended around the entire five country area, and a company that mixed a product in Nicaragua could sell it at the protected price in neighboring Honduras without having to pay a tariff to the Honduran government at the border.

Profits for the insecticide and fertilizer companies came from three sources. An ordinary merchant profit was earned on sales, an industrial profit was earned from the hiring of workers to mix and package the compounds, and an excess profit was earned owing to the favorable tariff structures. The source of the excess profit came not from the mixing and marketing of the compounds but from the activity of cotton growing. Profits of growers were transferred to the agribusiness supply houses because of the artificially high prices permitted by protective tariffs.

Companies whose earnings in Central America have been most closely connected with supplying cotton inputs are listed in Table A-5 in the appendix. Several corporations that made money from the cotton boom are omitted from the list because their earnings were so diversified. Major oil companies, for example, do not appear on the list, although they have supplied fuels and lubricants for tractors, trucks, and airplanes (ranking after pesticides and fertilizers in cash outlay by cotton growers), and they have supplied a wide variety of agricultural chemicals from their petrochemical divisions in Central America.[53] Major chemical companies, like DuPont, Dow Chemical, and American Cyanamid, do not appear on the list because their earnings in

Central America have not been primarily linked to cotton, even though they do supply some agricultural chemicals. Another multinational corporation that has been omitted because of its diversified investments in the region is Bayer. Well known throughout the world for aspirin, Bayer also supplies Nicaraguan growers with insecticides. The companies that have been listed earn their profits primarily from the production and sale of agricultural chemicals, and many appear on *Fortune*'s list of the five hundred largest firms. Some retain complete ownership and control over their Central American subsidiaries, but many formed joint ventures with local investors and allow these investors to share in the profits.

In the short run the fortunes of the agribusiness supply houses may be made at the expense of the growers. When pests descend upon the cottonfields, business picks up at the Monsanto outlet. But in the long run these companies' profits are tied to the same forces that influence the profits of growers. Yields per acre must be kept above the world average, and wages must be held down if the industry is to survive the vagaries of the world cotton market.

Banks and the Cotton Boom

Cotton's dependence on large input purchases and its short crop cycle have produced opportunities for financial intermediaries to tap a portion of the cotton wealth. The cash needs of the various participants in the cotton economy fluctuate wildly over the course of a year, producing great bulges in the supply and demand for loanable funds in both local currency and foreign exchange.

During May and June there is a heavy demand for foreign exchange as inventories of fertilizer, seed, and diesel fuel are rebuilt in anticipation of the planting season, and the demand for foreign exchange further swells in anticipation of insecticide sales. The foreign exchange drained during cultivation is not replenished until after the harvest, when there is a huge inflow of foreign exchange from the sale of the crop. Between the withdrawal of cotton inputs from the world system and the time when the final product, laden with the value added from Central America, is injected back into the world system, there emerges a need for dollar financing. This need places holders of dollars in a position to collect a portion of the value added in production in the form of interest payments on dollar loans. Likewise, at every step where a transaction in domestic currency takes place, from the purchase of seed on credit to the advance sale of the crop to the ginning company, there emerges the possibility of collection of a portion of the cotton wealth in the form of interest. The cotton boom has thus spawned not only input supply houses, growers, ginning companies, and export houses, but also banks.

Initially, government banks, with backing from multilateral lending agencies in Washington, took an active role in removing the financial obstacles to the development of cotton as a viable export crop. But once the cotton boom began, private banks rushed into the cotton-finance business.

In Guatemala following the CIA overthrow of the Arbenz regime in 1954, the new government hastened the shift to private-sector finance not only by providing private banks with favorable rediscounts for cotton loans but also by inviting foreign banks to participate in the cotton bonanza. In 1958 the Banco del Agro, a bank owned by Guatemalan nationals, was established to serve the large agriculturalist, and four years later the Bank of America began collecting interest from cotton and other expanding sectors.

In El Salvador lending to cotton growers was promoted by government loans to existing private banks and the Cotton Cooperative. As opportunities in cotton and other activities expanded in the 1950s, three new private banks were set up by Salvadoran nationals (two in 1955 and one in 1957).

Even in Nicaragua, where the government-owned Banco Nacional continued to be the most important lender to cotton growers, three new private banks formed in the early 1950s, each of them jointly owned by large international banks and prominent members of the Nicaraguan agricultural elite.[54] Major cotton growers were principal shareholders of these banks and served on their boards of directors. In fact, the Banco Nicaraguense (BANIC) was almost exclusively a cotton growers' bank.

Lending to cotton growers had its risks. In the late 1960s, when low cotton prices and insect damage bankrupted growers, private banks suffered losses. Some of them, however, were able to transfer problem loans to the government development banks that had stimulated cotton finance in the 1950s.

Vegetable-Oil Factories and Textile Mills

The cotton boom provided business opportunities for domestic industries involved in producing by products from cotton, for a local supply of cottonseed and cotton lint was made available at prices that did not include port fees, export taxes, and the costs of long-distance transport.

The processing of cooking oils and margarine experienced some expansion in the 1950s, but in the 1960s, with the rapid expansion of a regional market for wage goods,[55] domestic investors and multinational corporations invested in this branch of food processing. Among the most important foreign investors to claim a share of this lucrative new market were the international fruit companies. By the middle and late 1960s three fruit companies had acquired oil-processing plants in the region. Castle and Cooke bought Industria Aceitera of Honduras in 1965, and about the same time Standard Brands purchased similar factories in Guatemala, Nicaragua, and Costa Rica. United Brands joined the others by setting up margarine factories in Honduras (1968) and Guatemala (1973), and by acquiring 77 percent of an already established cooking-oil factory in Nicaragua.

As discussed in Chapter One, the domestic textile industry was an important buyer of Central American cotton, and the mills of San Salvador and Guatemala City competed vigorously in the regional market when free trade was introduced with the foundation of the Central American Common Market in the 1960s. The fortunes from the rapidly expanding textile industry, unlike those from vegetable-oil processing, were closely held in Central American hands. Nevertheless, some foreign investors did penetrate the textile business. A French firm and a Japanese firm established plants in El Salvador; Bemis, a large U.S. firm, built mills to produce sacks and other textile products in Honduras and Nicaragua; and Bartlett Collins, another U.S.-based multinational, built a mill in Costa Rica.[56]

Neither the vegetable-oil business nor the textile mills relied exclusively on the cotton economy for raw materials. The fruit companies began cultivating African oil palm as an alternative to cottonseed, and the textile mills imported synthetic fibers to blend with domestically produced cotton. Nevertheless, by the late 1960s virtually all of the cottonseed produced in the region was ending up in the frying pans or the butter dishes of Central American households, and the textile mills were absorbing one tenth of the lint grown on the Pacific coastal plain.

In contrast to the other activities of the cotton economy, however, the profits of the textile mills and the vegetable-oil factories varied inversely with the world price of lint or cottonseed. When growers, agribusiness supply houses, landlords, gins, and export houses were pleased with high world prices of cotton, the textile manufacturers and margarine producers complained. The opposite occurred when world prices of lint and cottonseed sank. Some investors, however, were able to benefit regardless of the whims of the market.

Cotton and the Cotton Elite

Numerous business opportunities emerged with the cotton boom. The profits taken by suppliers, growers, ginners, and exporters, the rents collected by landlords, and the interest claimed by banks all became tied to the world cotton market. Along with these business opportunities came a host of new jobs for tractor drivers, labor contractors, mechanics, gin operators, foremen, agronomists, airplane pilots, chemists, accountants, truckers, salespeople, managers, and other skilled workers. Above the bustling activity of the coastal plain, however, arose a group of investors whose origin as an elite predates the emergence of cotton.

Initially, as noted above, the largest growers in Central America made their profits from cotton by turning portions of their family haciendas into cottonfields. As fortunes from cotton growing were created, members of the largegrower group proved flexible in dealing with government agencies, private and public banks, and multinational corporations. This group perceived any phase of the cotton economy where profits were to be made and invested accordingly. Thus, members of the group became principal stockholders and sat on boards of directors of companies connected with various aspects of the cotton economy.

In Nicaragua the cotton elite protected itself from the volatility involved in growing cotton by forming financial institutions like BANIC and the smaller Financiera de Occidente (in León).[57] In turn, these financial institutions invested not only in the various phases of the cotton economy but also in other sectors of the larger economy.

BANIC, for example, got its start from the flush of cotton earnings around the time of the Korean War. Of the ten principal directors of this financial group only three were not from families with large cotton holdings. BANIC's investments included an agricultural chemicals company (EXPASA Química), three cotton-export houses (EXPASA, Desmotadora "La Virgen" [also a ginning company], and Industriales Nacionales Agricolas), a ginning and cotton-services complex (Central de Algodoneros), a textile corporation (FABRITEX), a cottonseed-meal plant (GEMINA), a cottonseed-oil complex (AGROSA), a machinery and transport equipment company (VIMSA), and stock in a chemical group holding company (INQUISA) that, in turn, held stock of a turpentine company (ATCHEMCO), a chlorine manufacturer (PENNSALT), and a company that combined turpentine and chlorine to form the insecticide toxaphene (HERCASA).[58] Other major cotton-growing families owned ginning and servicing companies outright, formed joint ventures with multinational agribusiness supply companies, and invested in other financial groups.

In Guatemala the Alejos family, whose ownership of coffee farms and coastal haciendas dates back to the 1880s, saw the opportunities in cotton very early and became major growers. Family members also invested heavily in ginning companies (Desmotadora Champérico, Desmotadora Nueva Linda, Algodonera Retalteca), and they owned a vegetable-oil factory (Aceites Esenciales). Similarly, the Aycinena family, whose vast holdings date back to the colonial period, when indigo was Guatemala's major export, and who planted coffee in the late nineteenth century, invested in cotton growing and in two cotton-ginning companies: Desmotadora Horqueta and Algodonera Retalteca. The Herrera family, who became major coffee growers in the late nineteenth century and who acquired cattle and sugar estates along the coastal plain long before the cotton boom, further expanded their wealth by turning extensive cattle haciendas into cottonfields in the 1950s and 1960s. The Herrera family has invested in almost every sphere of the Guatemalan economy, including cotton textile mills and the Banco del Agro. In Guatemala some of the cotton elite derived their wealth from manufacturing and diversified their investments when the cotton boom hit. The Ibargüen family started the first modern textile factory in Guatemala in 1884 near Quetzaltenango. In the 1950s and 1960s the Ibargüens not only expanded their textile investments but also acquired a fertilizer factory, two cotton gins, and stock in the Algodonera Guatemalteca. The Kong family initially owned a soap and candle factory in 1911, but by the 1960s family members served on the board of the Desmotadora del Sur, a large ginning company, and had acquired a cottonseed-oil complex in Escuintla. Similarly, the Zimeri, who initially established a weaving factory in the 1930s, became owners of numerous yarn and textile mills in the 1950s and 1960s and have invested in cotton-ginning and vegetable-oil companies.[59]

The Salvadoran cotton elite has been more successful than the elites of other countries in avoiding the sharing of cotton profits with multinational corporations. This success has partially resulted from the Cotton Cooperative, which has maintained a monopoly on the marketing and ginning of Salvadoran cotton since the 1940s, thereby preventing profits from falling into the hands of foreign export houses and ginning companies. In Guatemala the California-based Bank of America has been able to drain a portion of cotton earnings through its collection of interest on cotton loans, but in El Salvador cotton lending has been dominated by the Cotton Cooperative and several private-sector banks, which, until recently, were owned by members of the cotton elite and other members of the Salvadoran oligarchy.

A list of Salvadoran families with a thousand bales or more of cotton harvested in 1972–73 (Table A-6 in the appendix) reveals that the cotton elite was for the most part a landholding elite with origins in previous export booms. Particularly noticeable is a prevalence of English, German, and Italian surnames, along with a sprinkling of Spanish surnames, a result of the tradition established in the nineteenth century of welcoming enterprising foreigners from Europe and North America to help develop the country's export trade. The majority of the top cotton-growing families in El Salvador fall within the top thirty land-owning families, and all of those on the list, with the exception of Wright and Nottebohm, fall within the top fifty coffee-exporting families.[60] Many, including the Wrights and Nottebohms, have sugar estates, and five of those on the list have large cattle ranches. At least half of these large cotton grower families have diversified their investments in cotton by acquiring stock in textile, fertilizer, seed, or insecticide companies. Most of those on the list have still other other industrial and commercial investments.[61]

As shown above, cotton growers rely heavily on the availability of credit. In El Salvador the cotton elite, because of its extensive investments in financial institutions, has exercised considerable control over the availability of credit. With the exception of the Dalton family, all of those listed in Table A-6 were primary stockholders of El Salvador's commercial banks (ten of them had stock in the Banco Cuscatlán) in the late 1960s and early 1970s, and most of them had family-related financial corporations. Members of this elite not only owned the banks, so that they were entitled to collect dividends on bank stock, but also played active roles in bank management. Thus, the Guirola bank, Banco Salvadoreño, had Carlos A. Guirola as its president in the early 1970s. The president of the Banco de Comercio was Miguel Dueñas; the president of the Banco Cuscatlán was Roberto Hill. All of these are on the list of prominent cotton growers (Table A-6).

At the top of the credit pyramid in El Salvador is the Central Reserve Bank (Banco Central de Reserva). As we have seen, public funds from this state institution were lent to the Cotton Cooperative and to commercial banks at a subsidized rate for the purpose of promoting cotton, an arrangement that provided Salvadoran growers with some of the lowest borrowing rates in the region. In the early 1970s, of the six private-sector directors of the Banco Central de Reserva, three were major cotton growers: Hans Homberger, Julio C. Salaverría, and Prudencio Llach.

The Salvadoran family whose fortunes have been most closely associated with cotton appears at the top of the grower list. In 1972–73 the Wright family achieved a harvest representing 7 percent of Salvadoran cotton exports that season, nearly twice the size of the harvest of the second-most-important grower group, the Salaverrías. The basis of the Wrights' wealth is their approximately ten thousand acres of land, including the Hacienda La Carrera, where the cotton fortune began. The Wrights' major family holding company is called Rait, S.A., the Spanish pronunciation of the English surname. Rait, S.A., holds one-fourth of the stock of the textile company Textilera del Pacifico, owned jointly with other cotton-grower families. Other industrial holdings include stock in Insecticidas de El Salvador, an insecticide company, and Productos Agroquímicas de Centroamérica, producer of agricultural chemicals. The family has a financial investment company, Raul Avila Inversiones, and holds stock in the Banco Cuscatlán, along with numerous investments in transportation and commerce. In the early 1970s Juan T. Wright Alcaine, president and manager of Rait, S.A., not only represented the family's private holdings in various other companies but also represented the family's interests in "cooperative," public enterprise. In 1972 three of the five board members of the Cotton Cooperative were from major grower families, and the president of the board was Juan T. Wright Alcaine.[62]

Ecological Consequences of Cotton

The cotton boom was proof of man's ability to control nature through the purchase of modern imported technologies. In the short run, practically any problem confronting the grower could be solved with the appropriate chemical mix or mechanical device. In the long run, however, nature proved less manageable. The extension of the cotton economy soon overstretched the bounds of the coastal ecology, depleting the rich soils, encouraging the growth of harmful insects, and contaminating the air, land, and water of the coastal plain.

The stress on the soil from cotton is particularly severe. Although landlords realize quick profits from one-year cash rentals, this practice leads to land abuse. Furthermore, the law requires that all growers clear the fields of stalks immediately after harvest and plow them under to destroy a potential breeding ground for cotton pests. This practice helps control insects, but it leaves the light, volcanic soils vulnerable to wind erosion for the remainder of the dry season. With the cotton boom, dust storms began to appear along the coastal plain.[63]

The greatest destruction of the soil, however, does not occur until the rainy season. Growers need to be ready to plant during the lull in the rainy season in July or August; the timing of the sowing of seed makes a great difference to the health of the cotton stand later on. The fields are plowed at the end of the dry season in February, March, or early April so that little extra soil preparation will be needed when the rains let up four months later. Year after year some of the best soils of the region are exposed to the heavy thunderstorms of May and June. Rivers during the rainy season become thick with silt from the fields. Although growers know that the planting of leguminous cover at the beginning of the rainy season reduces erosion, the costs of long-run prevention are not likely to be borne by short-term renters, and growers of all types have been reluctant to run the risk of missing the best time to plant.[64]

Finally, successive plantings of cotton on the same plot can seriously deplete nitrogen (in which the soils of the coastal plain tend to be relatively deficient), phosphorus, and other nutrients. In analyzing the Guatemalan cotton boom in the 1960s, Adams concludes that cotton "is currently bringing important agricultural lands to a state of ruin."[65]

The most dramatic ecological change along the coastal plain, however, was generated by the protracted use of modern insecticides. Until recently, when the escalation of pesticide prices forced growers to modify their thinking, they followed a strategy of total eradication of cotton pests. In the 1950s and early 1960s increased yields were achieved by growers who adopted this strategy and laid out the cash for DDT and other chlorinated insecticides. The short-run success of the total-eradication strategy, however, turned into a long-run disaster, for two reasons. First, the insecticides were indiscriminate: they killed not only cotton pests but also the natural enemies of cotton pests. The removal of these natural checks from the environment meant that the number of economically important cotton pests increased with each growing season. Before 1950 there were only two important pests with which Nicaraguan growers had to contend; fifteen years later there were nine; today there are fourteen.[66] Second, total eradication of an insect species is close to impossible because mutant strains within a species will be immune to the insecticide. It is not cost effective for growers to apply the insecticide to adjacent fields or woodlots. The genes of the insecticide-resistant survivors of the sprayed fields rapidly spread through the larger population that escapes the spraying, and over the years a more resilient strain of the original pest evolves.

In response to continuing problems, chemical companies urged growers to apply larger doses of more toxic mixes. When the whitefly and other pests played havoc with grower profits after 1965, chemical companies began promoting organophosphate compounds. By the early 1970s it is estimated that cotton growers in Central America were dumping more than forty pounds of insecticides on an acre of cotton, and for Guatemala in 1974–75 the average exceeded seventy pounds an acre.[67]

After years of insect evolution in an insecticide-laden environment, others along the coastal plain were affected besides the cotton growers. Natural enemies of corn and bean pests were killed off by the cotton poison, and there were infestations of secondary pests in nearby corn and bean fields. The incidence of malaria showed a dramatic drop during the early years of the cotton boom,[68] but strains of DDT-resistant anopheles mosquitoes began to appear, making malaria control through insecticide application more and more costly for governments.[69]

Further, the insecticides dumped on the cottonfields became part of the material composition of plants and animals inhabiting the coastal plain and the coastal waters. Chlorinated compounds decompose slowly and they are fat soluble, so that they are highly adept at climbing the food chain. A 1974–76 study of the coastal ecology by the Instituto Centroamericano de Investigación y Technología Industrial (ICAITI) found DDT and other chlorinated compounds in samples of well water and river water. Samples of pasture grass, corn, beans, rice, sorghum, fruits, and other plant life revealed higher concentrations of the toxic substances than were present in the water samples. The study also found that samples of fish and shrimp taken off the shores of major cotton districts were more contaminated than samples taken from other waters.[70]

In Guatemala the researchers sampled milk of dairy cows and fatty tissue of beef cattle and found that the three major cotton departments had extremely high concentrations of DDT in both categories.[71] The high concentrations of DDT in beef fat and milk are not surprising considering that in Guatemala, and elsewhere along the coastal plain, less fertile soils adjacent to cottonfields are frequently used for pasture, so the water supplies, the grass, and the animals themselves sometimes get doused along with the cotton plants. In Guatemala, especially, many of the large cotton growers are major cattlemen as well. Spray from their own crop dusters has resulted in a loss of profits when their beef is returned to Central America stamped "contaminated" by the USDA.

The long-range impact of chlorinated insecticides on human health is not fully understood, but the highest concentration of these substances is found deposited in human fat tissue. In 1975–76 the ICAITI study team found DDT levels in human adipose tissue to be twice as high in the cotton zones as in other areas of the three major cotton producing countries; in Honduras, where cotton is least important, the samples showed significantly lower DDT levels than in El Salvador, Guatemala, and Nicaragua, where the cotton boom hit much harder.

The long-run consequences for human health may not be understood, but there is yearly proof that large doses of cotton poison make people sick. From 1972 through 1974 an average of 4,000 cases of cotton poisoning were reported each year in Central America, cases that resulted in an average of 13 deaths a year.[72] These estimates are very low because they count only those who entered health clinics. The poor typically cannot afford these clinics, and they tend to avoid them except in extreme cases. In a study of 243 cases of insecticide poisoning in Nicaragua in 1973, more than half the victims were between sixteen and twenty-five years old (the largest age group for cotton workers), 90 percent were men, and 70 percent were day laborers.[73] The chlorinated compounds require large doses to be immediately noticeable, and they tend to attack the digestive system, whereas small doses of organophosphates can damage the central nervous system. In the late 1960s in Nicaragua, when the shift to organophosphates began, there was an epidemic of poisonings, probably owing to a lack of understanding of the immediate effects. In 1968–69 several hundred people died there from organophosphate poisoning.[74]

Summary

The wealth generated by the cotton boom was divided among growers, landlords, bankers, ginners, exporters, suppliers of inputs, textile manufacturers, and vegetable-oil processors. Some of the beneficiaries were multinational corporations and some were urban professionals, but the greatest concentration of wealth went to several dozen families who were already wealthy before the cotton boom and who were in a position to benefit from cotton because they owned large haciendas along the coastal plain. When roads were built through their properties, the best lands were planted in cotton. Some of the earnings from cotton growing were invested in other phases of the cotton economy, and so the families with the largest cotton holdings also came to own gins, insecticide dealerships, textile mills, vegetable-oil factories, financial corporations, and other related companies. Successive years of investing in cotton, however, led to declining profits for the investors themselves as soils were depleted and insecticides poisoned the coastal ecology.

3. Cotton and the Common Man

From several thousand acres to more than a million, cotton came to claim the best farmland along the Pacific strip, bringing with it the most advanced applications of science and technology. We have seen how landlords, growers, insecticide companies, tractor dealerships, ginning companies, export houses, and banks responded to the fresh opportunities of the cotton economy. But how did this remarkable boom affect the day to day lives of the rural majority?

The Cotton Boom and the Opening of Fresh Cropland

Before cotton became a viable export crop, portions of the Pacific lowlands had already been settled by peasants who had come down from the crowded highlands in search of land. Great sections of the strip, however, were still in forests or unimproved rangeland. The lands nearest the sea were considered by the peasants to be ridden with malaria and other tropical diseases, and large landowners who wanted to develop their haciendas commercially sometimes found it difficult to attract peasants to the area because of its reputation as bad for the health.[1]

The cotton boom, however, brought DDT and government-sponsored malaria-control programs that made the zone, for a while, at least, more desirable to peasant colonizers. The boom brought roads that opened up previously inaccessible lands. It injected cash into the coastal economy, placing speculative pressures on existing cropland and creating an incentive for the development of fresh cropland.

All up and down the coastal plain, new lands were drawn into cultivation. In the eight most important cotton-producing *municipios* of Guatemala, 52,000 acres of fresh cropland were created between 1950 and 1963–64. In the eight most important cotton-producing *municipios* of El Salvador, at least 70,000 acres of cropland were developed between 1950–51 and 1970–71. In Nicaragua the land area devoted to seasonal crops doubled in the two most important cotton producing departments between 1952 and 1962.[2]

The evidence suggests that a portion of the new cropland was carved from the forest, but this pattern of change in land use was not evenly distributed. By most accounts, the strongest conversion from forest to cottonfield occurred along portions of the coastal plain in Guatemala. A 1963 USDA report includes a photograph of a cotton plantation in coastal Guatemala, with the caption reading: "Scene near Tiquisate, Guatemala, illustrates conquest of jungle for cotton culture. Fields of cotton recently cleared reach from jungle in background up to gins."[3] Guatemala's two agricultural censuses support the view presented in the Tiquisate photograph; between 1950 and 1963 Guatemala's eight most important cotton-producing *municipios* lost some 380,000 acres of forest.[4] The census data suggest that the bulk of this forest reserve (220,000 acres) was turned into pasture, but the best tracts were converted into cottonfields.

The sections of the coastal plain that became El Salvador's cotton belt were already in an advanced stage of deforestation by the early 1950s. According to the first agricultural census, only one-fifth of the farm area surveyed was still in forest in the eight *municipios* where cotton became king. After two decades of commercial development almost no forest cover was left, and a significant portion of the land that had been in pasture in 1950–51 was in cotton and other commercial crops by 1970–71.[5] A geographer who compared aerial photographs of the coastal plain taken in 1949 and 1965 noted the same process picked up by the censuses and observed that by 1965 "nearly all of the forest was gone in all sections of the coast. The remaining forests were being cut into. Pasture had been greatly reduced and cropland had been extended to all areas not inundated along the mangrove swamps."[6]

The information available for the cotton zones of Honduras and Nicaragua shows that by the mid-1960s deforestation had reached the stage of coastal El Salvador a decade earlier. The five most important cotton-producing *municipios* of Honduras still had forest cover on about one-fifth of the area surveyed by the 1965–66 census.[7] In coastal Nicaragua the five most important cotton-producing *municipios* had one-fourth of the area still in forests by the time of the 1962–63 census, but in the most remote section of the cotton belt, to the far north, forest reserves still covered about two-fifths of the area surveyed.[8]

To the extent that cotton stimulated the felling of forests, it created fresh opportunities for landless peasants to gain temporary access to prime cropland for the cultivation of subsistence crops. While the most capital-rich cotton developers may have used bulldozers and other heavy equipment to clear the jungle quickly, it proved to be much cheaper to clear land in the traditional way: by turning land-hungry peasants into the area. After slashing and burning the forest cover, peasants were allowed to plant corn on the clearing for one or two seasons, time for the stumps to rot enough so that the land could be plowed with a tractor. At that time the peasants would have to move from the area to make way for cotton.

Peasants flowed in large numbers into sections of the coastal plain where forests were converted into cottonfields. In contrast, areas that had been deforested before the cotton boom experienced outflows of peasants when cotton was introduced.[9]

Cornfields to Cotton

Not all of the cottonfields took root on lands freshly carved from forests. Popular folklore and census data alike reveal that the first lands to become cottonfields had been worked as cropland long before cotton became profitable. Some of this established cropland was already producing export crops like bananas in Tiquisate, Guatemala, and sesame in Guatemala, El Salvador, and Nicaragua. The bulk of this land, however, was used for growing the number-one staple of the peasant diet: corn.

Just as the conversion of forest to cottonfields was uneven, so too was the transformation of cornfields into cottonfields. Before the cotton boom, peasants of Nicaragua referred to the band of rich earth located in the departments of León and Chinandega as *el granero* (the granary). The soils of *el granero* were of mythical reknown throughout the country. It was said that they could be planted year after year, two seasons in a row, and "they would not lose their force."

In 1947, when cotton claimed only a thousand acres of the coastal plain of Nicaragua, corn farmers in the department of Chinandega averaged 5 bushels per acre compared with average yields of 3.7 bushels per acre in the highland corn department of Matagalpa.[10] The *municipios* of Nicaragua with the highest corn yields in 1947 became the cotton belt in the 1950s.

During the 1950s and early 1960s the displacement of corn by cotton took place at a faster rate than the opening of new cropland, producing a relative and absolute decline of corn acreage as the cotton boom progressed along the Pacific. In 1952 one-fourth of the cropland of the coastal departments of León and Chinandega was already claimed by cotton,[11] and by 1958 cotton claimed two-fifths of the cropland, almost as much as the 128,000 acres still in corn.[12] By 1963 the cottonfields of León and Chinandega spread over 196,000 acres, claiming three-fifths of the land in annual crops and reducing corn to less than one-fifth of the available cropland.[13] In this fashion, El Viejo, the northernmost *municipio* of the Nicaraguan coastal plain was transformed from Nicaragua's second-most-important corn-producing *municipio* in the late 1940s (out of a total of 125 *municipios*) into the number-one cotton-producing *municipio* by the early 1960s, with 80 percent of its cropland in cotton and 20 percent of all the cotton in Nicaragua at that time.[14]

In coastal El Salvador cotton displaced corn, but not to the extreme degree that occurred further south in Nicaragua. Between 1948 and 1950–51, when the first agricultural census was taken, corn plantings dropped by more than 8,000 acres in El Salvador's eight most important cotton-producing *munici-pios*. By 1950–51 cotton already claimed more than 20 percent of the cropland, and corn 50 percent. Twenty years later corn had been reduced to a third of the cropland and cotton had expanded to more than one-half. El Salvador's experience was analogous to that of Nicaragua; the two largest corn-producing *municipios* of El Salvador in the early 1950s (San Miguel and Jiquilisco) were transformed into the two largest cotton producers by the early 1970s.[15]

In Guatemala the three coastal departments of Escuintla, Retalhuleu, and Suchitepequez, where most of Guatemala's cotton came to be raised, experienced an enormous increase in corn production at the time when cotton was expanding. The 66 percent expansion of corn output between 1950 and 1963 suggests at first glance that cotton did not displace corn. However, when the more detailed *municipio* data are examined, the pattern of cotton displacing corn appears much the same as elsewhere in Central America. In 1950 the 8 *municipios* (out of 178) that were destined to grow more than 90 percent of Guatemala's cotton a decade later, had some of the finest cornland in the country, achieving average yields of 50 to 100 percent more than the national average.[16] During the thirteen year span between the two censuses, total cropland in these eight *municipios* expanded by 52,000 acres, much of it coming from tropical forest. Despite this enormous increase in land under cultivation, cornland registered a decline of 25,000 acres; cotton expanded by 192,000 acres, commanding 70 percent of the zone's cropland by 1963–64.[17]

Cotton and Peasant Access to Land

The displacement by cotton of some of the best cornland in Central America might not have mattered much if the persons who ended up raising cotton were the ones who used to raise corn. The switch would have represented merely a purchase of corn for family consumption with the money from cotton sales. The switch to cotton, however, did something different. For corn producers along the strip, cotton became another word for eviction.

Before cotton became a profitable crop, landlords did well to have peasant families living on their haciendas. Peasants were a source of labor for cutting firewood, caring for the landlord's livestock, clearing land, putting up fences, and tending to the landlord's crops.

Before cotton, plows were drawn by oxen on the great haciendas of the coastal plain. Oxen required care and skill in handling, so that if a landlord were to raise cash crops on any scale, he needed to keep peasants who worked well with oxen and who would care for the beasts year round. Considering the large, permanent work force required by ox-drawn cultivation, and considering the preference of peasants for life in the highlands, where malaria and other tropical diseases were not so severe, landlords with haciendas along the Pacific sometimes suffered labor shortages. In order to attract and hold an adequate labor force, they usually allowed peasants access to small plots of land so that they could raise food crops for family consumption. Frequently they permitted peasants access to larger plots of land in return for a specified share of the crop, a few sacks of corn, or a number of days of labor on their own fields.

Sometimes peasants were able to secure access to land in ways that avoided direct day-to-day control by landlords. Sometimes the land they settled was already legally titled in the name of the owner of the nearest hacienda, but the lands were so difficult to reach that effective control by the landlord was not worth the trouble. In other areas the land was not yet legally titled, so that peasants were in effect squatting on national government lands. In yet other sections of the coastal plain, peasants over the years obtained access to cropland through what is called the "ejidal" system.[18] These were lands legally held by the township or municipality, which peasants were allowed to cultivate if they paid the municipality or township a small user fee, called a *cañon*.

The ways that peasants gained access to cornland before cotton varied greatly from one location to another, depending on the legacies of prior settlement, the timing and spacing of hacienda formation, and the particular histories of land struggles in the area. However, when the possibility of raising cotton on those lands pushed their market value up, the corn producers had to be moved one way or another. The logic set in motion by cotton was the same everywhere, regardless of the forms of land tenure that had evolved. In places where peasants had illegally squatted on lands that were to be opened to cotton, they were evicted, sometimes by force. Untitled lands lying near proposed roadways were quickly titled and brought under the control of cotton growers or others with privileged access to the land-titling institutions in the capital city. Where ejidal forms came in the path of the cottonfields, the rights were transferred from municipalities to private landlords through all sorts of trickery and manipulation. On private haciendas with lands suitable for cotton cultivation, access rights were switched from traditional forms like sharecrop or other in-kind rental payments to money rents paid in advance, rents too high for peasants to afford.

Reports from the cotton belt in Nicaragua and Honduras attest to the bitterness of the peasants who were robbed of ejidal lands. In the municipality of Chinandega, Nicaragua, peasant protests flared up in 1958 when large landowners attempted to force peasants out of an area by closing off the roads leading into it; the lands in question had been worked by peasants under ejidal arrangements granted by the municipality, which had received legal title to the lands from the national government in 1915. In 1958, peasants just fifteen miles down the road protested the illegitimate eviction from their lands, accusing the mayor of Posoltega of acquiring for his own private estate seventeen hundred acres of what the peasants considered to be municipal properties. Another twelve miles down the road, near León, tensions over evictions mounted to such an extent that "more than 200 campesinos from the indigenous community of Subtiava, organized in armed squads, took over the lands which they considered usurped."[19]

Five years later only 28 percent of the land area in the cotton-belt *municipios* of León and Chinandega was still governed by traditional forms of peasant access. The remaining 72 percent was being worked as legally titled private property, either on an owner-managed basis or rented for money. In the noncotton *municipios* of these same two departments, traditional peasant forms of land tenure still prevailed, representing 65 percent of the census area.[20]

A similar story is told in the coastal plain of southern Honduras, where landlords, enticed by profits from cotton and cattle, extended their estates onto what had been municipal or national lands. At the same time, landlords began switching from sharecrop to money rents on the lands they already controlled. White found that the peasant movement in southern Honduras in the late 1960s had its origins in the struggles surrounding those earlier evictions. His interviews of peasants reveal the brutality of the evictions and a strong belief that, even after many years, the lands which had been either national lands or ejidal lands were still rightfully theirs.[21]

In coastal El Salvador the ejidal form of land access had already been destroyed before cotton became a viable crop. The abolition of ejidal rights was accomplished through a combination of coffee expansion onto ejidal lands in the late nineteenth century (in the piedmont) and a series of repressive measures that followed the mass slaughter of peasants in 1932. By the time cotton became commercially attractive, most of the land suitable for it in the Salvadoran portion of the coastal plain was already carved up into legally titled private estates. In El Salvador corn producers were removed from the land in a manner identical to the one used to remove peasants from legally titled estates in Guatemala, Honduras, and Nicaragua.

The typical cotton eviction proceeded as follows.

As a road neared completion through a rich agricultural area, the landlord would notify the peasants that they could remain on the land and continue to cultivate it. However, the method of payment of rent would change from kind to cash: no longer would payment be made as a share of the crop or a fixed number of sacks of corn at the end of the harvest; it would have to be made in cash in advance of the growing season, when peasants were most strapped for funds.

From the perspective of the landlord, this shift of the rules of access made good business sense. After all, the land could be easily rented to a cotton grower on those terms. In the mid-1960s a landlord who sold his share of corn under the traditional arrangement could expect between six and ten dollars an acre, depending on the quality of land, the weather, and the price of corn. If the landlord rented the property to a cotton entrepreneur, he would receive two to three times that amount, and the cash was immediate. Furthermore, renting for money to a grower meant avoiding the yearly problem of ascertaining whether the peasants were hiding part of the crop, and it reduced the uncertainties owing to weather or low corn prices.[22] Another advantage of eviction through a switch to money rents was that it appeared fair and open-ended; it placed the decision to stay or move on the individual peasant family and thereby avoided the costs of hiring an eviction squad and antagonizing other peasants in the area.

The peasants unlucky enough to be cultivating prime cropland along the route of the highway saw an immediate change in the rules governing their survival as cotton made them landless. But the logic of cotton production did not conquer the entire coastal plain overnight. During the first decade of the cotton boom, there remained a labor shortage in sections of the coastal plain, and some landlords continued to attract peasants to their estates in the traditional way, by granting use rights to small plots of land. In return, the peasants were obligated to plow the landlord's cottonfields with the traditional oxen, to clear forests, to construct farm roads, and to dig drainage ditches. Over the first decade of cotton's expansion, Guatemala and El Salvador experienced a dramatic rise in the number of permanent workers with subsistence plots (*colonos*) residing on estates in the cotton belt.[23]

This relatively favorable situation for peasants did not last long. With the cheap credit being pumped into the cotton economy, growers found it to be much more practical and profitable to mechanize certain stages of the cotton cycle. The once-familiar sight of oxen trudging through fields in monotonous straight lines, each team requiring a driver, was replaced by the spectacle of great tractors turning under many rows at a time, gliding effortlessly through the rich volcanic earth. Whereas platoons of workers had been needed for planting, with one worker per row plodding across the field depositing seeds, the same tractors used for plowing had attachments that could plant many rows at once, drawing thin lines of chemical fertilizer in the same sweep. Even though machete teams were still needed to thin the young plants and to chop the weeds that had grown up between them, the weeds in between the rows could be eliminated with either a cultivator attachment or an attachment for spraying herbicide. The teams of men with tanks over their shoulders hand spraying insecticide were replaced: a tractor attachment could do the job faster (up to a certain plant height), and an airplane could do it even faster. Only the first weeding and the harvest resisted mechanization.[24]

When it became clear to growers that the labor market could provide them with their peak labor needs, it was no longer necessary to maintain a large number of permanent residents on the estates. With mechanization, housing for a few administrators, a handful of tractor drivers, and several mechanics sufficed. As it turned out, even the services of the tractor drivers and mechanics did not necessitate the provision of houses and small pieces of land on the plantation. As commercial activity increased, these services could be purchased from the market. Private contractors with fleets of tractors and assorted attachments began to flourish in the cotton belt.[25]

In the 1960s permanent residents were expelled from the estates in droves.[26] The trigger mechanism for the expulsion of *colonos* in El Salvador was the passage of a law in 1965 that extended the minimum wage to permanent agricultural workers. The underlying pressure to expel the *colonos* was already present, but after the minimum wage law was passed, the retention of unskilled workers on the land appeared even more absurd from the perspective of growers. Why should a grower be expected to continue to provide subsistence parcels, housing, and weekly rations to *colonos* when the same money wage held for day laborers? In Guatemala, likewise, a trigger to the mass expulsion of *colonos* was the passage of national legislation that extended social security deductions to permanent agricultural workers; the national legislation became an excuse for eviction.[27]

The people evicted by cotton began to swell the rocky riverbeds, the edges of mangrove swamps, and other areas unsuitable for mechanized agriculture. They tacked up their cardboard shacks wherever the threat of eviction was not immediate. Shantytowns of the landless sprang up along the national road rights-of-way near the cotton farms, and slums formed around the villages, towns, and cities of the Pacific coastal plain. Other peasants left the coastal plain to seek refuge in the slums of the capital cities, where they mixed with the people streaming in from other areas. Those who were most unwilling to give up their accustomed way of life as corn producers had to settle on lands ever more remote from the reaches of the market. Some migrated all the way to the steaming jungles of the Atlantic frontier.[28]

Cotton and the Creation of a Wage-Labor Force

Cotton changed not only the physical locations of people but also the way they made a living. The best lands were no longer available for cultivating corn and other subsistence crops, so an ever-increasing portion of a family's food needs had to be purchased with cash. At the same time, denial of access to land dried up traditional sources of cash: sales of fruits, vegetables, firewood, chickens, pigs, and milk. Thus, the only remaining source of cash for many peasant families was wage work, and the biggest source of wage income along the coastal plain was the cotton plantation.

From the newly created clusters of poverty, men went out daily in search of odd jobs, or they waited at the customary crossroad in hopes that a truck would arrive and take them for a day's work on the nearby plantation. The women made do by selling some sort of service in the pores of the cotton economy. In the towns and cities they could sometimes find domestic work in the homes of growers, merchants, and other prosperous townspeople. They took in washing and sewed, or nursed the children of the rich. Others cooked soup, patted out tortillas, fried plantain chips, peeled oranges, sold refreshments, or provided some other service in the marketplace.

Directly or indirectly, people found themselves dependent on cotton wages. For those with personal connections or those able to acquire skills useful to cotton, wage incomes could be high and steady. Airplane pilots, managers, accountants, foremen, tractor drivers, mechanics, and mixers of cotton poison fared relatively well in deriving cash income, and sometimes special privileges could be exacted with the job.

For the uneducated bulk of the population with neither valuable skills nor connections, cotton was more fickle. Seasonal availability of wage work fluctuated wildly. At thinning and weeding time, plantations would take on men to chop. During picking season, especially at the peak in December, wages could be earned every day even by women and children. At other times of the year, however, wage work was hard to get, and without injections of wage money from cotton, it became more difficult to sell beverages and prepared food in the marketplace.

Wage work in cotton fluctuated not only from season to season but also from year to year and from place to place. When growers' profit expectations were high, even marginal lands were drawn into production, and wage opportunities would rise, giving buoyancy to the service jobs in the cotton towns. But when insect pests, interest rates, or world prices dampened growers' hopes, people along the coast would become desperate for work. Added to the seasonal and year-to-year insecurities was the workers' helplessness with respect to growers' decisions about technology. At any time another phase of the production process that provided jobs for unskilled laborers could be taken away by modernization, as had occurred earlier with the shift from oxen to tractors.

Chart 3-1 indicates the instability of cotton as a source of employment at harvest time, when the largest numbers of laborers are needed. Jobs picking cotton are generally available from mid-December through mid-March, although the peak demand differs slightly in different places along the coastal plain. The average picker is able to contract for about seventy days of work during a normal season,[29] and payment is made on a piece-rate basis, the unit of measurement usually being 100 pounds of lint. Some workers can pick as many as 140 pounds a day, others can pick only 40 or 50. The average for a normal adult male under normal picking conditions is approximately 75 pounds a day.[30] Based on average picking conditions, the number of jobs in the cotton harvest grew from 15,000 in the early days of the boom to over 350,000 when the boom peaked in the mid-1960s. With the problems of insects and poor price expectations among growers, this source of seasonal income collapsed by more than 100,000 picking jobs by 1971. When cotton rebounded in the 1970s, the number of jobs in the harvest expanded once more and passed the 400,000 mark, mainly owing to the upward thrust of Guatemalan and Nicaraguan production.[31]

Where do all the pickers come from?

A portion of the picking force lives close enough to the cottonfields to go to and from work on a daily basis. Those living along the riverbeds and the roadways can walk to the fields when the nearest plantation is hiring. Those living in the villages along the coastal highway are sometimes picked up in the morning and returned in the evening by trucks owned by the plantations; others must get rides from independent truckers or ride buses, paying the transport costs out of their wages.

During harvest season the slums of the large cities near the cottonfields provide a vast supply of cotton pickers,[32] but the coastal economy, geared as it is to mechanized agriculture, does not provide enough permanent jobs to support the entire harvest force year round. The work force needed for the cotton harvest has been shown to be so large at times that it exceeds the entire

Chart 3-1

Number of Jobs Harvesting Cotton, 1950–1978

Jobs
(thousands)

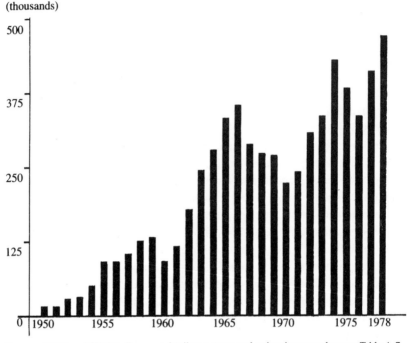

Sources: USDA and SIECA. For more detail on sources and estimation procedure see Table A-7 in the Appendix.

Note: Jobs are defined here as seventy-day harvest contracts. See n. 30 to this chapter for further details.

economically active population of a country's cotton departments.[33] It is difficult to gauge the exact numbers, but certainly more than half of the seasonal work force must be imported to the coastal plain for the duration of the harvest, only to be exported when there is no more cotton to pick.[34]

Owners of the plantations have makeshift barracks erected at little cost, and migrant workers spend the evenings in these crowded quarters for the duration of their contracts.[35] Those lucky enough to have relatives living near the cottonfields migrate to the coastal plain and stay with their relatives for the duration of the harvest, seeking work in the fields day by day and thereby avoiding the squalor of plantation housing.

Workers who migrate to the coastal plain for the duration of the harvest come from various locations. One important source of harvest labor is the capital city, where squatter settlements have grown up. The slums of San

Salvador are fifteen miles from the cottonfields, and workers can commute to and from the fields on a daily basis, but the slums of Guatemala City and Managua are too far from the major cotton zones to make daily commuting possible. Nevertheless, Guatemala City provided the coastal plain with approximately 10 percent of seasonal migrants in 1965–66 and 15 percent during the 1968–69 harvest.[36] One-third of the cotton-harvest workers of Nicaragua come from major metropolitan areas,[37] and large contingents from Managua go down to the coast every year for the harvest.[38]

The slums of the capital cities and other metropolitan areas have provided a cheap labor pool for the plantations at harvest time, but an even cheaper pool, albeit more scattered geographically and more cumbersome to tap, exists on the margins of the peasant economy. Over the years, as commercial agriculture has claimed the best lands, peasants have sought refuge in zones where they can grow their corn and beans with minimal interference from large landlords. The areas to which they have flocked tend to have rockier soil, to be more subject to erosion, and to be more difficult to reach than the export zones. In these mountainous areas, with their intricate patchwork of small fields, some people have been able to prosper on a year-round basis without having to leave their communities in search of work elsewhere. These relatively prosperous peasants usually have access to larger holdings or better land, or they produce crafts for sale on the peasant market. Others are not so lucky. As the peasant population has grown, overcrowding has occurred in the already settled areas, and the less prosperous peasants have had to move either to the city or to more remote areas with even poorer soil. The size and yield of the subsistence plots of the less prosperous cannot sustain them for a full year, so family members must seek wage work elsewhere. The most destitute people from these peasant areas are thus obliged to make yearly pilgrimages to the Pacific coast to harvest crops.

Every country of Central America has its zones of peasant refuge. There is great diversity between zones and within zones. Some peasant communities are so prosperous that no one has to migrate to the coast for harvest. In other communities 70 to 80 percent of the work force must migrate to find work. Except for a few fertile river valleys, the northernmost section of El Salvador, constituting one-fifth of the country's surface area, is one zone of the latter type. The soil is rocky, the mountaintops have long been deforested, road networks are poor, and in the pockets of soil between the rocks, people plant corn, beans, and sorghum. During the dry season they migrate to the coast to pick export crops, only to return in time to plant their own subsistence crops when the rains begin.[39]

In Nicaragua the mountainous areas in the departments of Nueva Segovia and Madriz and in parts of Estelí, up toward the Honduran border, have provided seasonal migrants to the Pacific coast. Except for some rich river valleys, the soils in these areas are liberally interspersed with pieces of granite and other metamorphic rocks. During the Nicaraguan cotton boom, labor contractors were sent by the plantations to these poor, remote areas to recruit seasonal workers. In the early 1960s contractors were paid a flat rate of approximately seven cents a head for delivery of pickers at the plantation, and sometimes recruiters were able to entice whole villages to go down for the harvest.[40]

Until recently, more than three-fourths of the seasonal migrants of Guatemala were recruited from the Indian highlands of the northwest.[41] Most come not from the relatively prosperous central market towns, where cottage industry and truck farming flourish, but from peripheral zones of the highlands. In 1966 approximately 52 percent of the seasonal migrants of Guatemala came from the far northwest departments of Huehuetenango and Quiché, and by 1969 the proportion had risen to 62 percent. Those two peripheral departments sent more than half of their economically active population to the Pacific coast for the 1968–69 harvest.[42]

A sophisticated system of recruitment has evolved that ensures a cheap flow of harvest workers from these peripheral areas. It is reported that in July, only a month before the corn harvest, when household inventories of grain and cash reach their lowest levels of the year, labor contractors representing plantations of the Pacific coast offer the peasants an advance on harvest wages in return for signing contracts for a specified number of days of harvest work on the coast when the export crops mature. The contractors may be merchants, usurers, or political leaders from the towns in the highlands who are in a position to know the peasants in the surrounding villages and who are able to pressure them to comply with the contracts when they come due. In the 1960s it was not unusual for the advance to equal half a month's wages (fifteen dollars). At that time the cotton plantations tended to pay workers for only one day's labor after half a month, with the rest used to reimburse the contractor for the advances made and for the costs incurred in transporting the workers to the coast. In 1965–66 a sample of migrant workers showed that three-fourths of them had received advances and were under such contracts. By withholding wages until the end of the contract period, plantations could effectively prevent workers from moving elsewhere in search of easier picking conditions, better pay, or better treatment. Also, the withholding of pay ensured that the labor contractors would get their cut, which at that time amounted to 10 percent of the wages earned.[43]

Comparative studies of Guatemalan seasonal work in coffee, cotton, and sugar reveal that cotton workers are typically recruited from the most destitute of the peasant households, from the families with the least land and livestock, and from the poorest and most remote of the mountaintop villages.[44] The living conditions they face on the coast are worse than those on coffee and sugar plantations: they have more meager rations, no pay for legal holidays or Sundays, inferior lodgings, and poorer sanitation facilities. The cotton workers face a higher risk of catching malaria and suffering from dysentery, and they often suffer from symptoms of cotton poisoning.[45] Despite the greater health risks of working in cotton, cotton plantations very rarely offer any sort of health care for seasonal workers, whereas most sugar and coffee farms have clinics or are at least visited by teams of health workers periodically.[46] For all these reasons cotton picking has a bad reputation among the seasonal workers, and money wages paid in cotton tend to be higher than in coffee or sugar in order to attract workers in sufficient numbers.[47]

The yearly flow of seasonal migrants from areas of peasant refuge to the export zones is not a phenomenon contained by state boundaries. Over the years increasing numbers of people have found their conditions for survival so precarious that they are willing to risk the brutality of border guards as they migrate from one country to the next in search of harvest work.[48]

The most abundant pool of internationally mobile harvest labor has been produced by the extremely poor and overpopulated peasant zone of northern El Salvador, where the conditions of survival are among the worst of any of the peasant zones of the five-country area. Cotton growers in Escuintla, Guatemala, show preference for hiring these hardworking Salvadorans; in the late 1960s Salvadorans made up one-tenth of the picking force for Guatemalan cotton.[49] Before the 1969 war expelled Salvadoran peasants from Honduras and border security was tightened on the Honduran side, many thousands of Salvadorans migrated on a seasonal basis to pick crops in Honduras. Some of these seasonal workers were imported by rich Salvadoran growers who had extended their cotton operations over the border into the Honduran portion of the coastal plain.[50] Before the fall of Somoza and the worsening of relations between the government of El Salvador and the Sandinista government in the late 1970s, large numbers of workers were imported from El Salvador to relieve the shortage of harvest labor faced by Nicaraguan growers. Most of these Salvadorans made their yearly journey by boat over the Gulf of Fonseca, but some were smuggled through Honduras in covered trucks. After the harvest they were deported and sent back to El Salvador to scratch out a living for the remainder of the year.

The Irreversibility of Cotton

The cotton boom, as was shown in Chapter Two, demanded ever-increasing amounts of pesticides and fertilizers for profitable yields. The rising costs of production were supported in the early 1960s by a period of rising cotton prices, but after 1964 world cotton prices entered a period of slump.[51] Declining world prices and unusually severe insect infestations turned the boom into bust. Marginal growers were forced into bankruptcy or into the cultivation of other crops. Nearly three hundred thousand acres of Central American cotton-fields were released for alternative uses before world prices stimulated another boom in the early 1970s.

Some of the lands taken out of cotton were planted, once again, in food crops, but traditional modes of farming and rights to land did not return. Ejidal properties or national lands that had been claimed by the cotton boom were not restored when cotton lost its appeal but endured as privately titled properties. Private estates that had been worked before cotton by sharecroppers, *colonos*, or peasant renters came to be worked by wage labor. The tractors and assorted attachments purchased for cotton were not sold and converted back to oxen and the single plow but were adapted to whatever crop was considered the most profitable. The growers, who had become accustomed to relying on bank loans, miracle seeds, fertilizer, imported equipment, and wage labor, did not revert to traditional practices but continued to borrow money and to purchase the inputs needed for cotton's substitute. The masses of landless people produced by cotton's rise remained landless when cotton fell.

The landowners' decision not to switch back to the previous mode of production made sense on economic grounds. Banks, public and private, continued to lend them money; the agribusiness supply houses continued to supply them with seeds, fertilizer, and equipment; and the wage-labor force was still seeking work. But the decision to continue to deny peasant access to land was not one based on narrow profitability calculations alone: it carried with it a logic of a more fundamental nature.

Peasants evicted from lands rarely left without a struggle, and once lands were lost, they did not forget the experience. In the 1960s they began to organize around the issue of land reform. At this time a number of social institutions became more sensitive to their plight, especially in marginal parishes of the Catholic church and in sections of national governments connected with Alliance for Progress reforms. Wherever peasants perceived the opportunity, they pushed for recovery of their lands.

The growing peasant movement frightened landowners. Once a landowner had fought to clear the land of peasants to make way for cotton, he or she was unlikely to invite them back onto the estate just because cotton was no longer profitable. Such a move would have reduced flexibility in switching crops. Moreover, it would run the risk at a later date of peasants' claiming the land as theirs on the grounds that they were working it, a typical procedure when national governments become open to the pressures of land reform. Better to leave the land clear of this risk, regardless of the crop.

Cotton to Cattle

Opportunities for the production of other exports presented themselves just as cotton waned. The beef-export business continued to expand throughout the 1960s and 1970s, making it attractive for some growers to convert former cotton lands into pasture. The trend to raising beef cattle was especially strong in Guatemala, where cattle and cotton had been raised from the start on the same large estates, but this change also occurred in other places along the coastal plain. When the cotton-to-cattle switch occurred, it usually meant a shift into the most technically advanced form of cattle ranching, with improved breeds, imported varieties of grass seed, improved wells and fencing, and so forth. The switch from cottonfield to cattle pasture preserved the economic logic of cotton, but not cotton's appetite for a large labor force.[52]

Cotton to Sugar

Sugarcane also expanded into what had been cottonfields. As the world price of cotton declined, that of sugar increased, climbing at an average rate of 5 percent a year from 1965 to 1971.[53] During this period 160,000 acres of land were drawn into sugar production.[54]

The major factor in deciding whether to switch from cotton to sugar was the proximity of a sugar mill. Without a nearby sugar mill, the costs of transporting the cane to the mill could quickly erode a farmer's margin of profit. Unlike a cotton gin, a sugar mill is a huge fixed investment that cannot be moved easily. In Guatemala some of the cotton areas were not within easy reach of a sugar mill, so that the switch from cotton to sugar was less attractive there than in other places.[55] In El Salvador the switch from cotton to sugar was more difficult than in Guatemala, because the sugar mills are located either in the upper piedmont, or further away in the river basins of the northern portion of the country. The shift from cotton to sugar did occur in Guatemala and El Salvador during the cotton slump, but not nearly so strongly as in Honduras and Nicaragua.

The proximity of a sugar mill was not a problem in Nicaragua because the San Antonio sugar complex, with the largest mill in Central America, is located between León and Chinandega in the middle of the cotton belt, and Nicaragua's fourth-largest mill at that time, Monte Rosa (now Germán Pomares), is located in the most important cotton *municipio*, El Viejo, in the department of Chinandega. Both of these mills own vast tracts of land where sugar is cultivated on a permanent basis to ensure a supply that will keep the mill running, but farms within proximity of the mills can enter contracts to sell cane to the mills at harvest.[56] During the Nicaraguan cotton slump these two mills expanded their own sugar lands by 32 percent, from 19,000 acres in 1967 to 25,000 acres in 1971, but the independent producers supplying these mills with cane expanded their sugar acreage two and a half times, from 7,000 acres in 1967 to 18,000 acres in 1971. When the cotton boom resumed after 1971, the mills continued to cultivate and even expand their own acreage in sugar, but the independent producers cut back their sugar planting dramatically.[57]

In 1967 the first sugar mill in southern Honduras, the Los Mangos complex, was completed. It was located in Marcovia, the most important cotton-producing *municipio* in Honduras, where one-fourth of the country's cotton was grown.[58] The shift from cotton to cane has been more thorough and permanent in Honduras than elsewhere along the coastal plain, and today this stretch of road boasts two sugar complexes and more than 22,000 acres of cane.

The switch from cotton to cane has provided a more stable market for the middle-sized farms in the area, but it has meant an even greater concentration of economic power in the area than when cotton was produced. An interview with a top-level manager of one of the complexes revealed that nearly half of the land in sugar was owned by the two mills.[59]

Some of the tractors and airplanes that were used in cotton cultivation in the 1960s are still being used in sugar cultivation, and little has changed in the way production is organized. Sugar, just like cotton, relies on wage labor. The permanent work force is slightly larger now than when cotton was cultivated, but sugar, like cotton, calls for a large number of workers during the harvest. The larger of the two complexes in 1982 hired 750 permanent workers, but 3,000 additional workers were needed for the 1982–83 harvest.

A manager of the larger complex said that the bulk of the permanent work force lived in nearby Monjarás, a town of shacks located on the very edge of the sugar lands where the rich, well-drained soils give way to coastal swamp. According to the manager, the seasonal work force is recruited from the slopes of the mountains that rise above the coastal plain. "Fortunately," he said, "the best time to harvest cane is in the dry season when corn is not being cultivated. The minute the rains begin, there goes our labor force." He said that at the time of the harvest, company trucks would be sent before dawn to depot points where the workers congregate, and the trucks would return them to these same points after dark.[60]

Cotton may not dominate southern Honduras as it once did, but cotton's mark is indelibly etched on the landscape.

Cotton to Basic Grains

Even when traditional food crops replaced cotton, the cotton revolution proved irreversible. In certain sections of the coastal plain, growers recognized that greater profits could be realized by planting corn or rice or sorghum, even though the destination of these crops was not primarily the world market but the market in Central America itself. The cotton boom stimulated the growth in money demand for basic grains in several ways. When the best lands were permanently removed from small subsistence farmers, fewer households could raise their own food, so they had to purchase it from the market. At the same time cotton provided money to buy food with, especially during the harvest season.

By the late 1960s, when cotton production declined, large-scale, modernized corn production began to appear in the cotton zones of Guatemala and El Salvador.[61] One observer pinpointed precisely the origin of El Salvador's modern corn farms. He described them as being "on flat land, using tractor pulled plows to prepare the earth, mechanical sowers, herbicides, and even mechanical harvesters; these technically advanced corn farms are the exception today and were born of the cotton crisis, when large landowners had to return to corn production utilizing part of the machinery left idle by the declining acreage in cotton."[62] Some of the fields in every cotton-producing country were returned to basic grain production when cotton lost its appeal, but by far the strongest shift from cotton back to basic grains occurred in Nicaragua.

The Somoza business group of Nicaragua, along with some other astute Nicaraguan business interests, recognized the new opportunities created by the growing domestic grain market. Investments in modern grain farms were made, but in an attempt to monopolize Nicaragua's grain trade, an even larger amount of capital was channeled into grain processing, storage, and marketing. In convenient locations, close to the grain-producing areas, these business interests built large centralized granaries, with the most modern facilities for unloading the grain from trucks, blowing it free of chaff and debris, drying it, and storing it in bulk.

Production of grain on a commercial basis, like cotton production before it, was stimulated through easy credit to growers. Large irrigation projects were begun in order to encourage the cultivation of wet rice. The year before cotton acreage in Nicaragua peaked, the Banco Nacional de Nicaragua and the national banking system as a whole began to scale back lending for cotton cultivation, as loans to marginal growers began to apear on the "nonperforming" list. Between 1965–66 and 1967–68 the banking system discontinued finance for some thirty-eight thousand acres of cotton, but financing for the cultivation of basic grains more than took up the slack.[63] Through government promotion programs, corn, rice, and sorghum—traditional crops of the peasantry—became yet another investment outlet for large, mechanized agriculture, and the peasants were not made better off. In fact, the return to grain production meant a loss in jobs. When cotton acreage expanded again in the 1970s, the picking jobs returned, but on the marginal cotton lands the switch to mechanized grain was more permanent.

Cotton and the Social Fabric

The revolution in agricultural practices that cotton came to symbolize was thus not limited to that one crop: cotton growers found that sugar, rice, corn, and many other crops could be raised in much the same way with minor adjustments. Nor was the revolution limited to the flatlands. By the mid-1960s new varieties of coffee had been developed and chemical herbicides began to be introduced, so that coffee farms could go without the large permanent work forces they were accustomed to. Very much like the shift from oxen to tractors in the cottonfields, this application of modern technology to coffee resulted in the denial of peasant access to subsistence plots and the switch to wage labor.

For many reasons cotton takes the credit for modernizing Central American agriculture. The cotton plant's vulnerability to insect damage required the application of modern pesticides. Its need for fertile soil and sweltering heat limited its cultivation to zones that were easily adapted to tractors. Its short growing season made it attractive for short-term bank financing. Thus, cotton captured the imagination of the urban and rural elites and provided a pragmatic blueprint for dragging primitive agriculture into the modern era. As yields per acre and money profits increased for growers, something less favorable was happening to peasants.

The cotton revolution stripped the rural majority of some traditional protections. Peasants were denied land on which they could raise food. Traditionally, one's patch of cornfield, however meager, at least absorbed some of the stress of market fluctuations. With cotton's advance, the numbers of rootless peasants increased, and they moved wherever the labor market called them. The survival of this group became critically linked to the availability of wage work and the purchasing power of the current wage.

With reduced access to land in the countryside, the traditional ways in which women contributed to the maintenance of the family collapsed. No longer were there chickens, pigs, and cows to tend. No longer was there produce from the farm to work up for family consumption. No longer were there eggs, milk, fruits, and vegetables to take to market. The cotton revolution retained some jobs for men in the countryside, but the women had to migrate to urban areas to find employment to compensate for the loss of the family plot. Only in the towns and cities was there wage work for dishwashers, floor scrubbers, cooks, nurses, and seamstresses. This geographical split in the availability of wage work produced a dramatic rise in the number of female-headed households in the urban areas, while males roved the countryside in search of plantation labor.[64] In this way the cotton revolution pulled apart the peasant family.

As the traditional glue that had held the peasant family together came unstuck, so too did the glue that once held social classes together in the countryside. Landlords and peasants alike sometimes reflect glowingly on better days in the past. Peasants tend to look back and remember times when it was still possible to obtain access to pieces of land on which they could raise corn, whereas landlords tell of the days when peasants respected them.

A closer look at the actual conditions faced by the two groups tarnishes the glowing image sometimes presented in these memories. First, before the coming of roads, credit, and agribusiness supply houses, large landowners were not nearly so rich. Second, peasant access to good land, within reach by oxcart, was almost always conditional upon entering some sort of exploitative arrangement with the largest landlord in the vicinity.

The obligations that bound peasants differed from place to place, but there was a universal requirement in addition to the rent, regardless of the form the rent took. Peasants were obligated to bow their heads in the proper way and to salute the landlord as "Don Carlos" and his wife as "Doña Maria" when they passed. If this posture was not assumed, it was grounds for eviction, even if all other obligations were fulfilled.

What is sometimes overlooked is that the landlord faced certain obligations as well in this earlier arrangement. If a tenant family came under unusual stress for any reason, the landlord was expected to find some way to relieve it. If the stress involved a conflict between two tenants, the landlord was expected to settle the dispute in a just manner. If the stress took the form of illness, the landlord was expected to call in a doctor. If the stress was a shortage of corn, the landlord was expected to release provisions. If a peasant got drunk in town and ended up in jail, the landlord was expected to intervene on his behalf and bail him out. The mutual obligations that bound peasant to landlord and landlord to peasant were hardly written in tablets of stone; they assumed the more pervasive texture of an attitude, a fact of life, a religious view of the natural order of things. For the peasant, meekness and acceptance of one's place on earth would bring reward in the kingdom of God. For the landlord, it was a duty ordained by God to be charitable and to show mercy in looking after one's flock.

The cotton revolution struck at the foundation of this established order. The large numbers of tenants that a landlord had needed to keep an estate prosperous in the era of oxen were obstacles when the tractors came. Landlords who ignored this change and who tried to retain the peasants and the oxen found themselves displaced by younger entrepreneurs who obtained favored access to credit and the miracle seeds, fertilizers, and equipment that it could buy. The old attitude of paternalism toward one's subjects still made sense for the handful of tractor drivers, mechanics, and managers that were kept permanently on the farm, but toward those dirty, anonymous faces that showed up once a year at harvest time, the old attitude appeared increasingly naive and sentimental. The pickers came from afar, perhaps even from another country, and once the harvest was over and the wage paid they would migrate somewhere else, never to be seen again. To treat these transients with the same personal attention expected by the permanent staff was an absurdity. As the cotton revolution spread, the complex web of landowner obligations was reduced to a single duty: the payment of a money wage.[65]

From the perspective of the wage laborers, the old attitudes appeared even more absurd in this changed setting. How could one display the old posture of respect when one's contacts were with a labor contractor and a hired boss instead of the owner of the plantation himself? Why should one show duty toward landowners when access to their land was no longer part of the bargain? Why should one feel loyalty when the employer shed all responsibility upon the payment of the wage and was neither protector nor provider in times of stress?

In the context of spreading cottonfields, the old-time religion began to fall on deaf ears, and a new one began to sprout, raising the spirits of the dispossessed. Where the old religion taught patience in the here and now in return for everlasting life in the hereafter, the new one raised the hope of bringing the kingdom of God to this earth. Where the old-time religion interpreted the landowner's property as part of God's natural design, the new one viewed that property as a denial of human life and therefore a denial of God's law. Instead of defining duty as meekly accepting one's place, the new religion defined it as taking action to change the situation. As the cotton revolution did its work, the pockets of the dispossessed became fertile ground for the spread of a new faith. Instead of looking back glowingly on the past, the new faith offered hope for a radical change in the future.

Summary

Emanating from the zones of flat, rich earth, the cotton revolution wove a pattern on the rural landscape. Once an area was brought under its sway, there was no turning back. Its compelling logic left little room for the subsistence plot, the peasant family, or the paternalism of yesteryear. More and more people found themselves uprooted and homeless, exposed to the caprice of an unpredictable market. Wherever the cotton revolution could not go, the common man sought refuge. But even the areas most protected in the past by poor soil and bad roads were soon to be opened, as the coming chapters will explain, to another sort of commercial venture: the cattle ranch. At first the successes of export-led growth hid what was happening, but as cotton proceeded on one side and cattle on the other, the entire social fabric was being progressively weakened so that it was ill prepared for the shocks that were to tear through the region in the seventies.

Part Two: Cattle

4. The Beef-Export Boom and Its Primary Causes

Cattle have grazed in Central America since the Spanish first established their haciendas in the sixteenth century, but until recently the beef trade was limited to on-the-hoof sales within local and regional markets. The link between the pastures of the region and the world beef market was forged in the late 1950s. In 1957 the first modern USDA-approved packing plant was completed in Managua, Nicaragua. Shortly thereafter a steer was slaughtered, deboned, packed into boxes of sixty pounds, frozen, trucked to port, loaded on a refrigerated vessel, shipped through the Panama Canal, unloaded in Miami, passed through inspection, and trucked to a processing plant. Within a week, the steer that had been eating grass on the Pacific strip of Central America had become so many more hamburgers in the booming U.S. fast-food business.

By 1960 Honduras, Costa Rica, and Nicaragua had export-packing houses, and the region's herd of approximately 4 million cattle yielded some 30 million pounds of boneless beef a year for North American fast-food chains. Beginning in 1961, the Alliance for Progress boosted Central America's beef-export business. Export quotas to the United States were increased, and all sorts of promotional efforts were undertaken to stimulate the trade and to modernize beef production. After a little more than a decade of export promotion, even tiny, overpopulated El Salvador had an export-packing house. By 1973 the region's twenty-two packing plants exported 180 million pounds of beef a year, and the region's cattle herd had doubled in size to approximately 8 million head.

The oil crisis, the interest-rate explosion, and the worldwide recession between 1973 and 1975 drained the region of foreign exchange, and governments responded by promoting beef exports further. Between 1973 and 1977, when the second wave of worldwide inflation hit, six more export plants were approved. By 1978 Central America's herd of 10 million provided the United States with 250 million pounds of beef a year, representing 15 percent of U.S. beef imports.[1] Another worldwide slump and a revolutionary crisis in the 1980s once more left the region drained of foreign exchange. In 1984 the Kissinger Commission noted the success of export promotions of previous decades and recommended the further extension of Central America's beef quota as one of the measures to alleviate the crisis.[2]

Central America's beef-export boom did more than expand the herd 250 percent, raise yearly foreign exchange earnings by $225 million, and catapult Central America into third place as supplier of beef to the U.S. market. Behind these quantitative leaps was a qualitative change in every phase of beef production from breeding cattle on the ranch to retailing in the United States. The beef-export boom dragged a colonial enterprise into the twentieth century.

Practices before the Export Boom

When the first modern packing plants were built in Central America, the practices of beef production were found in a primitive state, ill suited to the needs of the world beef business. The dominant breed of cattle was an inferior beef producer, pasture management was crude, animal hygiene was poor, transport to slaughter was wasteful, slaughterhouses were unsanitary, and marketing networks were medieval.

The dominant breed roaming the Central American range at that time was the criollo, a scrawny creature descended from Spanish stock brought over during the colonial period. The virtue of the criollo was that it could survive with little care, but from the perspective of the modern beef business it had little to offer. Weight gain on criollo cattle was notoriously slow compared to North American breeds, an undesirable characteristic in a business demanding yearly increases in beef exports. Furthermore, on the same pasture the pure criollo steer took two to three years longer to reach mature slaughter weight than the hump-backed Brahman or Zebu, the breed that later became the criollo's competitor. The lengthy maturation period tied up capital longer, a decided disadvantage once bank credit and interest payments intruded into cattle ranching. When mature slaughter weight was finally reached at age 5 or 6, the criollo weighed 140 to 200 pounds less than a 3- or 3½-year-old Zebu. This light weight at maturity translated into a lower yield of beef at the slaughterhouse. From the perspective of the modern beef business, with its logic of maximizing the rate of beef formation and speeding up the turnover of capital, the wiry, slowly maturing criollo was an impediment.[3]

Before the export boom of the 1960s, cattle managed Central America's pastures. Fencing was rarely used to control overgrazing. Rather, herds were permitted to roam wherever they pleased. After grazing out one area, the herd naturally moved on to another.[4] If the grazing area on a hacienda was large and varied in terrain, with some low-lying creek bottoms suitable for the dry season, the cattle got fed. But there were several drawbacks to this practice. The cattle expended a great deal of energy just looking for food, which lowered the rate of beef formation and yielded a product full of gristle. Secondly, the cattle overgrazed the superior grasses, leaving behind a healthy stand of weeds and thereby lowering the long-run feeding capacity of the range.[5]

Like the criollo cattle, the native grasses could survive with little care, but their productivity was low. An FAO ecologist visiting Nicaragua in 1959 reported, "The production of feed from almost all of the pasture land in the area is far below the land potential. The native pastures produce relatively small quantities of feed compared to the improved pastures."[6]

The practice of allowing the herd to fend for itself on extensive ranges of unimproved pasture produced the interrelated phenomena of malnutrition, insect infestation, disease, and infertility. In the late 1950s one observer in El Salvador reported: "Malnutrition is responsible for sterility in 10 percent of the cows and for a slow rate of sexual maturation, and contributes to the low (40 to 45 percent) annual calving rate. Calf mortality rates of 35 to 40 percent are the product of malnutrition as well as intestinal disorders, umbilical infections, and neglect. Mastitis and brucelosis are prevalent in a majority of herds. Few herds are free of tick or screwworm."[7] This condition of the cattle herds extended from Guatemala to Costa Rica, with the exception of a handful of "progressive" farms scattered throughout the region.

Traditional cattle-raising practices cannot be attributed entirely to ignorant ranchers. At least by the 1930s it was well known that arsenic dips killed ticks, vaccines prevented blackleg and anthrax, and worm medicine dislodged internal parasites. By the 1940s it was widely understood that pastures planted with Jaragua, Pará, Guinea, Pangola, and other imported seeds produced abundant yields of animal fodder. By the early 1950s it was no secret that the beefy Zebu was as resilient to the tropical climate as the bony criollo. But with few exceptions, the traditional practices persisted.

To make sense of the slow diffusion of superior technology, it is necessary to look beyond the ranch to the marketing networks and slaughterhouses of the period. From the accounts of observers at the time, a steer suffered a grueling journey from the ranch to the roaster.

Before the export boom of the 1960s, the majority of the cattle were driven on the hoof to their slaughter. Typically, a cattle-driving team would arrive at the ranch several days before market day to purchase the cattle from the rancher. The cattle were "driven day or night, with little allowance for browsing, rest, or watering."[8] They were sometimes driven long distances. For example, it was not uncommon for cattle to be herded all the way from ranches in Honduras to the market plaza in San Salvador,[9] or from the ranches of the coastal plain in Costa Rica to the highland market plaza in Alajuela.[10] Although instances of rail transport of cattle to market were reported in the 1950s, and by the late 1950s transport by truck was beginning to appear in Costa Rica, Nicaragua, and Guatemala, even by 1959 the "cattle were still transported on foot, for the most part."[11] The consequences of this method of transport were losses from death along the way, weight losses of up to 10 percent of the hoof weight on the ranch,[12] "waste of fat and meat, dehydration of the animal, fevers, contusions, damages to the feet,"[13] and hides that were ripped or raw.[14]

Near the central marketplace, the tired beasts would be watered and briefly rested; then they were taken to the marketing plaza, where they would be purchased by contractors for sale to butchers or bought by the butchers themselves and driven once again, this time to the local township where they would be slaughtered. The market for meat was limited to residents of the *municipio* who could afford it, but the municipal slaughter business was protected from competitors by inadequate roads, the lack of refrigeration, and local monopoly laws.

From all accounts, the business environment of the municipal slaughterhouse was that of a regulated monopoly, with laws designed to prevent the entry of beef from outside the jurisdiction of the *municipio*. It is unclear precisely how this institution arose. Perhaps it had something to do with the health hazards of rotten meat. It is not difficult, however, to find reasons why this legal setup lasted once it was in place. The local butchers were not likely to protest the lucrative arrangement. Nor were municipal governments likely to take the initiative to change the law when the slaughter tax was an important source of revenue. Although local governments required health inspections of live animals and sides of beef, according to one observer they were "hardly more than a gesture."[15]

Considering the small, protected business environment, it is not surprising to find that the slaughterhouses of the pre-export days characterized as "typically . . . small, poorly illuminated, unscreened structures of some antiquity. Tools, facilities, and techniques are rudimentary; and disposal of waste usually involves a rear wall, buzzards, and dogs."[16] One observer described the slaughter procedure in some detail: The animals are first

dropped to the ground, then blooded, skinned, and cut up on the same spot. The entire operation is carried out by only one person, or with the help of a single assistant. With this system a division of labor and specialization cannot be achieved. Besides, the butcher works in a tiring position that does not permit rapid and precise movements. It takes a long time to position the animal in exactly the right spot to put him down. Many of the animals when they are brought to be slaughtered end up trampling meat of the others that have come before, a fact that by all concepts is inconvenient from the point of view of sanitation.[17]

From the municipal slaughter shed, the sides of beef were carried to the public marketplace in the center of town. By the late 1950s trucks were beginning to be used to take the beef to market in some of the larger towns in the region, but the most likely mode of transport was still a wheelbarrow, a large basket, or the back of the retailer himself.

The clean, higher-priced specialty stores and supermarkets that cater to the rich in Central America today did not exist at that time. Everyone who could afford beef bought it in the public markets. From descriptions of beef retailing at that time, little has changed over the last two decades in the meat section of the public market. Meat vendors were clustered together, each occupying a stall. Slabs of beef were draped over metal or concrete counters or hung from poles, within easy reach of potential customers and flies. The meat was kept in large hunks to retard spoilage, and cuts were not made until a customer decided on a particular piece. One noticeable difference between today's marketing and previous descriptions is that today the more prosperous meat vendors in the markets of the largest cities boast a refrigerated display case, but in those days old meat was dried or salted before severe spoilage set in.[18]

The ordeal the steer experienced from the ranch to the dinner table had an economic as well as a physical dimension. In order to make the long, hard drive, the *corretero* paid a low-enough price at the ranch and received a high-enough price at the auction to compensate his hired drivers, to pay for the use of the horses, to cover the loss of an occasional animal on the way, and to pocket a reasonable profit. Despite the poor condition in which the animals arrived, the markup per head from ranch to market could be considerable. Figures reported in El Salvador at that time were $30 to $100 per head paid at the ranch, compared to $80 to $150 paid at the central market, and observers in other countries showed similar astonishment at the size of the markup.[19] The markup per pound in percentage points was much larger than the markup per head, considering the loss of weight and deterioration of the quality of the average animal by the time it reached the market. To the costs of transportation were added those of waste, price gouging, and taxation afforded by the municipal abattoir's local monopoly. Finally, vendors received some compensation for waste owing to normal spoilage, and a competitive merchant profit was extracted at the final stage as well. These successive markups resulted in a large differential between the price the cattleman received and the price the consumer paid.

Because of the inefficient and costly methods of transport, slaughter, and retailing, the rancher experienced great difficulty recovering cash invested in herd or pasture improvement. Within the marketing context of the period, it made more sense from a business point of view for ranchers to avoid cash outlays wherever possible: why pay cash for fences, fertilizer, improved seeds, imported livestock, veterinary medicines, and the like when compensation at the time of sale would not justify the expenditures? Better to let the beasts fend for themselves, find grass where they might, and reproduce at their own pace.

In such a retarded cash economy, it is easy to ask why cattle raising was so widely practiced by large landowner and middle peasant alike. The evidence suggests that in the days before the export boom, there were other motives for holding cattle besides their eventual sale for beef.

For a peasant family of modest means, the good fortune of a bountiful harvest had to be converted into some store of value that could be used in case of disaster. In the event of a prolonged drought, for example, stocks of corn and beans would not be sufficient to ensure a family's survival to the next harvest. A family with livestock could meet the deficit by selling off first the chickens, then the pig, and finally the cow. The family with livestock could avert the disaster of losing access to land, having to move, and being forced to look for work as day laborers. There were advantages of cattle over cash as a store of value. Young animals would mature and gain weight, thereby increasing their market value over time. Calves could be sold, and cows could continue to be milked.

For the large landowner the threat to physical survival was not the issue, but the preservation of the family's wealth was an ever-present concern. Because idle land in Central America is subject to invasion by the landless, a herd of branded cattle in an area marked the extent of the family property and guarded it against the planting of corn by squatters. In addition, a substantial cattle herd was itself a sign of family wealth and status. The sale of mature steers was a source of cash enabling the large landowner to maintain a relatively high standard of living, but wealth was accumulated not so much through the rapid weight gain of one's animals as through the increase in the size of the herd from which the steers were culled.

Large landholders expanded their herds in two ways: natural increases in the herd and purchases of animals from peasants. For purchases, it was best to wait until the dry season, when peasants came under duress and had to sell. At that time livestock prices would usually drop and acquisitions required a minimal cash outlay. Large ranchers, who typically controlled the creek bottoms and other low-lying areas, would turn their herds into these wetter areas for the duration of the dry season and avoid losing animals to the drought, a luxury most peasants could not afford.

Despite the difference in motivations of peasants and large ranchers, the general purpose of owning cattle in the days before the export boom was not so much for turning a quick profit as for serving as a store of wealth. The possibility of selling an animal for beef at some point in its career supported it as a worthy instrument of hoarding, but the central focus of attention was not on this final step in the animal's life. An informal rural market consisting of large landholders and smaller holders existed for the purchase and sale of cattle; the buyers did not intend to drive their purchases to a distant slaughter but made each acquisition more as a time deposit to be drawn on at some occasion in the uncertain future. In the interim cows produced offspring and milk; calves matured and gained weight; and for the large operator, the whole herd maintained claims over extensive land areas that might otherwise have been vulnerable to peasant colonization.

These other motives for holding cattle resulted in slaughters late in life. John Thompson, reporting on El Salvador in the 1950s, estimated that 60 percent of the cattle slaughtered were cows or oxen ten to fourteen years old and that half of the bulls slaughtered were more than seven years old; accounts of other countries suggest that there was a tendency to slaughter steers long after mature weight had been reached and the possibility of further weight gain diminished.[20]

Viewed in the economic context of the time, the criollo breed had certain advantages. A steer's late maturity was no great drawback when he was likely to be passed from one member of the community to another until his useful life as a store of value had deteriorated. His abilities to scrounge for grass on brush-infested pastures and to survive with minimal care were attractive characteristics in a cash-starved setting. From the perspective of the peasant family, the criollo may not have been the greatest beef producer, but compared to the specialized breeds developed by the modern beef industry, the criollo cow was superior because she yielded interest in the form of milk.

Considering the marketing context of the time, the practices of cattle raising were far from irrational. But little did the practitioners know that many of the age-old ways would soon be rendered obsolete. A combination of forces stronger than the local monopoly was busy at work. The time-honored traditions were soon to be caught in the whirl of the international beef market.

The Demand for Beef in the U.S. Market

Following World War II and until the early 1970s, the world system witnessed the longest wave of prosperity since the Industrial Revolution began in the eighteenth century. Under the political, economic, and military leadership of the U.S. government, trade channels were created, financial networks were spun, and institutions were founded to facilitate the movement of capital and commodities on a world scale. War-torn Europe and Japan were rebuilt in the 1950s, and by the 1960s the hum of capital accumulation had become a roar. The postwar boom was more than a mere quantitative increase in growth rates of GNP. It brought with it changes affecting where people lived, how they transported themselves, and their means of communication. It also changed what they ate.

With rapidly rising incomes, North Americans demanded more red meat. By 1961 the average U.S. citizen consumed approximately 94 pounds of beef and veal in a year, already the highest per capita consumption in the industrialized world.[21] After another decade of suburban sprawl, backyard barbecue grills, and the roadside billboards of the National Cattlemen's Association, the average North American was eating more beef. By 1970 per capita consumption of beef in the United States had risen to 117 pounds a year, more than double the yearly average for Western Europe.

Part of this expanded consumption represented purchases by the newly affluent of the better cuts of grain-fattened beef, but the beef habit was by no means limited to those who could afford T-bones. With more North Americans scurrying to work in automobiles, more women pulled into the active labor force, and more baby-boom children becoming hungry adolescents, a market opened for already prepared food at a price within reach of the working family's budget. For those wishing to stay at home, hamburgers and frozen dinners became the rage. For those wishing to dine out, a new class of restaurant boasting golden arches and similar neon paraphernalia began to pop up along the superhighways and crossroads all across the land.

McDonald's, Burger King, and other fast-food franchises quickly discovered this market. In contrast to the low turnover and high markup of the better restaurants and steak houses, the hamburger chains' secret of success was in turning out a standardized product at a competitive price. In part this goal was achieved by mechanizing and reducing the skill component in the food-preparation process. Central processing plants stamped patties of exact size, weight, and quality into a form that would require little culinary prowess from the teenage work force behind the counter. High turnover was achieved through selective location of franchises at major thoroughfares, and the market was further boosted by nationwide advertising on television.

Mechanization, high turnover, and unskilled labor were important in this new business, but the essential ingredient to the success of both the hamburger chains and the frozen convenience-food corporations was a reliable, cheap supply of beef. Expensive cuts of grain-fattened beef, the specialty of the U.S. grain belt, were unnecessary for this newly expanding market. Lean, grass-fed beef, tough as it sometimes was, could be converted into an adequate meal with enough grinding, stewing, or tenderizing.

For grass-fed beef, U.S. producers faced higher costs because harsh winter weather meant increased expenditures for protection and feeding, and because land prices continued to escalate, as did labor costs.[22] The scale of beef purchases by the fast food industry was so large, and beef was such an important component of total costs, that the management could ill afford to stop at the U.S. range in its search for cheap meat. In the 1950s some of the largest users increased their orders of beef from abroad. They looked to well-established beef producers like Australia and New Zealand, and they scoured the earth for yet-untapped sources of supply. They even formed an industry group called the Meat Importers Council of America to lobby Washington for free trade.

The fast-food industry confronted some formidable obstacles to the importation of beef from lower-cost foreign sources. The Federal Meat Inspection Act, for example, required packing plants in other countries to pass the same sanitation tests as packing plants in the United States, and periodic inspections of packing plants and beef were required for USDA approval. Until modern facilities were constructed, the health laws were an effective barrier to importation of beef from most underdeveloped countries. A second obstacle to the importation of beef was the aftosa quarantine, a measure designed to prevent the spread of hoof-and-mouth disease to the North American herd. According to the USDA, the aftosa virus can be transmitted through fresh or frozen beef, so that beef from areas considered "contaminated" must first be cooked, a requirement that drives up the cost of production considerably. The entire South American continent from the Panama Canal to Tierra del Fuego is subject to this quarantine, which effectively prevents the cheapest beef in the hemisphere, that of the fertile plains of Argentina, Uruguay, Brazil, and Paraguay, from entering the U.S. market in fresh or frozen form.[23]

In addition, the National Cattlemen's Association of America over the years has been able to counterbalance the efforts of the fast-food industry by pressuring Congress for quota protection from cheap foreign beef. The first protective legislation came in the 1956 Agricultural Act. This act set the tone for later protective measures in that it took the form of voluntary export quotas, but subsequent legislation (1964 Public Law 88–481 and the 1979 Meat Import Act) contained teeth that the earlier law did not have. In the event that an exporting country violated the voluntary quota by a certain margin, the more recent acts provided for a real quota to be triggered by the Department of Agriculture. In that event the enforcement authority would be wrested from the government of the exporting country, and beef shipments could be turned back from the U.S. border.

The protection in force from 1964 through 1979 limited total imports of cheap cuts of beef to around 6 or 7 percent of U.S. production levels. As domestic production increased, so too did the volume of imports permitted the fast-food business. In the Meat Import Act of 1979, a more restrictive formula for setting quotas was established.[24] When the 1979 law was passed, the Meat Importers Council of America charged that the new law was written by the National Cattlemen's Association.[25]

The total volume of beef imports permitted to enter the U.S. market was primarily a contest between the fast-food industry and the ranchers, the two domestic business groups most directly affected. Once the total quota level was established, however, the distribution of quotas to the various exporting countries became subject to more complicated pressures from an array of corporations and private investors with profits tied to the disbursal of the quotas. Moreover, once the size of the overall quota was decided, the determination of the individual country quotas became open to the pressures of the foreign policy establishment in Washington.

Out of some fifty beef-producing nations, fewer than fifteen have received quotas at any one time. The beef quotas have provided U.S. trade negotiators a bargaining chip for opening the markets of the three advanced-country beneficiaries—Australia, New Zealand, and Canada—to U.S. exports. The beef-export quotas for the underdeveloped world became subject to foreign policy pressures resembling those that affect the U.S. sugar quota. After Castro's rise to power in Cuba,the Alliance for Progress began to promote the expansion and diversification of exports from Central America and the Caribbean as part of the development strategy for the region. Beef and sugar quotas could be manipulated by Washington to reward the obedient and punish the wicked. One of the first actions against the Castro regime was to cut the sugar quota and redistribute it to more "friendly" governments in the region, an action that was repeated with the cutting of the beef and sugar quotas for Nicaragua in the 1980s.

Ironically, the combined effect of the health and quota laws, measures that are protectionist in spirit, turned out to promote the exports of Central American beef to the United States. The aftosa quarantine has blocked South American beef from sharing the market, and the strategic concern over Central America has favored the increase in Central America's share of the quota on "developmental" grounds. Whenever the quota shares have been adjusted, Central America's portion of the total has been increased. A share that was only 5 percent of the total in the early 1960s was doubled in 1968 to 10 percent of the total. In 1971 it was increased to 11 percent. By 1979 the figure stood at 15 percent, representing 93 percent of the share of the quota that was doled out that year to underdeveloped countries.[26] In 1984 the Kissinger Commission recommended a further expansion of Central America's beef quota.

Central America's beef-export boom was favored by Washington's regulations on the demand side of the market, but success was not merely stimulated by demand. For Central American pastures to feed North American appetites, a host of supply conditions had to be changed. Modern USDA-approved packing plants had to replace the traditional slaughter sheds. Roads and bridges linking pasture to packing plant and packing plant to port had to be constructed. Refrigerated transport, beefier breeds of cattle, and modern pasture management had to be introduced.

The Vital Supply Link: The Modern Packing Plant

From the very beginning, the modern packing plant has played a lead role in Central America's beef-export boom. Even if the trade had not been regulated, the big buyers in the United States would have had great difficulty in purchasing beef from the hundreds of dirty little slaughter sheds in Central America. With the strict U.S. health laws and import quotas in force, the rush to build modern facilities was intense. It was soon discovered that the first step toward negotiating for a larger share of the U.S. quota was to build a packing plant that would pass USDA inspections. For this reason, the geographical spread of modern packing plants closely anticipated the exports of beef to the United States (Charts 4-1 and 4-2). As the packing plants multiplied and spread from country to country, so too did dollar revenues from the export of beef (Chart 4-3).

Like the traditional abattoir, the modern packing plant purchases cattle, puts them to death, skins and guts them, and sells the meat. Beyond these elementary functions, however, the two part company. From the scale of purchases and sales to the way the job is done, the two operations are worlds apart. A typical municipal slaughterhouse is pushed to handle more than 1 beast a day;

Chart 4-1

U.S. Beef Imports from Central America, 1957–1980

Pounds

(millions)

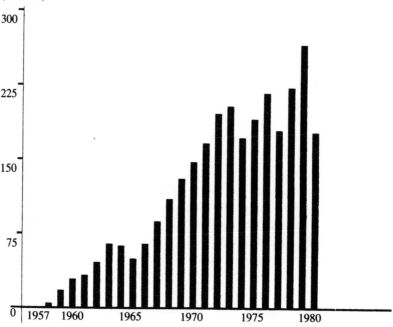

Sources: USDA and U.S. Department of Commerce. For more details on sources and individual country data see Table A-8 in the Appendix.

its modern counterpart is designed to process between 200 and 250, and some can do up to 500 per day. The traditional abattoir is a primitive shed; the modern packing plant is a gigantic concrete structure, sometimes two stories high, covering acres of land. The owner/operator of the traditional abattoir is personally involved in each step of the process from the purchase of live cattle to the sale of the carcass, and the operation is carried out with the help of rudimentary tools and one or two hired assistants. The modern packing plant hires hundreds of employees, assigns specific tasks, provides precise instruments to work with, maintains a sanitary environment, and has refrigerator storage chambers for the final product.

The thrust of modernization has projected beyond the packing plant. Through its purchases, the modern packing plant exerted pressure on the ranchers for improved livestock. The inspections at the plant corral determined whether the animal was deemed fit for export. Old, skinny cows,

Chart 4-2
Number of USDA-Approved Packing Plants, 1956–1978

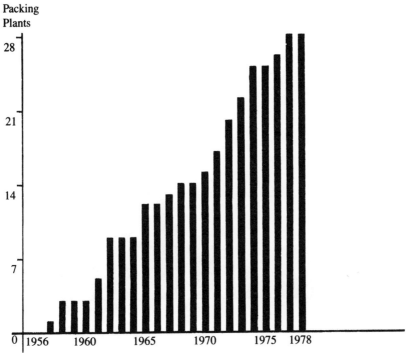

Packing
Plants

Sources: USDA; Slutzky, "La agroindustria de la carne"; de Lanuza, "La agroindustria de la carne"; and León, Barboza, and Aguilar, *Ganadería*. For more detail on sources and individual country data see Table A-9 in the Appendix.

animals with damaged hides and hoofs, diseased beasts, and those arriving in otherwise poor condition were either turned away at the gate or herded into the corral and labeled "domestic consumption." As the packing plants proliferated, the premium paid for export-quality animals was translated into transport to slaughter in modern trailer trucks instead of on the hoof, improved pasture management for rapid weight gain, the importation of beefier and quicker-maturing breeds of cattle, the use of modern veterinary supplements, and the introduction of other modern ranching practices from the United States.

Through its sales, the modern packing plants heralded a new era in the transport of beef to market.

Chart 4-3

Central American Beef Exports, 1960–1980

U.S. $ (Millions)

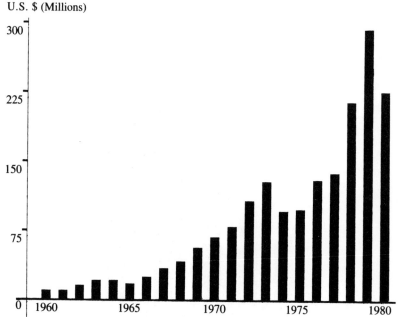

Source: SIECA. For more detail on sources and individual country data see Table A-10 in the Appendix.

Refrigerator Transport

Once the chilled or frozen beef left the loading ramp of the packinghouse, it had to be protected from exposure on its journey through the tropical heat. Without thorough protection there was little chance of a shipment passing the health inspector in Miami.

At first the method of transport was cumbersome and costly. The boxes of chilled or frozen beef were loaded into refrigerator trucks and driven to port. At port either the refrigerator trucks had to wait at the dock until a refrigerator containership was ready to receive cargo or the boxes were unloaded and placed in a refrigerator warehouse to await the arrival of the containership. Refrigerator trucks were tied up in extensive delays except in the few Central American ports that had sophisticated refrigerator warehouse facilities, like those of Corinto, Nicaragua. Once reaching Miami, the boxes would be unloaded once more and placed in cold storage at a warehouse or loaded directly onto refrigerator trucks for shipment to the wholesaler. Each step of loading and unloading raised the cost of the journey and risked exposure of the meat, and the service provided by the containerships was sporadic and expensive.

In the early 1960s the development of the "piggyback" trailer greatly relieved the transportation bottleneck. At the packing plant the boxes of frozen beef were loaded into a freezer compartment that fit neatly onto the bed of a trailer truck. The compartment had its own freezer unit and was designed so that it could be moved with a large forklift or hoist. The meat no longer had to be unloaded and reloaded with each transfer; instead, the already packed container unit was transferred from packing-plant loading dock to trailer truck to ocean vessel to trailer truck to meat distributor in the United States. This breakthrough meant that ports like Matías de Galvez in Guatemala, which did not have expensive refrigerator storage, soon became active in the beef trade, and the flow of beef did not have to rely on the irregular services of the refrigerator containerships. More important, the piggyback revolution meant that beef could remain frozen from the day of slaughter in Central America to the moment when it was tossed on the griddle in the United States.

Roads and the Beef Trade

As emphasized above, roads and bridges made previously remote areas in Central America accessible to the world market. Modern highways facilitated the trucking of freshly slaughtered beef to port. In Central America before the beef boom, there were only about 1,200 miles of paved roads, but by 1978 the paved road network had nearly quintupled, and with few exceptions the modern packinghouses located themselves near good roads that led to port.

Almost as important as the infrastructure linking the packing plant and the port were the improvements in the infrastructure linking packing plant and pasture. Practically the only feasible way to prevent the weight loss, hide and hoof deterioration, and death to cattle from an arduous overland drive was to put in a network of roads with decent bridges so that trailer trucks could be driven to the ranch. Some ranchers had been lucky or influential in getting modern highways to pass by their properties, but many more were put within reach of cattle trucks by all-weather roads topped with gravel, sand, or other materials. In 1953 there were some 5,000 miles of improved roads of this type, and by 1978 the network of improved roads had more than tripled to nearly 16,000 miles.

Connected to the improved roads were feeder roads made of dirt. During the long rainy season, roads of this type were little better than ox paths, but during the dry season they provided a valuable link between remote rangeland and the packing plant. Between 1953 and 1978 the network of dirt feeder roads had quadrupled in length, from around 7,000 miles to over 29,000 miles. Road development was so noticeable that a USDA report on the cattle industry of Central America in 1965 claimed that most of the cattle were being moved to slaughter by truck, stressing the great improvements in roads as the major contributing factor.[27]

State Promotion of the Beef Business

Road networks, refrigerator transport equipment, modern packing plants, imported cattle, veterinary medicines, barbed wire, improved grasses, and other modern inputs required dollar financing. Where did the money come from that turned Central America's traditional cattle sector into a thriving supplier of the U.S. market?

Private individuals and multinational corporations invested some of their own capital, but the primary financier of Central America's beef-export boom was the state. Financial resources were channeled into road building and cattle ranching in much the same way. Usually, a U.S. government agency or international development bank in Washington provided a grant or low-interest loan to a Central American government agency or development bank, which, in turn, would be responsible for administering the grant or loan.

If an institution capable of handling the promotional funds did not already exist in the recipient country, one was created. The seed money from Washington provided a foreign exchange base, and sometimes the donor agency developed a blueprint for the execution of a program, but in order to bolster the resources and participation of local institutions and people, the governments of the region were often required to pool matching funds from general state revenues or other sources in order to qualify for Washington finance. Once state promotional funds had been committed, the costs of beef production for private investors were lowered and the risks of loss were reduced as well. In this way, private financial resources were added to the total pool of capital available for beef.

Road Finance

Sometimes infrastructure loans have specifically targeted cattle development as a rationale, but more often cattle are a by-product of a road that was built for other purposes. For example, the road built in the late 1970s through northern Guatemala was primarily intended as a way to develop the oil and other mineral resources of the area, but once the road was built, cattle ranches appeared alongside it. Likewise, roads built for strategic purposes in Nicaragua opened up new areas for cattle grazing. Whether this outcome was in the minds of planners or not, roads have permitted inaccessible areas to be turned into grazing land.

Since World War II outside sources have provided more than half of the financing for Central America's roads. During the 1950s the primary concern of the U.S. government was not roads for development but roads for security. Most of the U.S. highway grants to Central America during that period went toward the construction of the strategic Pan American Highway, which ran through populous areas that did not necessarily have the best farmland. In contrast, the World Bank's highway program in Central America was targeted toward zones with the greatest potential for agricultural development, like the relatively undeveloped Pacific coastal plain.

With the Cuban Revolution and the Alliance for Progress, the U.S. government followed the lead of the World Bank and began stressing roads for development. In the early 1960s two more lending institutions were created that soon became active in promoting Central American roads, the Central American Bank for Economic Integration (CABEI) and the Inter-American Development Bank (IADB). During the 1960s and 1970s the World Bank, the CABEI, and the IADB became the primary conduits of outside financing of Central American infrastructure.[28]

Direct Promotional Finance to the Beef Sector

In addition to stimulating beef production through road building, Washington development institutions have promoted it more directly. For the World Bank, AID, and the IADB, beef was seen as a pragmatic, quick way to achieve export-led growth. Beef exports could be increased by expanding the existing herd and transforming traditional practices to fit the needs of the modern beef business. Because a basis for export expansion was already there, the beef business acquired an edge in capturing subsidized credit flowing from Washington.[29]

Chart 4-4 shows how seed money from Washington was dispensed to the cattle sector. Typically, loans were not made directly from the Washington source to the rancher but channeled through the central bank, a national development bank, or the ministry of agriculture. These recipient institutions would then pool national financial resources to augment the outside funds, and the entire pool would be administered either by the national government institution that received the foreign loan in the first place or by another financial institution. Once the cattle sector received priority status for state financing, private-sector funds augmented the financial pool even further. What may have started out as relatively small international credits of several million dollars here and there turned into a multimillion dollar flood of financing for the beef-export business. After a decade of beef promotion, more than one-fourth of private loans to agriculture and more than one-third of public loans to agriculture were going into the cattle sector.[30]

During the 1970s export revenues became crucial less as a way to finance development than as a way to make payments for inflated oil products and escalating interest rates. Beef had proved itself as an effective earner of foreign exchange in the 1960s, and bankers public and private continued to finance its production in the 1970s. For all five Central American countries, loans to the cattle business rose from around $150 million in 1971, before the first oil-price explosion hit, to between $200 and $230 million per year in the midst of the second oil-price explosion.[31]

Subsidized credit from Washington expanded the total volume of credit for beef by a multiplied amount because of the pyramiding of both public and private financial resources. The volumes of credit extended for cattle raising permitted a rapid increase in the size of the Central American herd, but seed money from Washington did more than expand production from a traditional base. It was aimed at transforming that base.

The evangelical spirit behind beef promotion can be seen in the project descriptions listed in Chart 4-4. The logic of the livestock projects was to reshape the traditional cattle sector into the image of the modern beef business. In a way that was quite at odds with the traditional attempt to spend as little cash as possible on one's herd, these loans promoted cash purchases of inputs, most of them imported inputs. In a distinct change from the traditional practice of letting one's herd fend for itself, these loans were predicated upon attention to and care for the livestock. These loans encouraged building fences, planting improved varieties of pasture, using irrigation, and actively intervening in other ways in pasture management, instead of letting the animals manage the pastures. Instead of operating from the perspective of cattle as a mere hoard to be sold sometime in the indefinite future, these loans were designed from the perspective of cattle as an instrument for making a money profit. The "improved" breeds and pasture-management techniques were intended to stimulate quick maturation and rapid weight gain, thereby maximizing the rate of beef production for the export-packing plants.

The Beef-Export Boom and Technology on the Ranch

While Washington was financing the development of modern cattle-raising practices, the packing plants were demanding bigger, younger, healthier animals from the ranchers. The combination of supply-and-demand incentives produced noticeable changes in Central American ranching. From the moment of conception to the final fattening before slaughter, not a single stage of the cattle-raising process was left untouched as herd and pasture management adapted to the needs of the world market.

Purebred Brahman and Santa Gertrudis bulls from Texas and Florida were imported to be bred with the native criollo.[32] At the same time, ranchers were improving their herds through the less expensive method of artificial insemination.[33] Especially successful was the cross between the Brahman (Zebu) lines and the native criollo, which produced a faster-maturing, beefier breed that had the added advantages of lower calf mortality rates and a high resistance to pests and tropical heat.[34]

Just as new bloodlines were being imported, so too were new methods of animal care. The companies that sold tubes of refrigerated semen also dispensed worm medicines, fly sprays, tick dips, vaccines, vitamin/mineral supplements, and other imported ingredients for improved animal health and sanitation.[35]

The boom transformed pasture management. High-yielding grasses were imported from tropical zones of Africa and South America.[36] Chemical fertilizers, a rarity on cattle ranches before the export boom, began to be used on improved pastures, especially on the ranches that fattened cattle for slaughter.[37] Tractors with mowers were imported, and after a decade of export expansion even herbicides were beginning to be imported, as ranchers moved away from reliance on the traditional machete teams for weed control.[38]

The boom stimulated the drilling of wells, the digging of ponds, and the placement of watering troughs within close proximity to the herd. It hastened the adoption of rotational grazing and other pasture control measures by providing cheap finance for the importation of barbed wire and the construction of fences.[39]

The combined effects of better breeds, better pastures, and better animal care produced younger, beefier, healthier animals for the packing plants.[40]

Chart 4-4

Major Institutions Dispensing Cattle-Promotion Loans

COUNTRY, Institution	Source and Date of Seed Money—Activities Targeted
GUATEMALA	
Bank of Guatemala (BG)	IADB (early 1970s)—promotion of all phases of livestock development in the Pacific zone through financial and technical assistance to the medium- and large-sized ranches[a]
Ministry of Agriculture and Livestock (MAG)	AID (early 1960s)—improvement of livestock industry through artificial insemination techniques and importation of frozen semen and purebred cattle[b]
	World Bank (1971)—with assistance from the United Nations Food and Agriculture Organization (FAO), credits and technical services to 300 ranchers for pasture improvement and better herd-management methods[c]
National Development Bank (BANDESA)	IADB (mid-1970s)—$17.2 million for pasture improvement and breeding stock, with emphasis on dairy improvement; some to other agricultural sectors[d]
EL SALVADOR	
Central Bank (BCES)	AID (1960s and 1970s)—small loans for supervised credit, livestock development, and irrigation projects[e]
Ministry of Agriculture and Livestock (MAG)	AID (early 1970s)—importation of pure breeding stock, experiments in feedlot fattening, improvement of sanitary and inspection organization[e]
HONDURAS	
National Development Bank (BANAFOM)	IADB (early 1960s)—$3 million for improved pastures, water facilities, and fencing; $1 million for purchase of purebred breeding cattle[b]
	AID—(late 1960s)—large-scale introduction of improved breeder stock, pasture improvement, increase in calving rate, decrease in mortality rate[a]
Central Bank of Honduras (BCH)	World Bank (early 1970s)—Livestock Office set up to administer original loan of $2.6 million (1970); enlarged by another $6.6 million credit in 1973; loans to cattlemen to finance pasture establishment, fencing, watering facilities, ranch buildings, parasite-control equipment, and improved breeding stock[c]

Ministry of Natural Resources (MRN)	AID (early and mid-1960s)—breeding improvements, animal sanitation, credit and marketing facilities; began as technical assistance from Interamerican Technical Service for Agricultural Cooperation (STICA, 1962), absorbed by MRN (1964) when AID began partial funding[b]
	IADB (1974)—$4.4 million to initiate a program to reduce the incidence of brucelosis and tuberculosis in the cattle population[f]

NICARAGUA

National Bank of Nicaragua (BNN)	IADB (early 1960s)—$9.1 million to increase rate of reproduction, reduce mortality rates, achieve higher meat yields, help prepare 95,000 hectares for pasture, construct 2.5 million meters of fencing, and construct wells, troughs, artificial ponds, drinking pools, silos, corrals, and dipping facilities for killing ticks[b]
	World Bank (1950s)—$3.25 million for purchase of machinery and equipment to stimulate mechanization of agriculture, opening of new lands, and improvement of pastures and acquisition of breeding stock; (1973)—financing of extension services, beef-marketing study, establishment of marketing centers for buying and selling cattle, a pasture-seed-multiplication scheme, and an artificial insemination center[c]
National Development Bank (INFONAC)	IADB (early 1960s)—$1.1 million for the purchase of breeding cattle in the United States[b]

COSTA RICA

Central Bank (BCCR)	World Bank (1950s, 1960s, 1970s)—agricultural loans channeled from BCCR to four state-owned banks to promote a number of activities, including the beef cattle industry[c]
National Bank of Costa Rica (BNCR)	IADB (1961)—$3 million for pasture renovation, purchase of livestock and equipment, and farm infrastructure; (1965)—$5.2 million to livestock and other activities damaged by Irazu volcano; (1972)—$6 million addition to original livestock programs[g]

[a]Rourk, *Beef Cattle Industries*, pp. 1–17.
[b]Gerrity, *Beef Export Trade*, pp. 1–11.
[c]IBRD, *World Bank Group*, pp. 1–105.
[d]IADB, *El BID en Guatemala* (Washington: IADB, 1980), p. 11
[e]Morgan, *Beef Cattle Industries*, pp. 1–26.
[f]IADB, *El BID en Honduras* (Washington: IADB, 1980), p. 10.
[g]IADB, *El BID en Costa Rica* (Washington: IADB, 1980).

Summary

Strong market forces operating independently of governments contributed to Central America's beef-export boom. On the demand side was an insatiable appetite for cheap beef created by the fast-food industry in the United States. On the supply side, Central America had some real cost advantages in the production of grass-fed beef. The link was further strengthened by a revolution in refrigerator transport in the early 1960s that lowered the cost of transport and reduced the risks of heat exposure along the way.

But the flourishing trade was not merely the work of technical break-throughs and the uncontrolled forces of supply and demand. From the start, the volume of demand was regulated by quotas and health restrictions set in Washington, D.C., a factor that favored the yearly expansion of demand for Central American beef. On the supply side, beef exports were stimulated by government programs initiated by development agencies in Washington. Roads were built into potential cattle zones, technical assistance was provided to ranchers, and subsidized credit was funneled into Central America's beef business.

Whether the source of the stimulus was public or private, the thrust was the same. Packing-plant purchases and government programs transformed traditional practices. The logic of the fragmented local market was progressively replaced by the logic of international business. Low turnover was replaced by high turnover in the slaughter and marketing of beef, and even the time honored hoarding motive, the hallmark of traditional cattle raising, was soon replaced by a new one: earning a quick money profit.

The results for beef technology were remarkable as ranching, transport, slaughter, and marketing responded to fresh incentives and reoriented themselves toward production for export.

From the development perspective of the World Bank, the IADB, and AID, Central America's beef-export boom was a success. The region's export earnings expanded rapidly, generating more foreign exchange for overall development needs. The export mix was diversified, so that the region became less dependent on the volatile coffee market for survival. Moreover, efficiency and quality were achieved by introducing modern technology into a backward area.

5. The Beneficiaries of Beef

In the previous chapter it was shown how governments promoted Central America's beef business. On the demand side, U.S. health laws discriminated against producers in South America and Africa, while Central America's portion of the U.S. quota was expanded from 5 percent in the early 1960s to 15 percent in the late 1970s. On the supply side, roads were built into zones showing the greatest grazing potential, cheap credit was made available for cattle raising and modern packing plants, and technical assistance was provided to ranchers. The private sector responded to the incentives, and beef became the fourth-most-important earner of foreign exchange, after coffee, cotton, and bananas.

For tiny Central America, the cash flow from the beef exports was considerable. Revenues climbed from approximately $9 million when the Alliance for Progress began in 1961 to over $100 million in the early 1970s. In the wake of the world economic crisis, more packing plants were approved to boost exports further, so that by 1979 Central America's twenty-eight packinghouses exported $290 million worth of beef, more than nine-tenths of it to the highly protected U.S. market.

The Source of the Beef Bonanza

The combined effect of the health laws and quota restrictions on imported beef caused U.S. prices to rise above the prices in the rest of the world. From 1964 through 1979 health laws and Public Law 88-481 effectively restricted imports of beef to approximately 6 or 7 percent of U.S. beef output, holding U.S. prices to more than double the prices received by producers in the lowest-cost areas, like New Zealand, and to one and a half times the cost of production in higher-cost areas, like Central America.[1] These laws yielded large profits for the lowest-cost U.S. producers, and they allowed higher-cost U.S. ranches to continue to operate behind a protective shield. These measures also created opportunities for earning excess profits by those fortunate enough to be granted access to the U.S. market.

Excess profits are created when the government grants particular interests monopoly rights to transfer a commodity from a low-cost source of supply into a market where the price is determined by higher-cost producers. The cost advantage that Central American producers have over North American producers is not primarily a result of cheap labor, although lower wages do create some Central American advantages in ranching and packing. Central America's most important advantages are that equivalent areas of ranchland cost much less in Central America than in the United States, and that Central American cattle do not have to be fed corn or hay during the winter months when the North American plains are under snow. For grain-fed beef, U.S. farmers need no protective quotas, but for lean, grass-fed beef the cost advantages in Central America are considerable.

The government policies described previously have further lowered production costs in Central America, but without the favorable health and quota laws Central American producers and U.S. producers alike would have their excess profits quickly eroded by even lower-cost beef from the fertile grasslands of New Zealand, Australia, Argentina, Uruguay, and Brazil.

One way to visualize the way a quota creates opportunities for excess profits is with the supply-and-demand analysis of Figure 5-1. Without the protective quota, U.S. ranchers would be competing directly with low-cost foreign producers and would not be able to sell in the United States at a price above the world price P_w shown in the figure. The low-cost domestic ranchers would be willing and able to supply only the quantity OA at that low free-trade price, and imports of foreign beef would equal AB. U.S. consumers would be buying the total amount OB at that low price. If the cattlemen are able to restrict imports of beef with a quota of CD, the price in the domestic market rises to $P_{u.s.}$ as the previous import levels are reduced to the level of the new quota. At that higher price U.S. consumers are willing and able to buy only OD: their consumption levels are reduced by DB because of the quota. With the higher price in the domestic market, higher-cost ranching operations find it profitable to increase beef production by AC. The excess profits taken by the lower-cost ranchers in the United States are equal to the shaded area $FEGH$, whereas the merchant profits earned on the imports of beef under the quota equal the shaded area $HIJK$, or the volume of imports times the differential between the protected price of beef in the U.S. market ($P_{u.s.}$) and the lower price of imported beef (P_w).

According to Figure 5-1, the "producer surplus" earned by the ranchers (area $FEGH$) and the "merchant surplus" (area $HIJK$) come from the U.S. consumers' having to pay more for less beef. Although beef consumers are the ones directly hit by the quota, some will be able to pass off the price increases to others by charging more, in turn, for the services they sell. Ultimately, the excess profits of the producers and merchants will be extracted from the

Figure 5-1
Effects of a Quota on the U.S. Beef Market

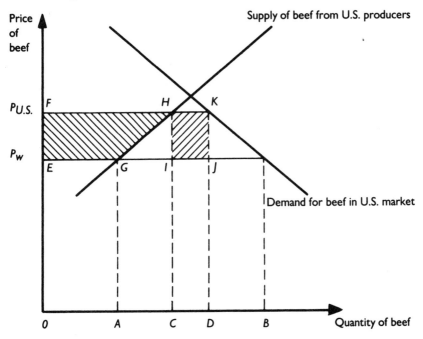

$P_{U.S.}$ = price of beef in the U.S. market after the quota
P_w = price of beef in the world market
OA = level of U.S. beef production without quota protection
OC = level of U.S. beef production with quota protection
OB = level of U.S. beef consumption without quota
OD = level of U.S. beef consumption with quota
AB = level of U.S. beef imports without quota protection
CD = level of U.S. beef imports permitted by quota
$FEGH$ = producer surplus because of the quota
$HIJK$ = merchant surplus to quota recipients

general wealth produced and marketed in the United States, where those with less market power, and therefore a lower ability to pass off the price increases to others, will end up paying. If the government issues a license to the import merchant and charges for the license, part of the merchants' excess profit can be collected by the government.

Under the actual arrangements of the beef-quota system, the monopoly access rights are issued not to the importer but to the government of the exporting country. That government then distributes the quota among the packing plants in the country.[2] Because of this institutional arrangement, the excess profit from the sale of low-cost Central American beef in the U.S. market does not all accrue to the beef importers, and none of it goes to the U.S. government. Instead, the excess profits are pushed back toward the source of supply, where the monopoly rights are being distributed. Beef importers in the United States may still be able to collect a portion of the excess profit by virtue of special arrangements with the packinghouses in Central America, and some of the excess profit may even accrue to the hamburger retailers in the United States by virtue of connections with the importers, but the greatest portion of the excess profit is collected by parties located in Central America.

How the excess profit has been distributed among Central American governments, packing plants, and ranchers has varied from time to time and from country to country depending on the institutional connections among the various parties. For a number of reasons, however, the packing plants have been able to tap the bulk of it.

The Packing Plants' Share of the Beef Bonanza

The greatest concentration of profits from beef accrue to owners of the packing plants partly because direct industrial profits are generated in the slaughter of cattle and the processing of the beef for market. More important, the monopoly rights to the U.S. market are issued directly to the packing plants, so that they are able to tap the excess profits from the sale of beef in the United States. National governments have restricted competition among packing plants by setting quotas consistent with the production capacity of the plants, and the building of new plants is not allowed unless the total national quota can be increased. Because of the quota licensing procedure, excess profits are not eroded by competition among plants in the marketing of beef. Likewise, in the purchase of cattle from ranchers, the packing plants have enjoyed certain market advantages, but the degree of market power exercised over the ranchers varies greatly depending on several factors.

Generally speaking, there are many ranchers and few packing plants, and so the packing plants are in a position to acquire cattle at a low price. Frequently only one packing plant serves an entire cattle zone, a situation that strengthens that plant's market power. Even when there are several plants in the same area, collusion among the packers holds down the prices paid for cattle. Often the largest plant will set the price to be paid for live cattle and other plants will follow suit, but when a certain plant is having difficulty fulfilling its quota it may break with the others and offer the ranchers more for export-quality cattle. Sometimes governments intervene to reinforce the market power of the packing plants, but at other times they intervene on behalf of ranchers.

Because of the different conditions of competition in the purchase of cattle, the profit shares extracted by packing plants have varied. In 1968, for example, packing plants from every country were receiving about forty-three cents a pound for boneless beef at Central American ports, but the prices they were paying the ranchers for boneless beef varied from a low of thirty-five cents a pound in Honduras and Nicaragua to a high of forty-one cents a pound in Costa Rica.[3]

The differential in prices paid by packing plants has created incentives for ranchers to market their cattle in low-markup countries, a practice vehemently resisted by packing plants in high-markup countries. Before the beef packers of Honduras passed a national head tax on the export of live cattle (1964), some Honduran cattle were being shipped to Guatemala for sale. Likewise, ranchers in southern Nicaragua found it profitable to sell their steers in Guanacaste, Costa Rica, despite restrictive laws banning the activity.[4]

The concentration of excess profits in the export-packing plants attracted the attention of investors, but because of the peculiar nature of the business environment, access was limited to a particular type of investor. Only large investors with international connections had the large block of capital and sophisticated technology required to build a plant that would pass health inspections. And in view of the way the quota licensing procedure worked, investors had to have political clout in Washington and in national governments to obtain access to the U.S. market.

From the very beginning, U.S.-based multinational corporations, especially those involved in the food-processing business, acquired packing plants in Central America. The first packing plant in Costa Rica and the first two in Honduras were foreign direct investments. Some well-known companies invested in Central American packing plants. For example, Borden, Inc., acquired Henderson Packing Plant in Costa Rica in 1965.[5] Tela Railroad Company, subsidiary of United Brands, the famous banana company whose 1978 beef sales were reported to be double its banana sales,[6] established a packing plant in its port town of Tela, Honduras.[7] International Foods, another famous food-processing company and a major U.S. importer of Central American beef, acquired two packing plants in Honduras, Empacadora Alus and Empacadora Rancho Lorenzo.[8]

At the other extreme from wholly owned subsidiaries of multinational corporations are some packing plants owned almost entirely by wealthy and politically prominent Central Americans. For example, a major stockholder in the first and largest packing plant in Nicaragua (IFAGAN) became the outright owner of a second packing plant, Productos CARNIC—Meat Products of Nicaragua.[9] This stockholder was none other than the dictator himself, Anastasio Somoza Debayle, who appears to have used international loans earmarked for the cattle sector to subsidize the purchase of refrigeration equipment for his plants.[10] Similarly, the list of shareholders of Mataderos de El Salvador, one of the two beef-export plants in El Salvador, contains the names Homberger, Quiñonez, Hill, Prieto, Salaverría, and Palomo, all of them members of the Salvadoran coffee oligarchy.[11]

The most typical pattern of investment that has emerged in the packing-plant business is a mixture of foreign and local capital. In a business context where connections with national governments, multilateral lending institutions, and the U.S. government determine the size of the market and access to cheap finance, it is not surprising that most packing plants are joint ventures or are owned by holding companies with a mixture of local and international capital. A good example of the way this process works is Agrodinámica Holding Company, a company that formed in 1971 with 60 percent of the stock owned by Latin Americans and 40 percent of the stock owned by ADELA Investment Company.[12] In turn, ADELA has been involved in the Central American beef business since at least 1966, when it received a regional development loan of more than $8 million from the IADB.[13] One of the founders of Agrodinámica is Alejandro Orfila, who at the time of incorporation represented ADELA Investment Company in the United States; later Orfila became secretary-general of the Organization of American States (OAS).[14] Among Agrodinámica's many other investments in the Central American beef business are included two packing plants in Honduras (Industria Ganadera de Honduras and Oriente Industrial).[15]

The modern packing business created opportunities for companies to service the packing plants. Companies like Weyerhauser and Crown Zellerbach, both West Coast-based multinationals, invested in cardboard box factories in

Central America and began supplying packinghouses with the sturdy, corrugated boxes necessary for shipping the beef. Hussman Refrigerator Company of Missouri and Clark Equipment Company of Minnesota began supplying modern refrigeration equipment, and Sea-Land, Inc., later acquired by R. J. Reynolds of North Carolina, began supplying the region with refrigerated piggyback trailers.[16] In cases where these servicing companies set up assembly operations, some of the excess profits could be extracted through the sale of commodities to the packing plants at a price protected by tariffs, while the service companies imported inputs for the assembly operation without having to pay duties on them.

The Impact of the Boom on Slaughter Sheds, Vendors, and Consumers

Modern packing plants prospered at the expense of traditional slaughterhouses, meat vendors in the markets, and Central American consumers. Yearly increases in export quotas drained beef from the domestic market. In the 1950s virtually all of the beef slaughtered in Central America was consumed domestically, but by the late 1970s three-fourths of the region's beef was being exported.[17] Because of health and quota laws, traditional slaughterhouses were blocked from the export trade, and by the mid-1960s the export-packing plants began selling beef in the domestic market as well.[18] The best beef went for export, with the meat from sick cattle, old cows, and contaminated animals left for domestic consumption.[19] Despite two decades of increased beef production, the average Central American was consuming less beef in 1978 than in 1957 before the first export-packing plant was built.[20]

Private Investment in Cattle Raising

Yearly increases in export demand exerted a steady upward pressure on cattle prices. The buoyant market demand combined with state promotions of supply raised the rate of profit in cattle raising in Central America. Unlike cotton growing, which is subject to wild swings in profitability, cattle raising soon gained a reputation as a sound, steady business.

The greatest profits in cattle ranching are claimed by ranches involved in fattening the cattle before slaughter. Typically these are large ranches, located on the very best pasturelands, with easy access to commercial centers and the export-packing plants.[21] Most of the cattle destined for export are purchased directly from these large operations, a system that enables the owners to have first claim on any excess profits that might pass from the packing plants to the ranchers.[22] In addition to excess profits that might be passed along, these ranches regularly collect the premium that is paid for larger animals. They operate by purchasing lean cattle, either from smaller operations that do not have access to prime pastureland or from very large, extensive cattle ranches located in peripheral areas. Because of their control over the best lands, their more favorable marketing position, and their connections with the packing plants, the large ranches involved in the fattening of cattle are the most likely recipients of bank financing, the most likely to introduce improved pastures and other modern cattle-raising practices, and the most likely to receive the benefits of government promotional efforts.

As in the case of cotton, many of the families who grew rich from the beef-export boom were members of an old elite who had long-standing titles to hacienda lands along the Pacific coastal plain before the area was fully developed for commercial agriculture. When opportunities from the beef-export boom came along, these were the families who controlled the lands suitable for the fattening phase of cattle ranching. Quite often members of this group became shareholders in the packinghouses or participated in their management.[23]

The packing corporations themselves have acquired some ranches near their plants in order to tap profits from the final fattening phase and to ensure a readily available source of cattle. When independent ranchers unexpectedly reduce their sales of live cattle, the packing company can keep the plant running at an efficient capacity by slaughtering its own cattle from nearby ranches.[24]

Substantial profits are earned from extensive rangeland in peripheral areas, where cattle are allowed to roam year round. Before the dry season mature animals are culled from the herd and sold to more-developed ranches near the packing plants. The families who already held title to land found themselves in a position to turn marginal zones into extensive grazing areas, but they also found that their properties could be extended into previously untitled areas. Their blocks of titled land were put up as collateral for subsidized loans. Livestock and barbed wire were purchased with the proceeds, and in this way grazing lands were extended into untitled areas. For example, in Nicaragua the Somoza family had already acquired fifty-one ranches before the beef-export boom, but by 1979, after two decades of export-led growth, the holdings of the Somozas and those closely connected had expanded to more than 2 million acres, more than half of which was in extensive ranchland.[25]

Multinational corporations with vast acreages of idle land before the beef-export boom also discovered the profits from extensive grazing. At the top of this list of recipients from the boom were the foreign-owned fruit companies, which held hundreds of thousands of acres of land in Central America. Some of the fruit companies were already raising cattle as a source of food for the sizable work forces on their plantations, but the beef-export boom made it profitable for them to expand their pasturelands. Some of the more accessible lands were developed into improved pasture areas for the fattening of cattle, and the less accessible and poorer lands were turned into extensive grazing areas. Today Del Monte, a subsidiary of R. J. Reynolds, raises cattle on its ninety-nine thousand acres of concessions in Guatemala and in Costa Rica.[26] Standard Brands, a subsidiary of Castle and Cooke, raises cattle on its concessions in Honduras and Costa Rica. In addition to a packing plant in Honduras, United Brands has improved pastures on its concessions in Costa Rica, and in northern Honduras its Tela Railroad subsidiary maintains fourteen thousand acres of improved pasture, and thirty-four thousand acres of extensive range-land.[27] The fruit companies are not the only foreign companies who were able to turn idle acres into money-earning pasture. For example, Goodyear Tire and Rubber Company's concession in Costa Rica was once a thriving rubber plantation; now it is a cattle ranch.[28]

Other multinational corporations with no previous foothold in the region were attracted by potential profits in cattle raising and acquired improved pasturelands as well as extensive grazing areas. Agrodinámica, a company whose grazing and packing operations have already been mentioned, is one example of a newcomer attracted by beef. Another instance of a company that emerged simultaneously with the beef-export boom is Latin America Agribusiness Development Corporation (LAAD), a Panamanian-incorporated multinational whose second-largest area of investment, after food processing, is beef cattle. According to one source, 62 percent of LAAD's herd grazes in Guatemala, Honduras, Nicaragua, and Costa Rica. Like Agrodinámica, LAAD works as a consortium of powerful interests. Its list of stockholders looks like a directory of multinational agribusiness; some on the list have already been mentioned as direct owners of packing plants and ranches. The LAAD stockholder list includes ADELA, Borden, Castle and Cooke, Bank of America, Cargill, Caterpillar, Chase Manhattan Bank, John Deere, Monsanto, Ralston-Purina, and eight other banks and agribusiness corporations.[29]

The beef-export boom expanded the wealth of those who already owned land and attracted fresh multinational capital, but like the cotton boom, it also created opportunities for a new group of urban based agriculturalists. In the cotton boom this group of urban professionals rented lands from owners of large haciendas. In the beef boom, however, this same group acquired ranches

in previously untitled areas.The advantage this new group of weekend ranchers possessed flowed from its urban base. Land titles and subsidized finance
for cattle raising were being issued from government institutions located in the
capital cities. Savings from professional incomes and connections with friends
in the government development banks helped secure cattle loans. With this
pool of capital, survey teams and lawyers were hired to establish legal title to
the land; barbed wire was purchased; fences were built; and herds were transferred to the properties. The development of such ranches meant driving long
hours over rough terrain after a forty-hour work week in the city. The weekend
consisted of working with a hired team to build corrals, fences, roads, and
other structures. Once the herd was established, the weekends were spent
rounding up the cattle, spraying them for flies, inoculating them, castrating the
young bulls, and managing the ranch. After the weekend the cattleman faced a
rough ride back to the city to start the professional week on Monday. The
payoff was greater than the earnings from the ranch, however. For doctors,
lawyers, government officials, army officers, and others with professional
incomes, the beef-export boom provided entry into the landholding class.[30]

The Collapse of the Small Holder

While large ranchers were expanding their herds for the export trade, peasants
were losing livestock. Before the export boom hit, approximately one-fourth
of all the cattle were held by peasants with farms smaller than twenty-five
acres. After a decade of export-led growth, small farmers had lost 20 percent
of their previous cattle holdings and owned only one-eighth of all the cattle in
the region.[31]

The loss of cattle by small farmers is an indication of generalized stress on
the peasantry, but the beef-export boom directly sped the process along. The
small cow/calf operators were at the lowest rung of the marketing hierarchy,
with the lowest degree of market power. When the packing plants began
demanding beefier breeds of cattle, the small holders were unable to acquire
the cash necessary to introduce the improved bloodlines. Moreover, the
humpbacked breeds demanded by the export trade were inferior milk producers and so were unattractive from the perspective of the peasant family. Instead
of buying criollo calves from the small holders, large ranchers began to
concentrate on the breeding phase themselves.

Beef-boom finance reinforced the dictates of the world beef market. Peasants had learned from centuries of experience to avoid the entanglements of
credit, and Washington finance promoted larger farms that were more likely to

purchase beefier bloodlines, veterinary medicines, and other modern inputs.[32] National financial institutions in charge of dispensing Washington beef loans were prone to favor the large operator as well. Located in the capital cities, these national lending institutions were in close contact with large ranchers and big-city lawyers, doctors, merchants, military officers, and other professionals. The traditional cow/calf operators tucked away in the countryside were naturally bypassed by subsidized finance, and private banks were even less likely to risk loans to small farmers. The end result was that the small farmer was unable to adapt to the new business environment and was replaced by larger holders who had more favorable relations with the packinghouses and the banks.

Profits from the Sale of Modern Inputs

Whereas cotton profits tapped by multinational corporations were concentrated in the sale of imported inputs, beef profits were more heavily concentrated in sale of the exported output. Nevertheless, the modernization of the cattle-raising sector called for increasing purchases of inputs from multinational corporations. Enriched animal feeds with veterinary supplements, improved grasses, fertilizer for pastures, barbed wire, purebred cattle, semen for artificial insemination, and the like began to be imported in larger volumes with the expansion and modernization of cattle raising.[33]

With the tariff and tax incentives offered by governments in the 1960s, a number of companies found it profitable to invest directly in Central America, import intermediate products and raw materials, and package the products in a factory in Central America. Fort Dodge Labs of Fort Dodge, Iowa, set up factories for the processing and packaging of veterinary products in Costa Rica, Honduras, and El Salvador. Ralston-Purina began producing and marketing veterinary products and animal feeds out of factories in Guatemala and El Salvador. Centrocom Enterprises (a subsidiary of Cargill) and Central Soya began producing enriched animal feeds in Guatemala. In addition to selling fertilizer and improved grass seeds to ranchers, W. R. Grace began selling frozen semen for artificial insemination from its distributorship in Nicaragua.[34]

Vertical Integration in the Beef-Export Business

A number of corporations and individuals found it profitable to invest in more than one phase of the beef business. For example, on the eve of the Revolution the Somoza family of Nicaragua owned many thousands of acres of unimproved pasture in Nicaragua and Costa Rica, thousands of acres of improved pasture in Nicaragua, two export-packing plants, a refrigerated warehouse at the port of Corinto, and a beef-import business in Miami. International Foods owns two packinghouses in Honduras and a beef-import business in the United States. United Brands controls many thousands of acres of improved and unimproved pasture in Central America; owns a packing plant, a railroad, and docks in Honduras; has a fleet of refrigerator ships; and until 1977 owned a major meat-packing and -distributing company in the United States.[35]

One of the largest investors in the Central American beef business is Agrodinámica Holding Company. The company controls thousands of acres of improved and unimproved pastures in Central America; it owns numerous packing plants, a leather tannery, and a meat retailing chain in Central America; and in the early 1970s it established United Beef Packers, a Miami-based beef-import house and wholesale distributor.[36]

Some very large U.S. companies have acquired stakes in the Central American beef business through the purchase of subsidiaries. For example, R. J. Reynolds owns thousands of acres of grazing land in Guatemala and Costa Rica through its subsidiary, Del Monte, and until recently it owned the piggyback containership company Sea-Land, Inc. R. J. Reynolds directly markets beef in a variety of frozen and canned convenience foods including Ortega brand beef tacos (Del Monte), Patio brand beef enchiladas (Del Monte), Chun King beef chow mein (Del Monte), and Del Monte Mexican Foods; and the company sells beef through Zantigo Mexican Restaurants (Kentucky Fried Chicken). If R. J. Reynolds's beef products are not enough, a consumer in the United States can preface the meal with a shot of José Cuervo Tequila (Heublein Spirits and Wine Company), douse the dinner with A-1 Steak Sauce (Del Monte), and digest it with the help of a Winston (R. J. Reynolds Tobacco Company).[37]

Summary

The beef boom is a prime example of how the private sector can bring about economic development when the government removes obstacles to trade and investment. The favorable access to the protected U.S. beef market pumped excess profits into Central America's traditional beef business. At the same time, the U.S. government, Washington-based development banks, and the governments of Central America reduced the private costs of beef production by building roads into potential grazing areas, providing technical assistance to ranchers, and lubricating the business with subsidized credit.

Multinational corporations responded to the profit incentives and tapped wealth from every phase of the business, modernizing as they proceeded. Agribusiness supply houses increased their sales of improved grass seed, barbed wire, fertilizer, pasture-clipping equipment, frozen semen, veterinary medicines, feed supplements, and other modern inputs. Fruit companies and other corporations with access to large blocks of land turned previously idle properties into money-earning pastures. Food-processing companies claimed some of the most concentrated earnings by investing in packing plants and improved grazing lands. Pulp and paper companies sold corrugated boxes to the packing plants, and refrigerator companies sold the packing plants modern refrigeration equipment. Profits were also earned both in transporting frozen beef from packing plant to port and then in shipping it to the United States. Finally, import businesses in the United States, producers of frozen beef products, and hamburger chains profited from the purchase of cheap Central American beef. Most of the multinational corporations involved in the beef-export boom invested in more than one phase of the business, and some corporations were found to be vertically integrated from Central American pasture all the way to North American burrito.

Multinational corporations, however, were not the only beneficiaries of the beef-export boom. Like the fruit companies, wealthy Central American families with large blocks of titled property before the export boom increased their wealth by turning marginal lands into pasture. Those with prime holdings, especially along the Pacific coastal plain, tapped some of the export premium by purchasing lean cattle from extensive grazing operations in poorer areas and fattening them on their modernized, improved ranches. A small group of very powerful families tapped profits from almost every phase of the beef business, from extensive grazing of cattle on marginal lands, to fattening operations, to slaughtering cattle in family-owned packing plants. From the beginning, government agencies and international development banks were an integral part of the business, a factor that influenced the patterns of investment in beef. More than cotton, the beef business came to be dominated by joint ventures or holding companies with ownership and directorships shared between wealthy, politically connected Central Americans and wealthy, politically connected multinational corporations.

The beef-export boom also created opportunities for a new group of weekend ranchers. As peripheral areas previously untouched by commercial agriculture were opened up for cattle raising, urban-based professionals with access to state finance and the titling press found in cattle ranching a way to move into the landed elite.

Some of the traditional participants in Central America's beef cattle industry lost in the transition. Export-packing plants drained business from the traditional slaughterhouses, and vendors in the public markets were left with lower-quality beef at higher prices for domestic consumers. Similarly, peasants who had specialized in cow/calf operations before the export boom lost livestock to larger ranchers who were better able to respond to the modernization incentives offered by the export-packing plants and the development banks.

Considering the rapid response to promotional efforts, the modernizing thrust of the business, the revenues generated by the trade, and the range and political clout of the beneficiaries, it is understandable why beef promotion has remained such a favorite development strategy in Washington.

6. Cattle and the Campesino

The beef boom was greedier for land than any of the export booms that preceded it. The expansion of coffee in the nineteenth century was held in check by biological constraints that limited its cultivation to fertile lands at altitudes between two and five thousand feet. Bananas could not be grown on a commercial basis except in wet, fertile, lowland river basins, and cotton proved to be unprofitable beyond the most fertile stretches of the Pacific coastal plain. Each of the previous export booms had profound effects on peasant life, but each was restrained by natural boundaries. The beef-export boom was different. Cattle could be raised wherever grass would grow.

Forest to Pasture

Before the first export-packing plant was constructed, Central America's cattle herd numbered approximately 4.7 million head and grazed on 8.5 million acres of pasture. After two decades of export-led growth, the herd numbered more than 10 million and occupied 20 million acres of land, an area exceeding that of all other agriculture combined.[1]

By most accounts, the pastures were carved from the Central American forest. Agricultural censuses point to a rapid rate of deforestation during the 1960s and 1970s, and the areas most heavily deforested were the zones where the cattle boom was most intense. By 1964 Escuintla was Guatemala's most important cattle-raising department, with one-fifth of the national herd. Before the export boom hit, 12 percent of the farm area of Escuintla was in pasture and 48 percent in forest, but by 1964, 42 percent was in pasture and only 16 percent remained in forest.[2] Similarly, in the most important cattle-raising department of Honduras (Choluteca), with one-tenth of the national herd in 1974, pastures expanded from 47 percent of the census area before the export boom to 64 percent in 1974, while forests declined from 29 percent to 11 percent over the same period.[3] In Costa Rica Guanacaste was the leading cattle-raising province throughout the period, with approximately 40 percent of the national herd. Pastures in Guanacaste climbed from 39 percent of the farm area before the export boom to 65 percent in 1974, while the farm area in forest collapsed from 34 percent to only 13 percent.[4] Direct estimates of forest reserves in Costa Rica show that in 1950 three-fourths of the country was covered with forest. By 1973 only half of the country remained in forest, and by 1978 forests covered only one-third of the national territory.[5] Figures 6-1 and 6-2 give a graphic image of what happened to Costa Rica's forest reserves. The areas that were forest in 1940 are with few exceptions now engaged in cattle ranching, and the destruction of the tropical forest continues as cattle ranching spreads into peripheral zones.[6] A more recent study of tropical forests found that in Central America "a strong trend toward cattle ranching . . . has greatly reduced primary forests, now believed to be two-thirds removed."[7]

Forest to Corn to Pasture

Only a small fraction of Central America's forest has been turned into lumber. The greatest portion of it has gone up in smoke.

Some accounts have noted the hiring of a team of men to clear the way for pasture. From interviews with Costa Rican farmers and forestry service inspectors, Lori Ann Thrupp reports the phenomenon of enterprising land speculators securing title to undeveloped forest, clearing the land with mechanized equipment, and then selling it to colonists, who later sell to ranchers.[8] Anthropologist Jefferson Boyer reports that ranchers in the cattle zone of Choluteca, Honduras, "simply hired labor to slash and burn the trees and brush, opening the land to grass production."[9]

The most commonly reported practice of converting forest to pasture, however, is not the most obvious one of hiring a gang of men to do the job. A more traditional method makes use of the natural inclinations of the Central American peasantry; it is the method that was used to clear land for coffee, cotton, and other exports that preceded beef.[10] This age-old method is nicely described by Robert A. White in a discussion of the cattle boom on the Pacific strip of Honduras: "Some large land holders used the rental of land to the small farmer as a means of clearing the hillsides of timber and preparing it for pasture for cattle grazing. The land was rented for a season or two to the smaller farmer, who was expected to clear the often heavy timber in order to prepare the land for seeding. Each year a new area was rented to be cleared so that gradually the whole area was prepared for pasture."[11]

An identical story of converting forest to cornfields and then to pasture is reported by observers in Guatemala, El Salvador, Nicaragua, and Costa Rica. Usually peasants are allowed to farm the land just long enough for the stumps to rot, at which time they are evicted to make way for cattle.[12]

Figure 6-1
Costa Rica: Area in Forest, 1940

Deforestation of Costa Rica
Forests 1940

PACIFICO SECO

ZONA NORTE

VALLE CENTRAL
OCCIDENTAL

PACIFICO CENTRAL

Area in Forest

Source: Sáenz Maroto, *Deforestación*, p. 29.

Ecological Consequences of
Forest-to-Pasture Transformation

Under certain conditions, slash-and-burn (swidden) agriculture practiced by
the peasantry allows for the regeneration of secondary forest growth after a
patch has been abandoned,[13] but when aggressive African grasses are planted
this secondary resurgence of forests is blocked.[14]

Some biologists have warned that an important filter for the earth's atmo-
sphere will be destroyed if the forests of Central and South America continue
to be ravaged. Others have pointed to the loss of genetic diversity that occurs
when forests that support many species of plants and animals are replaced by
open grasslands that support few.[15] With proper care, vast tracts of timber
could have been a source of lumber for centuries into the future, but with the

Figure 6-2
Costa Rica: Area in Forest, 1977

Deforestation of Costa Rica
Forests 1977

PACIFICO SECO

VALLE CENTRAL
OCCIDENTAL

PACIFICO CENTRAL

Area in Forest

PACIFICO SUR

Source: Sáenz Maroto, *Deforestación*, p. 30.

drive for more pasture, forest reserves have vanished. Watershed, valuable for subsistence agriculture and export agriculture alike, has been destroyed along with the forest canopy. Hillsides have become rutted with gullies, and the flatlands below have become subject to flooding. With the removal of the forests, drier areas along the Pacific have become more vulnerable to drought, and in some places dust storms have become a yearly occurrence.

The destruction of forest for pasture has proceeded without considering local soil conditions. In areas where soils are of limestone, new volcanics, or deep alluvial deposits, grazing is supportable indefinitely into the future with proper care, but under other soil conditions the lands that are cleared deteriorate quickly. In some areas soils have a high clay content, so that compaction by cattle soon turns the land to brick. In other areas the acid content of the soil is so high that after several years the only plants that will grow are noxious weeds. In still other areas the lush tropical forest is supported by a surprisingly thin layer of topsoil, so that within a few years after the removal of the forest canopy all the nutrients have been leached; what is left is a hardpan that will not support even the most aggressive pasture grasses. The indiscriminate spread of pastures may benefit cattlemen and packing plants in the short run, but in the long run even the direct beneficiaries of beef exports are harmed by the consequences.[16]

Impact of Forest-to-Pasture Transformation on Peasants

The group hit hardest by the conversion to pasture is the Central American peasantry. Traditionally, the forest has supplied firewood, building materials, game, fresh water, and other resources for day to day life. More important, the existence of vast untapped areas of forest has provided a crucial protection for the peasant system, a safety valve for a whole way of life.

As the peasantry has been herded off the richest lands by the expansion of export crops, and as population growth has made life increasingly difficult in marginal areas, peasants have migrated to the edge of the forest to clear the land, plant corn and beans, and continue life in the traditional manner.

Before the beef-export boom, peasants in frontier areas were unlikely to be bothered by commercial agriculture because much of the land was too remote or infertile to justify commercial development.[17] With the beef-export trade, however, these frontier areas became commercially attractive. As the cattle boom progressed, life on the edge of the peasant system consisted of being chased toward an ever-vanishing frontier.

The impact of the beef boom might not have been so severe on the rural majority if the conversion to pasture had produced jobs for the displaced. Compared to other export crops, however, cattle raising offers few prospects for employment (see Chart 6-1). The most conservative estimates indicate that cotton cultivation offers six times more employment per acre than cattle ranching, sugar offers seven times more, and coffee offers thirteen times more. Other estimates show cattle as comparing even less favorably with other export agriculture in the provision of jobs. (Chart 6-1)[18]

The tendency of cattle ranching to claim large areas of land without offering jobs has produced a repeated pattern of population movement in Central America. When forests are first being cleared, large numbers of people move into the area; but when cattle are moved in, people must leave. Studies of migratory patterns show that the most important cattle-boom departments in Central America exhibit strong outmigration tendencies.[19]

Chart 6-1
Labor Requirements for Key Exports

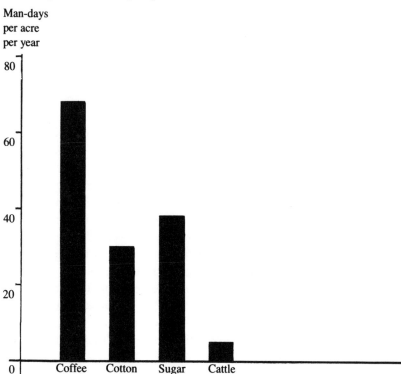

Man-days
per acre
per year

Source: SIECA, *El desarrollo integrado*, Vol. 5, Table 30, p. 74.
Notes: Data are for Central American farms larger than eighty-six acres in 1970. Cattle labor
requirements include pasture maintenance, cowboys, and other labor.

The Cattle Boom and Rights to Land Use

Deforestation has brought to light the fundamental incompatibility of two
systems of land use, one based on the production of commodities for the world
market and the other aimed at production for subsistence. By carving out fresh
territory for the export trade, the cattle boom has renewed an ancient conflict
between peasants and elites over rights to the use of land. The conflict takes its
most intense form at the moving edge of the forest, where the rights to land are
most open to dispute.

Behind the conflicts stand two diametrically opposed views about man's
proper relationship to land. These two views run deep in the consciousness of
people: They have accumulated over many generations, stretching back before

the conquest. They have been reinforced and embellished by centuries of agricultural practice. They exert a living force on the day-to-day decisions of individuals. They periodically justify the call to arms.

The dominant view of the elites of the isthmus is that the land is there for cultivation of commodities for export. Over the centuries the successful introduction of new crops for export has allowed Central America to import the latest technologies from the advanced world, and it has permitted the region to participate in the consumption patterns and culture of Western Europe and North America. In elite circles today, great honor and admiration are still bestowed on those forebears who took the initiative to carve from inhospitable territory the working plantations of indigo, coffee, and the succession of export crops that followed.

The elite view of the purpose of land is not just held by the oligarchs but is widely believed by merchants, professionals, state employees, and other educated townspeople and urban dwellers. It is heard in conversations with those who speak formal Spanish, it surfaces almost daily in the newspapers, and it is plastered on billboards: the purpose of land is for export and the increase in the national wealth.

The ultimate right to the land from the perspective of the ruling elites is defined by legal title, a document issued by the titling agency of the national government. Elites recall that in the latter half of the nineteenth century the issuing of title to the rich lands of the Pacific slopes made it possible to develop coffee on a commercial basis. Without title, the people with foresight at that time would not have risked making the huge capital expenditures necessary to raise coffee commercially.

For elites today, the titles to their properties have come to represent much more than the rights to land areas. Members of the elite recognize that if the titled estates are kept intact as working plantations, the income can be used to take European and North American vacations, to send children to college in the United States, and to import luxury goods. More important, however, land titles represent how family members of the past have contributed to the building of the country, and for this reason titles, more than money income, help define a family's relative social position. In short, from the elite perspective title means not only the good life, but also family heritage, national welfare, and civilization.

Perhaps the most beautiful physical embodiment of the elite view of land can be seen in the gemlike miniature of the Paris Opera House located in San José, Costa Rica. The craftsmen and the materials for its construction were imported with the revenues from coffee exports. The building was completed in the 1890s, a monument to the coffee aristocracy. On the vaulted ceiling of a staircase vestibule is an expansive triptych, painted by Italian muralists in rococo style. The large center panel shows the docks of Puerto Limón with the European merchant vessels, flags waving in the breeze in the background and bustling cargo activity in the foreground. Framing this port scene are two smaller panel scenarios, one depicting a huge black man shouldering a stalk of bananas and the second portraying blushing maidens of northern European origin engaged in the harvest of coffee. Decidedly absent from the ceiling are corn, beans, and rice. Land is for export.

Today's hero in these circles, the one currently being honored in Central America for taking the initiative to carve out fresh territory for the export trade, the one whose title connotes toughness and commands respect, is the *ganadero*.[20]

In contrast, the dominant view of the peasantry is that land is for human life. For peasants, the ultimate right to land is defined not by legal title but by whether or not the land is being used. If parents see their children starving and land standing idle nearby, it is their duty to their offspring and to God to move onto the land and make it produce corn. Once land has been put into use, however, it is considered a denial of life, a sin, for someone else to come along and claim possession of it.

The peasant view of land, like the elite perspective, takes on a religious dimension. Land is seen as a foundation for a way of life. The right to plant the land in *milpa* (maize) is equivalent to the right to live, to carry on the tradition of the ancestors, and to plant the seed for future generations. Rarely is the peasant view of land seen in print, but it is so prevalent in the spoken word, the oral tradition of the peasants, that it would require an ear severely deafened not to hear it. The voice expressing this view has become louder in the last two decades. It echoes from the churches in the countryside. It is chanted in street protests in the cities. It is the battle cry of peasant armies. *Tierra.*

Whenever possible, peasants attempt to secure titles to land they have settled in order to prevent takeover by those with better access to the titling press. However, the monetary costs and cumbersome procedures involved in titling in most cases make it practically impossible for peasants to secure legal title to the lands on which they live. Lands in remote areas unclaimed by commercial agriculture are not governed by legal title at all but by the traditions of the peasants who occupy those zones.

National governments over the years have been forced to bend the law to accommodate the practices of peasants. Lands that have not been claimed under private property or other legal categories are usually lumped into a large category called "national lands" or *baldios*. It is recognized in most agrarian legislation in Central America that squatters on national land can apply for legal title if they demonstrate that the land has been put to use for a specified period of time.[21] Such legislation explicitly recognizes actual peasant practices and has been viewed by peasants as legal justification for squatters' rights.[22]

Evidence of official recognition of peasant traditions can also be seen in agricultural censuses. Most of the agricultural censuses have land-tenure categories that do not belong to the tradition of private property. For example, one legally recognized category in the Honduran and Nicaraguan censuses is ejidal land.[23] Other forms appear that may not be considered legal but are recognized nevertheless. For example, the categories "occupied without title," "occupied by user," "precarious" tenure, "squatter," and so forth appear in the land-tenure tables of the censuses alongside legally accepted private property forms like "occupied by title holder," "rented," and "sharecropped."

Today, agrarian reform laws throughout the region have a single common element, regardless of the nature of the governments proposing them. All of them recognize the peasant perspective on land rights in that they do not attack properties that are in use, but they have provisions allowing for the expropriation and redistribution of idle properties.

The history of agrarian struggles in Central America can be understood as a clash between these two perspectives on the proper use of land. The pattern is that whenever opportunities arise for a new export commodity, governments have facilitated its development by providing infrastructure to service the area and by turning on the titling press for those who show promise in cultivating the export. Governments have also provided armies to dislodge peasants who resist the seizure of lands.

Large landowners, including the large fruit companies, have learned through many years of experience that constant vigilance is necessary to back up legal titles. Usually large estates will have only a portion of the total area in use at any given time, with the rest held in reserve for future use. Peasants, following their own view about the purpose of land, tend to move onto the idle areas. If a landowner does not take swift action against squatters, soon the estate will be swarming with peasants. After they have cleared the land and cultivated it, they are difficult to dislodge. Landowners who have lost control of properties to peasants in this way are the brunt of jokes at the opera house and the polo club. To prevent peasants from claiming idle lands, large landowners hire teams of armed men to patrol the perimeters of their estates or call on the services of the nearest unit of the army or the national guard.

For large landowners, the beef-export boom provided a way to increase earnings on lands already under their control, but it also provided a convenient way to validate claims on peripheral areas difficult to patrol. In the areas under the firm control of landlords, it was customary to permit peasants to live on the estates in return for some sort of rental payment, usually a few sacks of corn or services in kind. With beef exports, however, it became more profitable for landowners to put cattle into the areas previously occupied by peasants. The profits from beef provided an extra incentive to evict peasants from the peripheral areas of estates as well. Once cattle were turned onto those lands, peasants were less likely to invade because the land was in use. In this way Washington loans for barbed wire and herd expansion provided large landowners with a profitable substitute for costly squatter patrols.

The cattle boom extended beyond areas subject to preexisting property titles. Lands that had been previously recognized by legal authorities as open to peasant use—ejidal properties, municipal lands, and national lands—were quickly turned into ranches, along with lands that were being "occupied without title."

Peasants felt hardship from cattle evictions regardless of the previous tenure situation, but peasant responses to evictions differed depending on the degree to which they believed landlords had valid claims on disputed terrain. It is rare to find instances of peasant resistance in cases where the land in question was under firm and long-standing control by a landlord before cattle were introduced. In such cases the switch to cattle was similar to the typical cotton eviction. The landlord would increase the number of sacks of corn required, or the rent would be changed to a money payment that the peasant family could not afford. The move was just as difficult as in the case of a forced eviction, but the decision was placed on the peasants, and they did not feel they had been displaced from land that was rightfully theirs.

It was on land that had been outside the control of a landlord where conflicts occurred when cattle were introduced. Accounts by eyewitness observers in cattle-boom areas tell a story of clashes between ranchers and peasants. Variations in the story appear from one cattle zone to the next, but the typical pattern goes as follows.

Don Miguel, a local cattle rancher, gets a loan from the government development bank. He purchases barbed wire and hires a team of men to fence in an area contiguous to his existing cattle ranch.[24] The area includes a peasant settlement, with its cluster of palm-frond dwellings surrounded by cornfields. The peasants are notified that the land is Don Miguel's and that they must leave.[25]

The peasants have lived on the land for some time and have not previously been bothered by Don Miguel. They are the ones who cleared the area of forest, and from their perspective, the land is rightfully theirs.[26] They do not move from the settlement.

After repeated threats fail to budge the peasants, Don Miguel decides to wait until several weeks before it is time for the corn to be harvested. At this time he instructs his men to turn cattle into the peasants' cornfields. The cattle proceed to trample the crops and munch on the corn.[27]

The peasants drive the cattle from the fields. With barbed wire from a section of Don Miguel's fence they enclose the fields to prevent the cattle from reentering and further destroying the crops.

In retaliation, Don Miguel's men cut the peasants' fence and drive cattle onto their cornfields once more.[28]

By this time the peasants have formed an action committee and have notified peasants in neighboring communities as well as priests, schoolteachers, and other sympathetic people in the closest town.

If the peasants have not moved after the second or third trampling, Don Miguel sends for the police in the nearest town. The young men are arrested, roughed up, and imprisoned.

If the peasants do not move when the cattle are turned onto the fields at this point, Don Miguel has his men block the road or path into the peasant settlement to prevent people and supplies from passing. If the peasants still refuse to move, Don Miguel sends for the armed militia again. This time the militia arrives with reinforcements from the nearest army or national guard unit. The peasants are removed by force, and dwellings and cornfields are set afire. An armed guard is stationed day and night at the burned settlement to prevent the return of the evicted.[29]

The evicted move in with relatives in a nearby village. They enlist the support of sympathetic townspeople. They pressure the town government for the release of the imprisoned. They have a priest, a lawyer, or some other sympathetic townsperson who can read go to the registry of deeds to do a title search.[30] They have someone who can write literate Spanish help them draw up a list of grievances to submit to government officials.

In the meantime Don Miguel has united with other cattle ranchers in the vicinity. Peasants and persons sympathetic with the peasants are harassed by the police.[31] If direct harassment is not possible, a team of off-duty policemen is hired to intimidate the peasants and their supporters in an attempt to crush the movement before it goes to the next level.

The peasants, in turn, build a case to take to the land court or land-reform agency in the departmental or national capital. The list of grievances is submitted, and the peasants begin to seek out support for their case from national peasant organizations, churches, universities, labor unions, and other national institutions that may show sympathy toward their case.[32]

The cattlemen, in turn, gather their forces at a national level. They unite with other agricultural and business groups. They apply pressure through their allies in the military, and they do whatever they can to defeat the peasants and their sympathizers.

At any step the chain reaction may be aborted, or it may escalate until extreme levels of violence are reached. The paths taken by particular struggles have varied in important ways from one cattle-boom zone to the next depending on local and national conditions.

The Cattle Boom and Rural Conflict:
The Pacific Coastal Plain of Honduras and Costa Rica

Before the beef-export boom, the Pacific coastal plain was the most important cattle raising area in the region. When beef exports began, this area was the first to be developed for the export trade. Like those elsewhere in Central America, the coastal plain departments of Choluteca, Honduras, and Guanacaste, Costa Rica, have long histories of struggle between ranchers and peasants.[33] Conflicts intensified in the late 1950s and early 1960s when roads, packing plants, and promotional lending to cattle made previously marginal lands in these departments valuable for cattle raising.

In southern Honduras during the early phases of the beef-export boom, landlords were successful in evicting peasants, but by the late 1960s a national peasant movement gained momentum, and peasants at a local level saw the opportunity to reclaim lands. They began to move in mass onto lands from which they had been evicted years before. Interviews with participants in these land occupations led one researcher to conclude: "The brutality of many of the evictions caused a great deal of lasting resentment, and a deeply emotional hatred of the large cotton and cattle farmers began to build up among the small farmers of the coastal plain area. One cannot understand the motivation behind the land occupations and the great bitterness against the large landowners in the movement of 1969 to 1971 unless one goes back to the experiences of these evictions."[34]

Peasants also learned how to organize effectively as a result of earlier evictions. In the late 1950s and early 1960s local peasant committees gained experience dealing with the Honduran government and reaching out to sympathetic individuals in the church, the national university, political parties, and other institutions. When the national peasant movement emerged in the late 1960s, the local committees that formed to resist earlier enclosures regrouped to become affiliates of national peasant organizations.

Accounts of land disputes in coastal Honduras and Costa Rica document that local authorities are under the control of the largest ranchers in the area, and interviews with peasants reveal no confusion on this point. Interviews also, however, reveal a widespread belief among peasants that national authorities will deal with them in a just manner if appealed to in the proper way.[35] White was amazed at the tenacity of the peasants of southern Honduras in pressing their grievances at the national level, "making trips to Tegucigalpa, visiting lawyers, ministries of the government, and political leaders," even though "they were almost never given a sympathetic hearing."[36]

Despite their generally unfavorable reception, peasants in Costa Rica and Honduras have still been able to win some victories over local ranchers by pushing their cases at the national level. For example, in Guanacaste, Costa Rica, in 1972, a land dispute that had dragged on for years culminated in the death of a local saddlemaker who was supporting the peasants in their struggle. Immediately following the incident the local *guardias* hauled many of the peasants to jail, where they remained for nearly a month before bail was arranged by national-level agencies, ITCO and the Mixed Institute of Social Assistance (IMAS). The case was publicized in the national press in the Highlands, and the news was received with public outrage. It was discovered by the national land-reform agency (ITCO) that Morice, the local rancher, had only 613 legally titled acres out of a total of 5,797 acres claimed. Morice, who fled to Nicaragua after the incident, was tried in absentia for the murder of the saddlemaker. The national court found him guilty of the shooting, and he was sentenced to eight years in prison.[37]

In Honduras during the mid-1970s a spate of peasant land occupations forced the National Agrarian Institute (INA) to intervene in order to settle the disputes. When the occupied land was found to be legally titled and the peasants would not obey an order to move, INA sometimes instructed the army to expel the peasants from the land and throw the leaders in jail, but when property in dispute was found to be national or municipal land, peasants were often awarded rights to cultivate it. In certain cases, when peasants were extremely well organized, legally titled lands were turned over to peasants; in these cases INA settled the dispute by compensating the landlord for the property. During 1973 and 1974, 23,627 peasant families were awarded some 182,000 acres of land, one-fifth of which had been legally titled before the land was occupied by peasants.[38]

In Costa Rica national peasant organizations have not achieved the forcefulness of their Honduran counterparts. Nevertheless, land occupations on public and private properties have in many cases been pushed into the hands of the national courts and ITCO for settlement. As in Honduras, the national institutions have ruled in favor of the peasants on numerous occasions. One report claimed that between 1961 and 1975 ITCO had been involved in securing lands for some eighteen thousand peasant families. Some of these lands were state lands, but some were bought by ITCO from large landholders.[39]

Along the coastal plain of Honduras and Costa Rica, local security forces have frequently resorted to pressures like burning homes and cornfields, jailing leaders, and harassing peasant sympathizers, but rarely have conflicts in these more-established areas of settlement resulted in bloodshed. In peripheral areas, however, extreme levels of violence have been more frequent.

Olancho, Honduras: The Cattle Boom, the Peasant Movement, and Rancher Violence

The department of Olancho, in central Honduras, has been the scene of at least three massacres at the hands of ranchers since the cattle boom moved into the area in the early 1960s. In April of 1965 six peasants were killed in El Jute, one of whom was the leader of the peasant organization FENACH (Honduran National Federation of Peasants). The second massacre occurred in February 1972 in La Talanquera, where six peasants were killed, a number wounded, and others jailed after having participated in a land occupation.[40]

The most macabre of the three massacres took place on a large ranch called Los Horcones in June of 1975. The bodies found in the well of the ranch included five peasant activists who had been burned alive in a bread oven, two foreign priests who had been castrated and severely mutilated, and two women who were thrown in the well alive before the well shaft was dynamited. In the roundup before the massacre, five persons were shot to death by men wearing army uniforms.[41]

All of the victims of the Horcones massacre had been connected with the peasant movement in Olancho. Before knowledge of the slaughter became public, the army arrested thirty-two priests and had them expelled from the department.[42] It was discovered later that the ranchers had set a bounty of $10,000 on the head of the bishop (he was out of the country), and the commander of the army for Olancho province was paid $2,500 by the owner of Los Horcones for the murder of the Colombian priest. It was reported that the action had been planned two months before by Olancho ranchers who had garnered financial and political support from members of the National Federation of Farmers and Cattlemen (FENAGH) and other members of the Honduran business community.[43]

That the violence reached such extremes in Olancho has to do with the peripheral character of the department. By the time of the first massacre,

Olancho still had vast forest reserves to the north and to the east of the traditional ranching area located in the southwest corner near Tegucigalpa. Ranchers who wanted to extend their grazing lands faced the problem of what to do with peasants who were moving to the forest's edge from areas like Choluteca, where they had already been displaced by export agriculture.

The 1962 Agrarian Law, like its Alliance for Progress counterpart in the other Central American countries, contained a provision recognizing the rights of peasants to settle undeveloped national lands. This provision made the Olancho ranchers more vulnerable to a peasant movement than ranchers in previously settled cattle-boom areas where titled property was more developed. Even by 1974, half (49 percent) of the farm area in Olancho was still untitled national land, compared with one-tenth (11 percent) of the farm area in Choluteca.[44] Despite the relative vulnerability of the Olancho ranchers to peasant settlement, the Olancho cattle herd grew faster than the herds of other major cattle-boom departments, and by 1974 it rivaled that of Choluteca as the largest in Honduras.[45]

By the time of the first massacre (1965), the peasant movement had already begun to achieve some success in pressuring the national government to recognize the settlement provisions of the 1962 law. In response, the Olancho ranchers increased repression within the department and spearheaded a national movement of large landowners to counter the gains being made by the peasants. In 1966 Olancho ranchers helped form FENAGH.[46]

One of the most important activities of FENAGH has been to exert a counterpressure on INA, the agency in charge of settling land disputes. In cases where peasants occupied lands and issued appeals to INA for favorable rulings, FENAGH would counterpetition for eviction.[47]

In the late 1960s, when the national peasant movement began reclaiming lands, FENAGH counterattacked by pressuring INA to evict Salvadoran peasants from national lands. The ranchers argued that the 1962 agrarian law provided rights to national lands only to Honduran nationals. Not until 1969, however, did INA actually begin serving eviction notices to the Salvadoran settlers. The evictions by the Honduran army and the mass exodus that followed removed some of the pressure on actual or potential pastureland, and it divided the peasantry on national lines. The land-scarcity problem was temporarily redefined as a conflict between Honduran and Salvadoran peasants instead of as a struggle between ranchers and peasants. With the war between Honduras and El Salvador following the expulsions, all of Honduras seemed unified, and it appeared for a while that FENAGH had "succeeded in translating an internal problem of resource competition into an external one."[48]

Between 1970 and the end of 1972 INA "shifted to a conservative, even negative, policy toward the settlements of campesinos."[49] Much to the chagrin of the Olancho ranchers and other members of FENAGH, however, the Honduran peasants regrouped and resumed their tactics of land occupations and public protests over the government's failure to implement land reform. In an attempt to contain the "invasions," members of FENAGH increasingly resorted to terror at a local level. One of these actions was the second Olancho massacre (1972).

With renewed support from labor unions and elements of the church, the national peasant organizations continued to protest landowner brutality and government intransigence on land reform. At a time when the national government was becoming increasingly unstable, the National Association of Honduran Peasants (ANACH), with broad participation from other groups, staged a hunger march that brought tens of thousands of peasants to Tegucigalpa in early December 1972.[50]

At the same time, the Cruz government was deposed and the head of the armed forces, General Lopez Arellano, took power. One of the first actions of the new regime was Decree #8, which explicitly recognized peasant rights to national and ejidal lands and contained a provision for forced rentals of underused land on legally titled private property.[51] FENAGH attacked Decree #8 as encouraging land invasions[52] and escalated its harassment tactics in the countryside.

In January 1975 Decree #8 was superseded by Agrarian Law 170, a fullfledged land-reform bill that further enraged the Olancho ranchers. The new law set legal limits on the size of individual holdings, and it redefined "underutilized land" in a way that seriously threatened the extensive cattle operations characteristic of Olancho. In order to prove that land was functioning in a socially useful way, and therefore not subject to expropriation, the new law called for four times the number of cattle per land area than was required by the 1962 law.[53]

Confronted with a national government that it perceived as offering up its cattle range to the peasants, FENAGH threatened to take matters into its own hands if the land reform were not halted and respect for "private property" were not restored. In May 1975 the INA office in Juticalpa, Olancho, was seized by "700 armed men."[54] A month later, on the date of a national hunger march, came the ranchers' most spectacular and desperate attempt to paralyze the peasant movement in Olancho: the massacre of Horcones on 25 June 1975.

The Cattle Boom, Rural Guerrillas, and
Counterinsurgency in Nicaragua (1967–1972)

The Nicaraguan Revolution is sometimes portrayed as a revolution by the "proletariat" because of the powerful forces of insurrection that sprang from the slums and working-class neighborhoods of the major cities. Leaving aside for the moment the issue of the rural origins of that rebellious proletariat, the role played by peasants in the rural areas in their struggles with local landowners and the landowners' eviction force, Somoza's national guard, should not be overlooked. In his history of the Sandinista National Liberation Front (FSLN), George Black stresses the importance of the rural guerrilla in the late 1960s and early 1970s, prior to the urban uprisings that began to make headlines after the December earthquake in 1972.

The zone of the country that Black pinpoints is located in the eastern half of the department of Matagalpa, in the mountainous terrain of the *municipios* of Matiguás, San Ramón, and Matagalpa, shown in Figure 6-3. Black notes that the first guerrilla activity there centered around the mountains of Pancasán in 1967. The peasantry in the area supported the armed struggle by acting as "informers of National Guard movements, as mountain guides, cooks, suppliers of food and accommodation, purchasers of equipment. Many began to fight in small-scale harassment operations against the Guard, returning their weapons afterwards and going back to their farms."[55]

In August 1967 the guerrillas suffered a devastating blow from the guard. Somoza targeted the area as a zone for counterinsurgency operations, and "Guard units were drafted into the mountains on a systematic and unprecedented campaign against peasant sympathizers."[56] Among the losses were thirteen of the senior members of the FSLN.

Apparently the counterinsurgency efforts were not completely successful, for in 1969 minor skirmishes began in that same zone in the mountains of Zínica and El Bijao, not far from the site of the earlier activity. In early 1970 the minor skirmishes turned into a major guerrilla action. This time, however, most of the original leaders of the FSLN were absent. The guerrilla army of eastern Matagalpa "was almost exclusively made up of peasants."[57]

What was happening in eastern Matagalpa before Pancasán (1967) that made the peasants of the area so supportive of the FSLN, and what happened afterward that turned a small guerrilla column, composed primarily of urban youth, into an army of peasants?

Four years before the area was declared a counterinsurgency zone, the 1963 agricultural census showed eastern Matagalpa as the most important corn- and bean-growing area in all of Nicaragua. The 3 *municipios* of eastern Matagalpa

Figure 6-3
Departments of Nicaragua

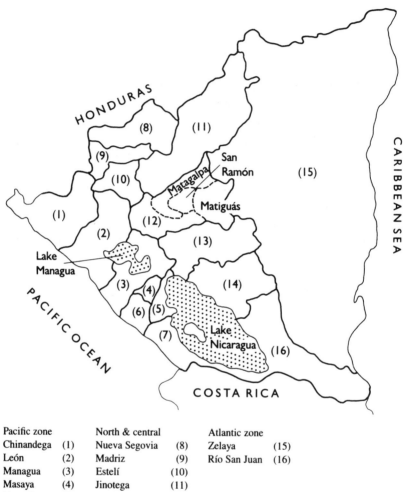

Pacific zone		North & central		Atlantic zone	
Chinandega	(1)	Nueva Segovia	(8)	Zelaya	(15)
León	(2)	Madriz	(9)	Río San Juan	(16)
Managua	(3)	Estelí	(10)		
Masaya	(4)	Jinotega	(11)		
Granada	(5)	Matagalpa	(12)		
Carazo	(6)	Boaco	(13)		
Rivas	(7)	Chontales	(14)		

produced more corn and more beans that year than any other entire department in the country. Out of 125 *municipios* in Nicaragua, the largest producer of corn and the second largest producer of beans was Matiguás, where Pancasán is located. The average corn farmer in Matiguás had a little more than eleven acres devoted to the crop, and the average area planted in beans was three acres. Like peasants in the frontier zone of Olancho, Honduras, the small farmers who had settled Matiguás held very precarious rights to the land. According to the 1963 census, Matiguás had one of the highest rates of precarious tenure in all of Nicaragua, with 68 percent of the land at that time "occupied without title," compared to 19 percent for the entire country.[58]

Cattle have traditionally been raised in the department of Matagalpa, but with the beef-export boom Matagalpa's herd experienced the largest absolute increase in Nicaragua. By 1963 it was the most important cattle raising department in the entire country.[59] Though cattle were scattered throughout the department, the three *municipios* of eastern Matagalpa had 62 percent of the herd. Matiguás had the largest share, with one-third of the departmental total. Judging from the census maps, the highest concentration of cattle in the department in 1963 was in the basin of the Río Blanco and Río Paiwas, just to the east of what was at that time the corn zone around Pancasán (see Figures 6-4 and 6-5).

Between 1963 and 1976 Nicaragua's beef quota more than doubled and a fourth packing plant was built. The process of change that had already begun in eastern Matagalpa was greatly accelerated. Where 30 percent of the land was forest in 1963, an agricultural survey in 1976 estimated that only 5 percent of the farm area of Matiguás remained forested. Where 8 percent of the surveyed area was in annual crops like corn and beans in 1963, the 1976 survey estimated that less than 1 percent of the survey area remained in annual crops. Pastures, on the other hand, spread from 39 percent of the farm area in 1963 to encompass 94 percent of the survey area a decade later.[60]

The cattle boom swiftly carved out new territory for private property. In the 1963 census 68 percent of the land was occupied without legal rights; only 2.5 percent of the area was so occupied in the 1976 survey. By 1976, 86 percent of the area surveyed in Matiguás had full-fledged legal titles, and 11.4 percent of the area was in land grants from the Somoza government.[61]

The process was observed in motion by a researcher who drove the road through Matiguás in April 1967, just four months before the guard routed the guerrilla column there. James Taylor was doing fieldwork on agricultural settlement in the frontier department of Zelaya and was curious why so many of the settlers he had interviewed there came from eastern Matagalpa. The stretch of road Taylor traveled went through the very heart of what was the

Figure 6-4
Department of Matagalpa, Nicaragua

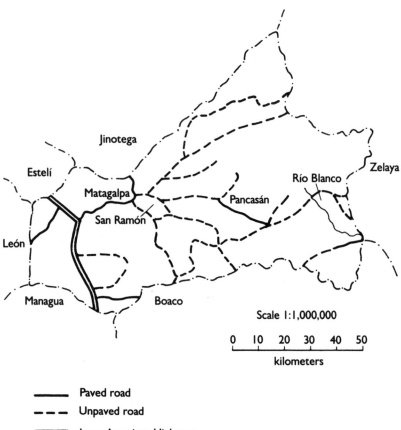

Scale 1:1,000,000

0   10   20   30   40   50
kilometers

——— Paved road
– – – Unpaved road
═══ Inter-American Highway
— . — Deparment boundary

Figure 6-5
Corn Cultivation in Nicaragua, 1963

Each point: 50 manzanas (83.5 acres)

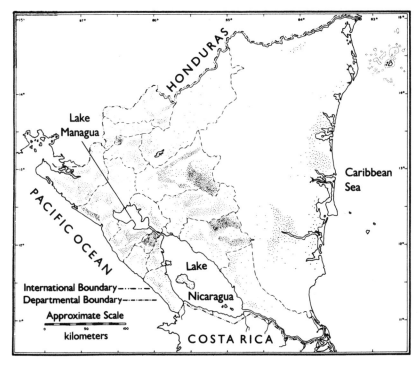

Source: DGECN, *Censos nacionales, 1963: Agropecuario*

Matiguás corn zone in 1963, between the towns of Matiguás and Río Blanco.
His report of this drive goes as follows:

Traveling from Boaco northeast to the town of Matiguás, then directly
east to Río Blanco, an obvious land use pattern was observed. Not until we
were about half way between Matiguás and Río Blanco were there any signs
of crop production; the land was almost entirely in pasture. A traveling
companion who works in the area purchasing livestock and dairy products
explained that a decade ago much of the area now in pasture was in forest.
By the time we reached Río Blanco there was little pasture to be seen, and
more of both forest and small areas that had been cleared for agriculture.
The informants with whom I spoke explained that agricultural production is
moving eastward with the advance of the road, then yielding to pasture.[62]

Only months after Taylor's visit to eastern Matagalpa, the process he recorded was sped up by the "counterinsurgency" policies of the Somoza dictatorship. Two strategic roads were built. One linked the city of Matagalpa with the town of Matiguás, passing directly through the 1963 corn zone around Pancasán. The second road ran from the city of Matagalpa to the town of Waslala, over the border in Zelaya, where the guard operated a concentration camp.[63] The 1963 census map indicates that the path of this second road went through another highly concentrated corn-growing area.[64] This second road passed over the Bijao River, which later became the locus of armed peasant resistance.

The ranchers of eastern Matagalpa must have been pleased with the designation of the area as a counterinsurgency zone. The roads and bridges built for strategic purposes could support cattle trucks as well as tanks, and the guard units could be relied on to remove the intransigent "rebel sympathizers" from the areas that had been cleared for corn. Furthermore, the local ranchers did not have to pay for the services rendered. Both the roads and the expense of the eviction force were financed by the Nicaraguan government, with a portion of the tab paid by U.S. taxpayers.

Local magistrates, guard officers, and peasant informers for the guard also appreciated the designation of the area as a counterinsurgency zone, for at last they had an opportunity to become landowners and ranchers themselves. The land was quickly vacated of corn producers as the "Communist guerrilla sympathizers" were rounded up, tortured, and shot. Many voluntarily fled the region to avoid reprisals at the hands of the guard. A large number were moved "for security reasons" to AID and IADB colonization projects in the tropical forests of Zelaya.[65]

According to the 1976 land-tenure survey, the second largest category of land tenure for the department of Matagalpa was a new one called "government land grants." This category consisted of about 110,000 acres, or 5 percent of the sample area. Two-thirds of the area in land grants was in the *municipio* of Matiguás. The recipients included 1,270 persons with plots averaging 7 acres; but 88 percent of the land area in grants went to 40 individuals, each of whom received a block of 1,670 acres (1,000 manzanas).[66] The spoils of war were sweet—for the while.

The First Phase of the Guatemalan Cattle Boom (1960s)

Guatemala's cattle boom began on the Pacific coastal plain where cattle had been raised since the colonial period. With improved roads and accessible packing plants, the boom moved from the central Pacific departments of Escuintla, Suchitepequez, and Retalhuleu to the north and the south along the coastal plain. By the mid to late 1960s, Guatemala's coastal plain had been largely deforested. During the 1960s intense violence occurred between ranchers and peasants and between plantation owners and seasonal workers who migrated to the Pacific to harvest the coffee, cotton, sugar, and other export crops that are concentrated there.[67]

As forest reserves along the Pacific coastal plain were being depleted, ranchers looked for grazing areas elsewhere in the country. The most important new cattle area during the 1960s was in northeast Guatemala, first in the departments of Izabál and Zacapa and later in the department of Chiquimula, as roads opened up new grazing lands.

In 1959 a paved road was completed between Guatemala City and the Atlantic ports of Matías de Galvez (the major beef port) and Puerto Barrios. The road ran through the middle of the rich Motagua River Valley in the departments of Zacapa and Izabál (see Figure 6-6). Between 1950 and 1964 Zacapa and Izabál experienced rapid deforestation and conversion to pasture: acreages in pasture tripled for Izabál and nearly doubled for Zacapa. Corn production declined over this period for Zacapa, as the better lands in the Motagua valley became increasingly devoted to ranching.[68] Between 1950 and 1964, out of twenty-two departments of Guatemala, the highest rate of herd expansion occurred in Izabál, and the combined herds of Izabál and Zacapa grew 45 percent over the period. In the mid-1960s the department of Chiquimula was drawn into the cattle boom when a road was completed that linked the departmental capital with the Motagua Valley road (Figure 6-7).

In the mid-1960s an armed guerrilla movement emerged in northeast Guatemala. The guerrillas operated out of the mountains to the north of the Motagua Valley, in the Sierra de las Minas and the Montañas del Mico ranges, and they established contacts with people in the towns along the main road and in the department capitals of Zacapa and Chiquimula. According to one account of the period, the guerrillas "began to establish the organisms of dual power through the formation of peasant committees in each village which disputed the real authority of the military officials and the vice-mayors, and administered justice outside the framework of bourgeois justice. By the end of 1966, the MR13 claimed to have 500 families organized into village committees." The guerrillas "were operating in a zone with mostly ladino small property owners, who for some time had been struggling against latifundistas trying to appropriate their land for cattle grazing."[69]

Before 1966 the Guatemalan army had great difficulties in its attempts to control northeast Guatemala, and ranchers had difficulties dislodging peas-

Figure 6-6
Departments of Guatamala

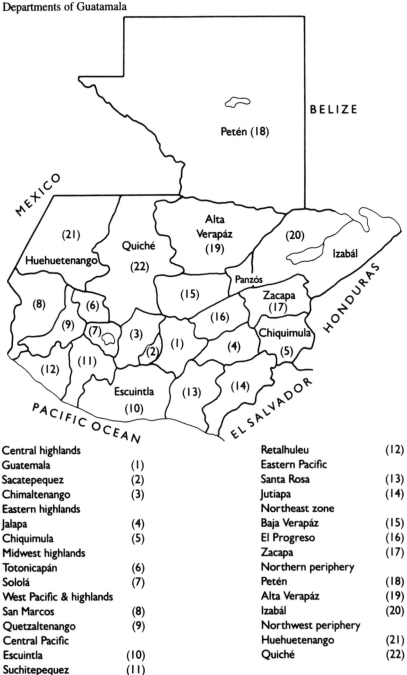

Central highlands		Retalhuleu	(12)
Guatemala	(1)	Eastern Pacific	
Sacatepequez	(2)	Santa Rosa	(13)
Chimaltenango	(3)	Jutiapa	(14)
Eastern highlands		Northeast zone	
Jalapa	(4)	Baja Verapáz	(15)
Chiquimula	(5)	El Progreso	(16)
Midwest highlands		Zacapa	(17)
Totonicapán	(6)	Northern periphery	
Sololá	(7)	Petén	(18)
West Pacific & highlands		Alta Verapáz	(19)
San Marcos	(8)	Izabál	(20)
Quetzaltenango	(9)	Northwest periphery	
Central Pacific		Huehuetenango	(21)
Escuintla	(10)	Quiché	(22)
Suchitepequez	(11)		

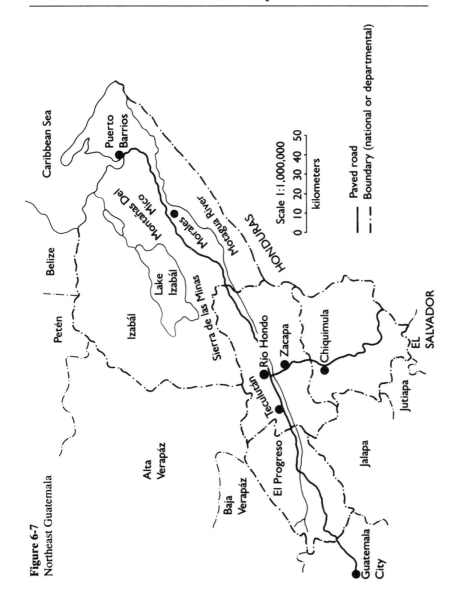

Figure 6-7
Northeast Guatemala

ants. In 1966, however, guerrilla successes sounded an alarm in Washington, and the northeast was declared a counterinsurgency zone. A network of informers and intelligence personnel was set up to locate guerrilla strongholds and to identify peasant troublemakers and people in the towns who were believed to be sympathetic with the peasants. Two death squads, La Mano Blanca (the White Hand) and Nueva Organización Anticomunista (New Anti-Communist Organization) were created to control the civilian population,[70] while men in uniform, assisted by a U.S. Special Forces team, directed attacks on the guerrillas and on villages believed to be sympathetic with them. Firepower was enhanced by U.S.-supplied helicopter gunships, T-33 fighter jets, and B-26 "Invader" bombers for dropping napalm. Flight training was provided by the U.S. Air Force.

Whole areas were swept clean of subsistence farmers as people fled to avoid reprisals. It is estimated that between 1966 and 1968 six to eight thousand persons were killed in a campaign that was designed to defeat a guerrilla force of approximately five hundred. The only peasants remaining were informants, participants in the army's "Civic Action" programs, and others who kept low profiles.

The counterinsurgency drive allowed ranchers to extend their pastures. Local officials, military officers, and paramilitary personnel were allocated the spoils of war commensurate with their positions in the hierarchy. It was during this period that the U.S.-trained commander of the counterinsurgency, Colonel Carlos Arana, earned the title "Butcher of Zacapa" and was granted a large ranch as a reward for services rendered.[71]

The repression apparatus that was created in 1966–68, with its network of peasant informers, its death squads, and its spoils system, was not dismantled after the sweep but remained to protect property rights and control the zone afterward. Following the 1976 earthquake, the first relief aid to the government of Guatemala was channeled through Arana's repression apparatus in Zacapa, even though that area was not the hardest hit by the quake.[72] In May 1982 more recent victims of the apparatus were interviewed by an American Friends Service Committee mission to the refugee camp of El Tesoro, Honduras, near the Guatemalan border. The report states:

> The Guatemalans at El Tesoro were also victims of government-supported persecution. Their stories gave no evidence of any armed insurgent movement in Zacapa province as exists elsewhere in Guatemala. The Guatemalans at El Tesoro were ladino small farmers who had been driven off in the interests of large cattle raisers or of local politicians who wanted the land for themselves. . . . One man we talked with had even become a trusted

foreman of a large foreign landowner. His employer told him that the army and the landowners of the area were going to finish off with the "Indians" because they had gotten the dangerous idea that the land should be theirs. Village "comisionados" attached to the army had hunted the rural poor and driven them from their homesteads. . . . Some mentioned that among the earliest victims of the violence had been delegates of the word, lay religious leaders with extensive training and deep local roots. . . . Most families had left all their worldly possessions behind as their villages were burned and their peers hunted down.[73]

The Second Phase of the Guatemalan Cattle Boom (1970s)

The cattle trails of the 1960s spun out from the traditional haciendas of the Pacific coastal plain. With the help of improved road networks they spread quickly into northeast Guatemala through areas inhabited by poor Ladino farmers. In contrast, the trails of the 1970s blazed their way through Maya Indian territory.

Before the possibilities of commercial ranching opened up, the lands to the north and west of Lake Izabál were deemed worthless for export agriculture. According to a 1963 transportation study, the departments of Petén, Alta Verapáz, Quiché, Huehuetenango and the portion of Izabál to the north and west of the lake, covering more than 60 percent of the land area of the country, had a combined total of eight miles of paved roads.[74]

A cattle study published in 1967 described the area: "The retarded zone is Guatemala's northern pioneer fringe, a heavily forested area where squatters, living largely in isolation, support themselves by shifting cultivation using the most primitive techniques. They keep few livestock, largely from lack of capital to purchase them, but also because of the depredations of wild animals. The boundaries of this region are slowly moving northward, as those in search of new land can only find it in the north."[75]

According to a 1965 USDA report, Guatemalan cattlemen already understood the grassland potential of this "retarded zone" and were pushing the government to take steps to open it up.[76] Spontaneous clearing of the forest was already being done by peasants who were moving there from the over-populated highlands, and two government agencies, INTA (National Institute of Agrarian Transformation) and FYDEP (National Corporation for the Development of the Petén), were further stimulating the clearing of the forest through a road-building program and colonization projects.

By the late 1960s government maps began to show northern Guatemala as the prime zone for future livestock development. In Figure 6-8, the whole of the Petén, part of northwest Izabál, and the northern half of Huehuetenango, Quiché, and Alta Verapáz are etched in as potential cattle-raising areas.

Estimates of herd size indicate that this area had already become a major cattle boom zone by 1973. The fastest-growing herd in the country between 1964 and 1973, according to these estimates, was that of the northwest periphery departments of Huehuetenango and Quiché, which together nearly quadrupled their holdings and expanded by 190,000 head over the period. The second-fastest-growing herd was that of the northern periphery departments of Alta Verapáz, Petén, and Izabál, which nearly tripled in size during the period, expanding by 135,000 head.[77]

What would be irony to an uneducated eye but is predictable after studying the cases of Nicaragua and northeast Guatemala in the 1960s is that the map of potential cattle-raising areas published in the early 1970s would serve with little alteration as a military map of Guatemala's "counterinsurgency" zone a decade later. As in the earlier cases, the transformation had to do with roads, fresh titles to land, cattle loans, and evictions of corn producers. But the scale of this latest thrust, the magnitude of the foreign and domestic capital employed, and the degree of state involvement in its planning and execution are several notches of intensity higher than in earlier cases. Beginning in mid-1978, the government effort to incorporate this peripheral area into the export economy was matched in vigor by resistance from the subsistence farmers living there.

The prospects of beef exports alone could not have drawn the hundreds of millions of dollars of international capital that have been sunk into the development of northern Guatemala. But the combination of nickel, oil, hydroelectric power, and beef made this zone a favorite of the IADB, the World Bank, AID, the U.S. Export-Import Bank, and private consortia. During the first oil-price explosion (1973–75), oil and nickel company executives, bank officials, and army officers alike came to refer to this area as the Northern Transversal Strip.[78]

By 1973 the eastern edge of the strip, from Lake Izabál all the way into the department of Alta Verapáz, had been conceded to the EXMIBAL nickel-mining and -processing operation, a $250 million investment.[79] After 1973, a major oil field was discovered in the thickly forested corner of the Petén and of Alta Verapáz near the Mexican border. By 1977 the first well began producing at the Rubelsanto field, and by 1978 seven international oil companies had received concessions in northern Guatemala.[80] In 1974 the first loan was committed to the largest single public investment project in Guatemala: the

Figure 6-8
Guatemala: Cattle-Regionalization Scheme, 1974

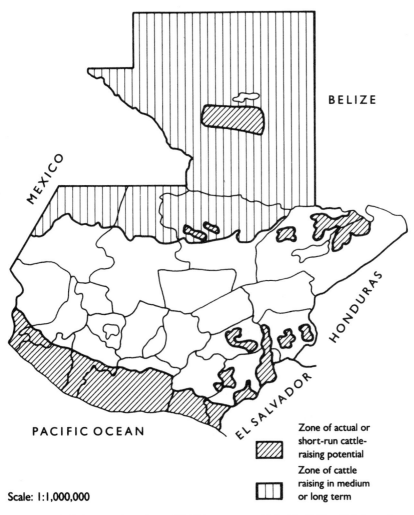

BELIZE

MEXICO

HONDURAS

EL SALVADOR

PACIFIC OCEAN

Zone of actual or short-run cattle-raising potential

Zone of cattle raising in medium or long term

Scale: 1:1,000,000

Source: ICAITI, *Comercialización*, p. 109. This map was published in 1974, with information taken from a 1968 Bank of Guatemala map, combined with information from three studies of the early 1970s.

Chixoy hydroelectric power complex on the Chixoy River, which defines the border between Alta Verapáz and Quiché.[81] A second hydroelectric project, the Chulac complex, to be located on the Cahaboncito River in Alta Verapáz near the EXMIBAL project, will be even bigger (475 megawatts, compared to Chixoy's 300 megawatts) and will cost more to build.[82]

The combined package of oil, nickel, hydroelectricity, and beef justified the financing of the largest road-building program of the 1970s and 1980s. A network of all-weather roads from population centers in the highlands down toward the projects in the lowland areas was begun by the Guatemalan Army Corps of Engineers. These highland-to-lowland roads were constructed to connect with the Transversal Highway, a two way, all-weather road being built through the center of the strip. At the same time, another road was begun that was to cut diagonally across the Petén, with one-lane feeder roads connecting with the diagonal. In addition, a pipeline was begun in 1978 to link the oil fields near the Mexican border with the nickel-processing plant near El Estor[83] and then with the port of Santo Tomás on the Atlantic.

For the multinational corporations, the main attraction of the roads was in facilitating the exploration, extraction, transportation, and processing of minerals. For army officers, government officials, and other Guatemalans close to the government, the roads meant the opportunity to become cattlemen.

Following in the tradition that created the coffee oligarchy in the nineteenth century, military officers and their friends and relatives showed cunning in acquiring properties. Speaking of the Northern Transversal Strip, an official of INTA said: "The government gave away or sold land titles to outsiders. It went to politicians, the rich, the military. They all grabbed what they could. There are large untouchable estates we call 'The Zone of the Generals.' "[84]

General Lucas García, who was in charge of the Northern Transversal Strip before he became president of the country in 1978, acquired a number of ranches and timber properties on the strip. Estimates of his holdings range from 81,000 acres to 135,000 acres. Some of Lucas's holdings were purchased from large landowners who already held title to sections of this frontier area, but some of the holdings were carved from the 125,000 acres of land that INTA had been settling as part of its peasant colonization program.[85]

The Cattle Boom and the Repression of Cooperatives in Quiché and Huehuetenango (mid-1970s)

Before the 1970s the areas of the country highly populated with Indians were not the areas most hit by violence.[86] However, beginning in 1975 and especially after the 1976 earthquake, Indian settlements in the Northern Transversal Strip and highland towns bordering the strip witnessed mass killings by the military and heightened resistance by the Indian population.

The first major military action against settlers in the Northern Transversal Strip took place in July 1975. Thirty-seven members of a settlement cooperative were abducted and carried away in a helicopter from the villages of Xabál Grande and Ixcán Grande in the peripheral *municipio* of Chajúl, Quiché. They were never to be seen again. Later the Ministry of Defense took responsibility for the event, claiming that it was part of an "antisubversive" action by the army.

This repressive action followed closely on the murder (June 1975) of the largest rancher in the area, José Luís Arenas Barrera, a man known by the peasants as the "Tiger of Ixcán." The Guerrilla Army of the Poor (EGP), at that time a small guerrilla group, claimed responsibility for the assassination. It is doubtful whether the members of the settlement cooperative or the Indian population in the proximity of the ranch were involved in the killing, but for several days following the event there was great rejoicing in the villages of the area.[87]

The assassination of Luís Arenas gave a short-run justification for the Guatemalan army's decision to turn its attention to the remote jungles of the Ixcán, but there were some longer-run reasons as well. Oil had been discovered forty miles to the east at Rubelsanto (see Figure 6-9), and there was already talk of a road to be built through the middle of the Ixcán. One problem in developing the area was that Maya Indians had been settling the Ixcán and believed it to be theirs.

At least by the time of the 1964 census, small farmers had begun to move into that territory, clearing the forest and planting corn wherever they settled. This colonization pattern can be seen by comparing the 1950 corn map (Figure 6-10), which shows very little corn being raised in northern Guatemala, with the 1964 corn map (Figure 6-11), which shows scattered corn production in the area.

Spontaneous settlement gave way to settlement of the area by cooperatives in the early 1970s. AID and Catholic relief organizations had been promoting cooperatives since the 1960s, but in 1974 the government of President Laugerud García gave official endorsement to the cooperative movement. In some of the poorest communities of the highlands, groups decided to move down to the wet tropical lowlands to clear the jungle growth and raise corn. They formed settlement cooperatives and took part in official colonization programs sponsored by the national government.

Most of the settlement cooperatives did not come from the more prosperous

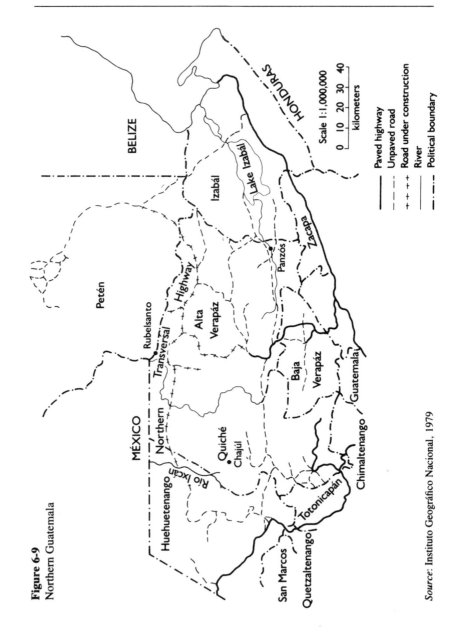

Figure 6-9
Northern Guatemala

Source: Instituto Geográfico Nacional, 1979

Figure 6-10
Corn Production in Guatemala, 1950

Each point: 100,000 pounds

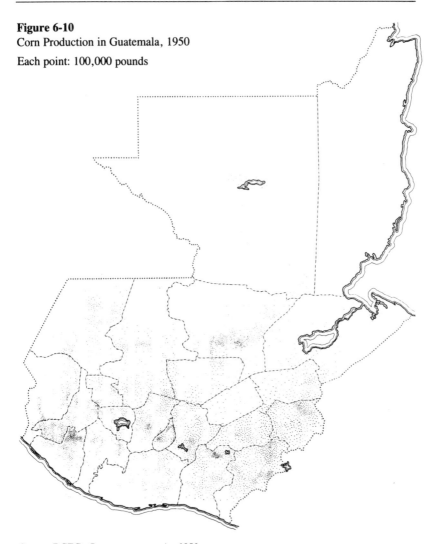

Source: DGEG, *Censo agropecuario, 1950*

villages of the central highlands. Rather, they formed in peripheral communities that had relatively poor land and relatively poor access to the central market towns. Because of poorer economic conditions, these communities were the ones that provided the bulk of the seasonal labor force for the plantations of the Pacific coast. According to Carol Smith's 1968–70 fieldwork, communities of the northwest periphery, especially in Huehuetenango, northern Quiché, and peripheral parts of San Marcos, typically sent more than half of their able-bodied adult males to the Pacific coast for the yearly har-

Figure 6-11
Corn Production in Guatemala, 1963–1964

Each point: 10,000 pounds

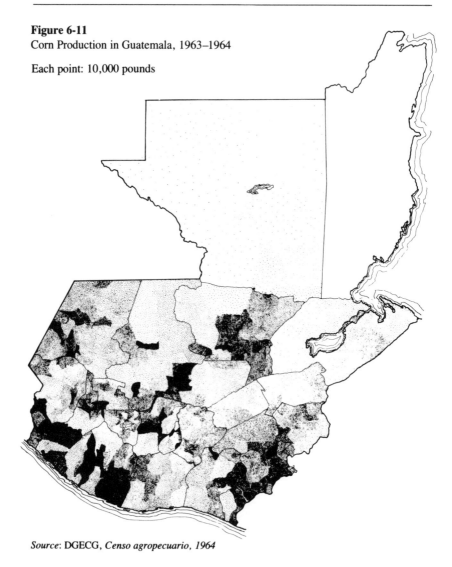

Source: DGECG, *Censo agropecuario, 1964*

vest.[88] Settlement cooperatives were seen by people in these peripheral highland communities as an alternative to the harsh conditions of wage work on the
Pacific coast plantations.

Father Bill Woods, a Maryknoll priest who died in a mysterious airplane
crash in 1976, was involved in a colonization project in the Ixcán region of
northern Huehuetenango shortly before his death. According to a Catholic nun
who was also working in the Ixíl Triangle (the highland villages around the
towns of Chajúl, Nebáj, and Uspantán) at that time, Father Woods had con-

vinced people in his highland community to move to the Ixcán as a way to avoid seasonal migration to the Pacific. He had obtained official endorsement for the colonization project in which his group participated. After the colonizers had spent more than a year of hard work clearing the jungles and fighting pests, the land was finally producing for them. One day an army unit arrived at the settlement and ordered the members of the cooperative to "plant grass seed in the cleared areas and then move." The embittered cooperative members returned to their highland community, and Father Woods was in the process of making their case known at a national level when he was killed.

During the first year after the earthquake, sixty-eight more leaders of settlement cooperatives were killed in the Ixcán region. An army base was set up in the center of the Ixíl Triangle, and twenty-eight community leaders in San Juan Cotzál, forty in the neighboring town of Chajúl and thirty-two in Nebáj were killed that year.[89]

Despite the increased frequency of forced evictions from the Ixcán and the corresponding repression of community organizations in the highland towns along the edges of the strip, it is curious that the form of resistance adopted by the Indian population at that time rarely included the use of arms. A small number of those who were directly hit by the repression responded by joining the guerrillas,[90] but at that time, a greater effort was begun to make the massacres known at a national level and to appeal to the national government for an official investigation of the killings and disappearances.

The difficulties of recruiting Maya Indians into the EGP changed dramatically after an event in May 1978.

The Cattle Boom, the Massacre at Panzós, and the Guatemalan Civil War

The twenty-ninth of May 1978 is a watershed date for the Guatemalan Civil War. Before that date Guatemala's Indian majority showed extreme reluctance to join the armed guerrilla movement. After the twenty-ninth the ranks of the EGP began to swell with Indian recruits, and communities of northern Guatemala increased their indirect assistance to the peasant army. The event that turned the tide took place in the town of Panzós (see Figure 6-9), located in the southeastern corner of the Northern Transversal Strip in the department of Alta Verapáz. Unlike similar events that preceded it, the massacre at Panzós made headlines in the national press and even received international attention.

There are several versions of what happened that day. The government issued its official statement on 30 May. In the days that followed, newspapers interviewed and published statements of peasant survivors, the mayor of the town of Panzós, and a medic who attended the wounded. Priests and other church people of the Diocese of Verapáz conducted a preliminary investigation on 30 May and published a document on 2 June that outlined its findings. Several years later taped testimony from a person who was to have read a government announcement to the gathering surfaced. This testimony has been published, along with a compilation of the other documents and newspaper reports of the event.[91]

The official government account interpreted the event as part of the tendency for

the peasants of the north of the republic to have been influenced by guerrilla groups to invade lands and private properties. . . . Unfortunately, today at 9:30 A.M., a large group of armed people unexpectedly arrived at the military post of the *municipio* of Panzós . . . attacking the guards, whom they seriously wounded, seizing the guards' weapons. In retaliation, the rest of the military personnel repelled the attack to contain the violence of the aggressors, recovering the arms that had been seized . . . the tragic result: 34 dead and 17 wounded of the aggressors and seven soldiers of the detachment gravely wounded.[92]

All of the other accounts point to more than a hundred persons killed by bullets, many more wounded, and a number drowned in the Polochíc River in an attempt to escape. All of the victims, except the wounded soldiers, were Kekchí Indians, small farmers from the villages in the Polochíc Valley in the departments of Alta Verapáz and neighboring Izabál. Their arms were sticks and machetes.

The testimonies of the survivors, the findings of the church investigation, and the arrival of an army detachment from Zacapa the day before the event provide evidence that contradicts the official claim that the peasants' arrival was unexpected. According to the other sources, those from one village had been "invited" several days in advance by a group of soldiers. Another village, which had applied for titles to the lands they had settled, was sent a written notice from the government to appear in Panzós to receive a document from the capital concerning its appeal for lands. Those from a third village joined the others to complain to the municipal government about brutality suffered two days before at the hands of a death squad, which left two of their village dead and several others badly beaten.

Estimates of the crowd that day range from six hundred to more than a thousand men, women, and children. The people were said to have been agitated as they marched into the central plaza, where they came face to face with the largest landowners of the surrounding area. Some of the Indians and the landowners exchanged harsh words. A scuffle ensued between one of the soldiers and one of the peasants. According to the church investigation this is when one of the soldiers was wounded in the leg. Initial shots fired by the landowners triggered a blast of bullets as the army detachment, the municipal police, and others lining rooftops and balconies joined in the slaughter. The church report claimed that even a member of the municipal council participated in the carnage. The person who was to have read the government statement to the peasants, but never got the chance, later reported that two more soldiers were wounded by machetes when they tried to block the streets to prevent the crowd from escaping.[93] According to the mayor, by late afternoon the corpses were already in a state of putrefaction, so the dead were buried at 4:00 P.M. in a common grave without identification. The story that floated through the Indian highlands following the massacre was that the grave had been dug by a tractor two days in advance.[94]

The gruesome details of this event often obscure the long-term buildup of tensions that set the stage for its enactment.

In 1950 the valley of the Polochíc River had not yet been settled. The corn and cattle maps from the 1950 census show very little activity in the part of the valley lying in Izabál or the part that passes through the *municipio* of Panzós. The valley of the Cahabón River, north of the *municipio* of Panzós, which leads up to the rich coffee zone of Cobán, was heavily settled and a major corn-producing zone at that time,[95] but subsistence farmers did not fill up the Polochíc Valley until after 1950.

The census maps contradict the peasants' testimonies that they had worked the contested terrain for more than fifty years. The church investigation seems more in line with the census data; it states that "for a number of years, groups of peasant families have come to occupy these lands for their plantings, unclaimed lands [*tierras baldías*] of the jurisdiction of Panzós."[96]

By 1963–64, the land use pattern had changed dramatically. Corn production (see Figure 6-11) had come to cover the whole eastern half of the department of Alta Verapáz, including the *municipio* of Panzós, the southeast corner of the department. Cattle were starting to make their way into the valley by the time of the 1963–64 census, but the major impetus toward cattle ranching did not come until later, when an improved road was completed from the nickel town of El Estór on Lake Izabál, along the southeastern rim of the nickel deposits, through the village of Cahaboncito, up the valley of the Polochíc, through the town of Panzós, and all the way up into the highlands. In the highlands this improved road linked up with a paved road to the packing plant in Guatemala City.[97]

By at least 1971 major ranching operations had begun in the Polochíc Valley. The 1971 portfolio of FIASA, an AID-sponsored private investment bank,[98] lists a loan outstanding to a corporation called Compañia Ganadera del Polochíc (Cattle Company of the Polochíc).

The church investigation of the factors leading to the events at Panzós points to a spate of supplementary titles issued to large landholders in 1978, and it is reported that the very week before the massacre large landholders had their gunmen intimidate and terrorize the villagers in an attempt to force them from the area. The ranchers must have known that the villagers were going to resist their eviction stubbornly; otherwise they would not have needed to call all the way to Zacapa for army reinforcements. Immediately following the slaughter, peasants still remaining in the villages were forced to flee, their homes were bombed with grenades, and the lands in question were cordoned off by soldiers.[99]

What makes the Panzós massacre different from the cattle evictions in Honduras and Costa Rica is not just the larger number of people killed in a single episode but the way the national government behaved and the way the peasants perceived that behavior. Panzós is no different from any other cattle zone in Central America as far as the behavior of the local government is concerned: the local police invariably serve the largest ranchers in the area. But when an appeal is pressed at the national level, rarely does one find in Costa Rica or Honduras a flat denial of peasant rights to land.[100]

According to the church report, some of the peasants of the Polochíc Valley had presented their claims to INTA, and "some had obtained promises; others provisional titles, and others permission to plant and harvest." Not a single one of the peasants was reported as having received legal property title.[101] The peasants who assembled in Panzós that day were appealing to justice higher up.

The delegation of large landowners standing in front of the municipal government building consisted of the largest ranchers in the area.[102] Adding to the symbolism of the ceremony, one of the most notorious ranchers, Flavio Monzón, made an announcement to the crowd assembled before him that day. The textual declaration of peasant survivors reported in the national news several days later described his speech: "Flavio Monzón, leader of the National Liberation Movement (MLN), told us that the President of the Republic and the Ministers of Defense and Governance had authorized our assassination."[103]

Whether the rancher actually made this statement is beside the point. This was the message confirmed by national army bullets the day of the massacre. This was the message that was published in the national news two days later.

More important, this was the tale transmitted with awesome speed in Pocomán to all the lands inhabited by the Kekchí. From Pocomán it was translated into Mam and other tongues as it shot westward over the length of the Northern Transversal Strip and made its way into the central market towns for distribution on market day.

The massacre at Panzós became the symbolic affirmation of what the Nicaraguan peasantry learned a decade earlier: there is no justice higher up.

Summary

For those with privileged access to the titling press and bank credit, the beef-export boom meant a quick way to expand family fortunes. For the millions of Central Americans who plant food crops for survival, it spelled doom. Unlike coffee, cotton, and sugar, which require very rich soils and special climates to be profitable, cattle raising did not stop when the relatively fertile soils of the Pacific strip had been claimed but spread wherever grass would grow.

Vast territories that had been worthless from the perspective of export agriculture became valuable as packing plants called for more meat, roads were built, and cattle loans were approved. Forested areas that had once provided survival insurance for the rural majority were blocked from peasant access by the relentless spread of pastures. Once the fences were built and the grass seed sown, the ranches offered few jobs for the dispossessed.

Barbed wire meant prosperity and prestige for ranchers, but for those who grew corn it came to symbolize a crown of thorns, the harbinger of crucifixion and death.

The peasantry did not accept slow death through starvation as inevitable but struggled against the ranchers at every step of the way. The receding edge of the tropical forest became the setting of a conflict between two incompatible systems of land use, one driven by the logic of the world market, the other driven by the logic of survival.

The early stages of conflict were the same practically everywhere in Central America, but the escalation differed in time and space. In Honduras and Costa Rica national governments intervened in ways that prevented the escalation of the conflicts into war. But by the late 1960s a different pattern had emerged in Nicaragua and Guatemala. There counterinsurgency forces supplied by Washington served as eviction forces for local ranchers, permanently altering the terms of the struggle in those countries.

There was ample evidence from the 1960s that beef exports produced rural unrest, but the cattle loans continued, the roads went on being built, and even tiny El Salvador, in a prophetic move, had its first export-packing plant approved by the USDA in 1972. By the time of the first oil-price explosion and worldwide recession (1973–75), the cattle zones of Central America had become drenched in blood. By the second wave of worldwide inflation and crisis, they had become staging areas for revolution.

Part Three: The Crisis

7. Cotton, Cattle, and the Crisis

Part One and Part Two showed how cotton and beef became the two most important new exports from Central America since the end of World War II. Both commodities helped expand and diversify the foreign exchange earnings of the region, and both expanded the tax base of governments. Both activities generated profits for multinational corporations and local investors, and both helped modernize agriculture. Along with prosperity, however, cotton and cattle produced ecological stress. Cotton farming poisoned the coastal environment, while cattle ranching irreversibly destroyed tropical forests. Far more devastating than their ecological consequences were their social consequences. Each boom in its own special way did more than the Soviets or the Cubans could have dreamed of doing in preparing Central America for revolution.

Cottonfields and cattle ranches claimed lands that peasants were using for food production. In this way the two placed similar stresses on rural people, who had to find other ways of making their livings. In increasing numbers, the people expelled by cotton and cattle flowed into the slums of the cities or migrated to ever-more-remote areas to sculpt cornfields in the rocky hillsides or to carve them from the forests.

In other ways, however, the two exports made different contributions to social instability.

Cotton and the Buildup to Crisis

Cotton required very rich, easily accessible, flat lands—requirements that limited its geographical expansion to the richest sections of the Pacific coastal plain or to unusually fertile upland river valleys. Because of their location and their fertility, most of the lands that became cottonfields had been worked for many years as haciendas. These haciendas had long-standing titles attached to them, and landowning families had exercised their rights to these properties for several generations.

In the atypical cases where cotton evicted people from areas that had not been controlled by large landowners, peasants resisted the takeover of their corn lands in ways that resembled responses to cattle evictions. In several instances peasants armed themselves and invaded the lands that had been taken from them, acts that ended in confrontation with national security forces. Most often, however, the switch from corn to cotton was peaceful. It involved the landlord demanding rent in cash instead of the customary corn, a rental arrangement that most peasants could not afford. The move from prime corn-lands placed peasants under duress, but it did not normally evoke their resistance because, in contrast to cattle evictions, it did not tamper with their beliefs about rights to land. The landlord had exercised a claim over those properties for years, and the choice to stay or move was placed squarely on the peasants.

Cotton claimed the highest-yielding cornlands in Central America, forcing those who moved to scrape harder for survival, but cotton's most important contribution to instability was not in the way it impoverished people. Cotton's contribution was more subtle and, in the long run, far more powerful. Cotton and the opportunities for mechanization that it brought transformed in the most fundamental way the relationship between the large landowner and his agricultural work force.

In the era of corn and oxen, the interrelationships between the owner of the estate and the large number of peasant families living permanently on the estate extended well beyond interchanges associated with work. A web of mutual obligations and duties, reinforced by religion, bound landlord to peasant and vice versa. Basically, the landlord was expected to be charitable and look out for his flock in times of stress; peasants were expected to be humble and to serve their master on earth so that theirs would be the kingdom of heaven in the hereafter.

With the cash influx that cotton brought to the flatlands of Central America, landowners found that much larger money profits could be earned by mechanizing. Bank finance was easy to obtain for cotton cultivation, and with financing, tractors could be bought. The introduction of tractors rid the landowner of the need for a large staff to care for oxen year round, and agribusiness suppliers offered all sorts of tractor attachments and chemical products that substituted for human labor at other stages of the cultivation process. Peasants who had once been viewed as essential for the prosperity of an estate began to be perceived as excess baggage. Landlords made far greater profits by retaining small permanent staffs of semiskilled tractor drivers on their estates and turning the peasant parcels into cottonfields. Large landowners who did not take the initiative to become growers themselves could double or triple their earnings simply by evicting peasants and renting the land to cotton growers.

Large numbers of unskilled laborers for weeding and thinning could be hired on a part-time basis from the pool of landless workers that began to appear in the slums of the coastal towns, along road rights-of-way, and along rocky river channels. At harvest time, when the local labor market became tight, cotton growers sent recruiters to the slums of the capital cities or to peasant zones in the least accessible and most barren sections of the country. Those recruited for the harvest from the local labor market returned home every night, but those imported from afar spent the duration of their contracts in makeshift barracks on the cotton plantations. In addition to the money saved from the harvest, many workers returned to their highland communities with intestinal parasites, malaria, and disorders associated with cotton poisoning.

The modernization process hit cotton first for a number of reasons, but it soon spread to other commercial crops like coffee and sugar. Once the shift in mode of production occurred and the peasants attached to estates as *colonos*, sharecroppers, or renters had been evicted, the process was irreversible. When cotton profits plummeted in the late 1960s and growers shifted to other crops, peasants were not invited back as permanent residents on the plantations, even when the shift meant a return to traditional food crops. Corn and rice, crops that had once been grown almost exclusively by peasants, began to be cultivated on the large fields in much the same way as cotton. The same tractors and the same airplanes were used, hybrid seeds and fertilizer were purchased from the same agribusiness supply houses, and temporary wage hands were hired whenever a large supply of labor was needed.

Landowners little understood that agricultural modernization meant more than an increase in money profits. With each tractor purchased came the potential for an expansion of money earnings, but only at the loss of the number of subjects under a landlord's direct control. Once the economic basis of paternalistic rule was destroyed, very soon thereafter there came a dissolution of the religion that had gone with it. Landowners continued to go to mass in the churches where the old-time religion was still preached, and they continued to exercise their old duties toward their house servants and permanent staffs, but no longer did it make sense to look out for the entire flock when the flock consisted of an unruly crowd of seasonal migrants imported for the harvest from afar, sometimes from a neighboring country.

Nor did it make sense in the new setting for migrant laborers to be humble and serve their masters when the master was no longer a person but a corporation, and corporate responsibility ended with the payment of a money wage. In the zones where the seasonal migrants came to congregate, in the slums of the coastal towns and capital cities, and in the barren stretches yet untouched by commercial agriculture, a new religion took hold. The new Christianity recognized the centuries-old peasant concept of the right to land for life, and it offered a hope for leaving the house of bondage and entering the promised land. The landlord's position in the celestial hierarchy changed. Instead of being seen by the peasants as a benefactor and protector located somewhere between themselves and God, the landowner moved into the position of a pharaoh. In the place of a reward to be received in heaven, the new religion promised that God's kingdom would be brought to this earth for those who took the initiative.

During the 1960s all sorts of organizations of the poor began to appear. Farm-worker organizations began to demand increases in the minimum agricultural wage and improvement in health conditions on the plantations. Slum-dweller associations began to demand water, electricity, and a halt to periodic evictions by the police. Peasant leagues began to press for land reform. Problems that had once been worked out in a personalistic give-and-take between landlord and peasant were pushed into the domain of the state.

In addition to dissolving the glue that once held the rural order together, cotton—and the mechanization that it came to symbolize—also increased the instability of the region by making landlord and agricultural work force both more dependent for survival on an unstable market. From the perspective of the landlord, not only was there the traditional worry about the fluctuating price of the harvested crop, but there was also worry about the costs of insecticide, fertilizer, seed, tractors, diesel fuel, parts, wage labor, and credit. From the perspective of the seasonal worker, no longer was there the security of a small plot to raise food on; survival became closely tied to the demand for wage labor, the wage rate, and the price of the foodstuffs, transportation, and other commodities purchased with the money wage.

During years of worldwide prosperity, the mounting tensions from cotton's advance went practically unnoticed, and governments had sufficient revenues for minor reforms and repression. It was not until the 1970s, when the world crisis hit, that cotton's contribution to instability was fully revealed.

Cattle and the Buildup to Crisis

Beef's contribution to instability in Central America was less subtle than cotton's. The beef boom placed greater stress on the rural population than cotton or any previous export boom. Coffee, sugar, bananas, cotton, and other export crops had very definite geographical limits outside of which production on a commercial basis was unprofitable. In contrast, cattle could be raised practically anywhere.

With very little starting capital and relatively little effort, ranchers could claim large expanses of land. Physical barriers to cattle ranching were temporary: forests were felled and roads were built. Cotton placed stress on peasants by claiming high-yielding lands from corn production, but cattle competed for the marginal lands as well. Moreover, cattle ranching differed from other export activities in that it offered little employment for the evicted.

Pastures impoverished more thoroughly than cottonfields, but economic stress was not the main reason why cattle raising became synonymous with rural unrest. The cattle boom, more than any previous export boom, tampered with something sacred: beliefs about rights to land.

Unchecked by biological constraints, cattle ranching spread into areas long protected from commercial agriculture by poor soils, tropical forests, and inaccessibility. For many centuries peasants had been permitted to colonize these national lands, clear the forests, and grow corn. As the zones unclaimed by export agriculture filled up with peasants over the years, spillover into yet-uncleared forest reserves had permitted the survival of the peasant way of life.

After World War II export expansion pushed peasants off prime cornlands. As the rocky peasant zones became overcrowded, the colonization drive intensified. Peasants migrated to the forest's edge and continued the corn cycle. First the remaining forest areas of the Pacific coastal plain were colonized; then the migration moved eastward toward the wetter, often less fertile tropical forest areas of the Atlantic side of the isthmus.

New pasturelands were created primarily at the expense of tropical forests, but the forest-to-pasture syndrome usually involved an intermediate step. Following a time-honored tradition, peasants were permitted and sometimes actively encouraged to move into a forested area, clear the land of brush and trees, and plant corn. Once the land was cleared and the stumps had had time to rot, the peasants were removed from the clearing and pasture grass was planted.

The removal of peasants from lands they had cleared was not always easy. Wherever the forest-to-corn-to-pasture transition occurred, there arose a clash between two incompatible systems of land use, and the people caught in the clash held equally strong views about why the land was rightfully theirs.

On the one side was the modern-day hero in elite circles, the *ganadero*, who through personal risk and private initiative was repeating the pattern of heroes past, contributing to the national wealth and the social status of his offspring by carving out new territory for the export trade. On the opposite side was the peasant, whose right to the land was governed by the tradition that had held sway over those areas before cattle ranching became profitable. Land was for life, and the right to land was for those who took the effort to clear it and make it productive.

The clash between peasants and ranchers rarely broke out into violence all at once, but more typically it followed a pattern of escalating steps of threat and counterthreat, with the stakes increased by each side at each step. Depending on the perceived strengths of the two sides, conflicts could be squelched at any point, or they could escalate to higher levels of authority. If local peasants could make their case known to national peasant organizations, university groups, church groups, labor unions, or other national institutions with sympathies for the peasant side of the conflict, pressure could be brought to bear on the national government. In Costa Rica and Honduras the peasants were able to win battles against ranchers, especially when national courts found that ranchers did not have legal title to the disputed territory.

As peasant groups gained momentum, ranchers began to form national organizations. Sometimes these, in turn, formed coalition groups with other landowner and business organizations. In the national government, ranchers followed the tradition established long before beef was a viable export: they called on the national security forces to back up their local claims. When national government institutions were staffed with officials sympathetic to peasants, rancher coalitions brought pressure to bear to oust those officials and to enact legislation and enforcement favorable to rancher interests.

By the late 1960s a pattern appeared in the most important cattle-boom zones of Guatemala and Nicaragua, one that became commonplace in cattle-boom zones elsewhere in the 1970s. Ranchers who were having difficulties evicting peasants were able to convince the national security forces that there were Communist threats in these areas. The national security forces were able to convince Washington of the same, so the areas of strongest peasant resistance were declared counterinsurgency zones. Local cattle ranchers in this way got free eviction forces, armed and trained at U.S. taxpayers' expense. The strategic roads that were built into the trouble areas further enhanced their viability as cattle zones. When peasants fled the gunfire and napalm, the lands they left were turned into cattle ranches, and officers in the national security forces became cattle barons as they shared the booty of war with local ranchers, local officials, and peasant collaborators.

U.S. Policy and the Buildup to Crisis

By the time the shocks of the 1970s hit, Central America was divided into two hostile camps. At the center of one camp stood the export oligarchy, changed by more than a decade of world-system pressures and technological adaptation, but clinging ever more desperately to a vision of civilization inherited from the past. At the center of the other camp stood the Central American peasantry, whose way of life and sources of survival had been radically altered by those selfsame pressures of agricultural modernization and export diversification but whose vision of civilization looked to a future free of the oligarchy, a future where uncultivated lands would not be denied and where rights to a living wage would at last be respected.

Throughout the 1960s, U.S. policy toward Central America nourished a monstrous contradiction. On the military front, the oligarchy was provided with a modern, well-equipped repression apparatus, capable of gathering intelligence and terrorizing the newly forming grassroots groups and their sympathizers. On the economic front, the wealth of the oligarchy was enhanced by the new opportunities for investment generated by export diversification and modernization.

On the other side, Washington's modernization and export diversification program helped create the class of landless peasants and slum dwellers that moved outside of the traditional day to day control of the large landowners, and it brought into open dispute territories that had long been claimed by peasants, thereby creating the conditions for the formation of peasant leagues and armed bands of peasants.

Even as a military-repression apparatus was being equipped and trained for the oligarchy, Washington went against the wishes of the oligarchy by funding social programs. Land-reform decrees were enacted that contained provisions recognizing the peasant perspective on rights to land. Peasant leagues and labor unions were sponsored by AID, and training programs for union leaders were established by the American Institute for Free Labor Development (associated with the AFL-CIO). Human rights organizations were given official U.S. support, and political parties that recognized the basic rights of the poor were encouraged.

Efforts to mediate the conflict between the two camps were made far more difficult by the natural and world-system shocks that hit in the 1970s. The shocks struck at the economic bases of both camps, reduced the economic space for compromise, damaged the fiscal capabilities of governments to respond, and unleashed fears and hostilities that had accumulated for years.

World-System Shocks: Impact on Elites

For the elites, the world economic crisis exposed the vulnerability of relying on imported inputs and international credit. During the 1950s and 1960s reliance on bank credit and tractors, hybrid seeds and chemicals, veterinary medicines and other purchased inputs produced rapid accumulation of wealth. When the crisis hit, dependence on the market spelled disaster.

The two oil-price explosions, 1973–75 and late 1977–81, sent world prices of fertilizer, pesticide, and tractor fuel spiraling upward, but prices of coffee, cotton, and beef were dampened by the onset of the most severe worldwide recessions since the 1930s. The acute anxiety that was felt by elites during the first wave of world crisis was mitigated in 1976 and 1977 by a recovery of prices of agricultural exports, but when the second round of oil-price inflation and recession hit in the late 1970s and early 1980s anxiety returned to the elite camp (see Table A-11 in the appendix). What made the profit squeeze unbearable was the behavior of interest rates. During both waves of world crisis, the cost of borrowing funds from the international banking system skyrocketed, a pressure that was quickly transmitted through the local banking systems.

The waves of crisis made the oligarchy more intransigent than ever on the issue of land rights. Many elites found themselves overextended and having to borrow more from the banks. In order to stay afloat, they had to mortgage more land. To get a mortgage on a piece of land in Central America, the owner must not only show the title to the property but convince the banker that the land is under the effective control of the owner. Otherwise, in the event of a default, the bank might end up with a piece of property infested with squatters. With the pressures for land reform building up, control over idle properties became particularly suspect from the point of view of bankers at precisely the time when landowners were demanding more credit.

World-system pressures, completely outside the control of local elites, reinforced to the point of passion their traditional view of land. Not only did the idle perimeters of their titled estates have to be more heavily guarded against peasant invasions, but land areas open to dispute had to be titled and brought under their control for use as collateral for loans.

The same world-system pressures that made elites cling to an absolutist position regarding land rights also reinforced an absolutist position regarding labor. A sense of helplessness spread through the elite camp as prices of oil, fertilizer, pesticide, tractors, and credit escalated. Practically the only commodity input produced locally, and therefore subject to landowner influence, was wage labor. Any move by farm workers, government agencies, or AID that might lead to a loss of landowner dominance over the local labor supply had to be resisted.

With the onslaught of the world economic crisis, the oligarchy felt desperate and cornered. To the elites, it seemed that to give up one square inch of territory under these conditions would be an invitation to the ill-bred to swarm onto the large estates. To make a single concession to organized labor, even in a sector other than agriculture, would be an invitation to the seasonal labor force to form unions and raise the agricultural wage. To give up in the slightest way their absolute right to control land and labor would be a move down the road toward Cuba. If any softening of these inherited rights were permitted today, not far down the road the elites would find themselves with no rights at all.

To hold onto their accustomed way of life, members of the oligarchy found it increasingly necessary to call on their traditional allies in the security forces. Encroachments by the poor had to be checked, lest the civilization inherited from the past fall into ruin.

World-System Shocks: Impact on the Poor

The world crisis hit the poor earlier than it hit the agricultural elites. It also hit them harder. The elites were able to pass on some of their rising input costs at first, before recessions lowered the prices of their exports, and when the recessions struck, the anxiety of elites could at least be temporarily relieved by bank loans. The average person was not so lucky. With access to land squeezed by two decades of export-led growth, the majority of the Central American population relied directly or indirectly on money wages for survival. Expulsions, mechanization, and rapid population growth produced a market for unskilled labor that was generally glutted. The pool of landless or nearly landless people overflowed national boundaries in search of work, making upward adjustments in wages difficult.

While money wages were being held down by excess supply on regional labor markets, the prices of some of the most important items of consumption were being determined on an inflationary world market. No longer were basic grain prices being controlled by local pressures of supply and demand. By the early 1970s grain production and the grain trade had become modernized and internationalized, much as cotton had been. If the price of corn on the world market exceeded the price a large grain warehouse could receive for corn on the domestic market, corn would be quickly diverted into the world market; the domestic price accordingly rose. Furthermore, with the best lands taken for export crops, Central America could no longer supply its own food needs; it had become a regular importer of grain from the world market by the early 1970s.

This internationalization of the market meant a rapid transmission of world food prices through the regional economy.[1] Glutted labor markets and inflated prices of basic necessities drove down real wages, the greatest reductions occurring during waves of world economic crisis or following natural disasters.[2] The precipitous drop in the purchasing power of the money wage placed greatest stress on those with the lowest wages and those with the least access to land, people whose money incomes were almost entirely spent on food and transportation, the commodities that showed the most dramatic price increases.

To avoid starvation, people who had become dependent on money wages were faced with a limited number of choices. One consisted of the traditional solution: moving onto idle properties to plant food crops. Another consisted of organizing for higher wages or for price freezes on basic grains, public transportation, and other purchased necessities.

Natural disasters did much the same thing in the localities affected as world-system shocks did across the entire region. The Managua earthquake in December 1972, the hurricane that struck the north coast of Honduras in September 1974, and the Guatemala earthquake of February 1976 disrupted food-supply and transportation networks, encouraged hoarding, and sent prices of basic necessities spiraling upward. The large numbers of people dependent on the purchasing power of wages responded to these natural shocks much as they responded to world-system shocks. In the areas affected, natural disasters sparked peasant land invasions, strikes by wage workers, and protests over the prices of food, public transportation, and other basic necessities.

The waves of unrest that shook Central America in the 1970s seem to have been triggered by natural and economic shocks of uncommon magnitude, but the way in which people responded to those shocks was not merely a product of the abnormal severity of the disasters. It is true that the shocks put large numbers of individuals under severe stress at the same time, but the responses to stress were conditioned by years of experience in collective action. Peasant leagues that had formed during the 1960s to resist enclosures of peasant lands used their acquired skills and connections to coordinate massive land occupations when the disasters of the seventies struck. Farm worker organizations that had sprung up with the shift to seasonal wage labor in the 1960s staged strikes and used their previously developed connections in church and state to pressure for wage adjustments when bursts of inflation hit. Organizations of slum dwellers that grew up along with the slums in the 1960s reorganized to provide earthquake relief when Managua and Guatemala City were leveled in 1972 and 1976.

People in the camp of the poor were armed not only with organizational skills acquired over the preceding decade but also with a new theology. If there were idle lands and people going hungry, the new religion saw it as God's will that people use those idle lands to favor life. If wages were no longer sufficient to cover basic necessities, it was God's will that they organize to raise wages. If earthquakes created shortages of food, it was God's will for people to organize to combat hoarding and speculation, to work to secure food, and to distribute the loaves and the fishes to the needy multitude. If earthly authorities stood in the way of life, it was God's will that the chosen people, the oppressed children of Israel, defy the authorities.

Summary

Triggered by natural disasters and world-system shocks outside the control of anyone, conflicts between the two great camps intensified. At precisely the time when elites were most threatened by the loss of lands to the banks in the city, the peasants were moving onto the lands in the countryside. At a time when profits were being squeezed by exploding prices of oil, fertilizer, pesticide, and credit, the labor force was demanding higher wages.

Similar pressures were felt by elites and the poor across the five-country area, but the way the authorities behaved differed substantially from one country to the next and from one wave of unrest to the next. The way governments responded to pressures had much to do with the way particular social crises unfolded.

8. Governments and the Crisis

By the early 1970s the five countries of Central America were exposed to the world system in much the same way. All five relied on a handful of agricultural commodities whose prices were to suffer from worldwide recessions. All five were dependent on imported inputs whose prices were to surge with uncharacteristic force. All five were habituated to borrowing from the international financial system whose interest rates were to explode. Most important, all five had social fabrics that had been weakened by more than a decade of agricultural modernization and export expansion.

People responded to economic blasts in the same ways throughout the five-country region. Peasants moved onto idle lands, wage earners demanded cost-of-living adjustments, and large landowners called on the services of the local police and the national security forces. What differed from country to country was the way national governments responded to the pressures from the different camps.

The Unfolding of the Crisis in Nicaragua

It is not coincidence that the country with the greatest success in expanding cotton and beef exports, and the country with the fastest economic growth rates during the decade of the Alliance for Progress, also broke out into civil war first. During the 1960s Nicaragua experienced growth rates in real per capita income double those of the region taken as a whole. This remarkable performance was achieved in large part by the fastest-growing export sector in the region. Cotton led the way. By the mid-1960s cotton had surpassed the traditional coffee as Nicaragua's leading export earner, and by the early 1970s, 45 percent of Central America's cotton exports came from Nicaragua. Nicaraguan beef exports began with Somoza's first packing plant in the late 1950s. By 1973 Nicaragua's four USDA-approved plants accounted for one-third of the entire region's beef exports.

The Nicaraguan government responded to economic shocks by promoting exports further. Three more beef-export plants were built after the first wave of world crisis hit, and by 1978, when the second wave hit and civil war had erupted, Nicaragua's beef exports had jumped another 40 percent above 1973 levels. Cotton exports were also encouraged as a response to the swelling external debt. By 1978, according to the most conservative estimates, one hundred thousand more acres had been pulled into cotton, and Nicaraguan cotton exports had increased another 30 percent over levels achieved in 1972 and 1973.

The tensions that had built from more than a decade of export-led growth were released in an increasingly revolutionary manner beginning in late 1972. The event that seems to have triggered the Revolution was the Managua earthquake in December of 1972. The earthquake destroyed the center of Managua, leaving six thousand people dead, twenty thousand wounded, and three hundred thousand homeless.[1]

Organizations of the poor that had formed during the 1960s mobilized for earthquake relief. The Somoza regime viewed this mobilization as a threat and attempted to prevent earthquake relief from being channeled directly to community groups. Instead, the national guard was given a monopoly on dispensing disaster relief. When popular organizations protested against the profiteering on relief supplies done by guardsmen, leaders of the organizations were thrown in jail or shot. Repression by the national guard forced organizations of the poor to go underground, where a fusion of diverse groups occurred. It was after the earthquake that church people who had been working in the slums became more open to working with the FSLN.[2]

The fusion of political opposition groups and the coordination of protests against the Somoza regime intensified as the world economic shocks hit the Nicaraguan economy. In 1973 and 1974, when cotton workers, hospital workers, and banana workers struck, and when slum dweller organizations, market traders, and other groups staged protest actions, the Somoza government tried to crush these organizations by disrupting protest actions and arresting the leaders. Along the receding edge of the forest, clashes between peasants and the national guard increased, and reports of rapes, disappearances, and the strafing of peasants by the national guard flowed in from these areas through church sources. In 1974, when two hundred students in the cotton town of León protested for the release of political prisoners, the national guard was sent in with tear gas and bullets to dislodge the students from the building they occupied.[3]

Following the taking of hostages by the FSLN in 1975, Somoza clamped on a state of siege that was not lifted for thirty-three months. During that period, counterinsurgency drives are said to have taken the lives of some three thousand persons. Black notes that between 1975 and 1977 linkups occurred between the armed guerrilla groups and the previously independent groups of urban workers, peasants, slum dwellers, students, rural wage workers, and

Christians.[4] When the state of siege was lifted under pressure from abroad, Somoza claimed that he had defeated the guerrillas, but shortly thereafter armed attacks on national guard barracks began. By late 1977 the second round of worldwide inflation was under way, and strikes, land occupations, and public protests broke out once more.

The Somoza government not only came under attack from organizations of the poor but also faced opposition from within the ranks of the business elite. From the perspective of the old wealth in Nicaragua, the Somozas were newcomers who had acquired properties through the use of state finance and control over the national guard. From owning little or no land before the 1930s, the Somozas and those closely connected with them came to acquire one-fifth of the arable land in the country, some of it taken from traditional elites during periods of economic hardship. When the earthquake leveled the center of Managua, the Somoza machine continued in its tradition of using disasters to expand the family's portfolio. Family-controlled real estate companies bought land around the periphery of the old city, and reconstruction funds were allocated to serve those areas, so that their market value was raised overnight. Somoza-owned construction companies were given contracts to pave streets and put in new water lines, and building materials were purchased from enterprises owned by members of the clan. In this way millions of dollars of earthquake relief filtered into the bank accounts of the Somoza dynasty.[5]

When opposition from business circles surfaced, Somoza adopted a no-compromise position. In 1974 Chamorro and Sacasa, members of the old landholding elite, were arrested and put on trial for encouraging abstention from elections.[6] Part of the thirty-three month state of siege included heavy censorship of *La Prensa*, the newspaper owned by the Chamorro family. Repression of political opposition only brought a buildup of opposition forces, and every attack by the Somoza government against these elites delegitimized the regime in Mexico, Costa Rica, Venezuela, the United States, and other countries.

The final fusion of opposition forces from the camp of the poor and the camp of the rich took place in January 1978, when Pedro Joaquín Chamorro, the most popular leader of the political opposition, was assassinated. Two days of riots followed this event, and Somoza-owned companies were stormed. The building housing Somoza's newspaper, *Novedades*, was set ablaze, and thirty thousand mourners attended the Chamorro funeral. A two-week general strike was called by the political opposition, private-sector business groups, and labor organizations.

After the death of Chamorro, the war took a new turn. Members of the old elite, some of them with names like Blandón, Montealegre, Robelo, and

Chamorro, names that appear on the list of large cotton growers, began to work in coordination with groups of the poor, which in turn were becoming more brazen in confronting the national guard and invading Somoza properties. Somoza responded to the mounting opposition by bombing the slums of the major towns, which had become the strongholds of the FSLN, but bombs were also dropped on factories and farms of members of the elite opposition. It is estimated that before Somoza was finally ousted in July of 1979, fifty thousand persons were killed, a hundred thousand more were wounded, and much of the country was left in ruins.

For a short while, elite participation in the overthrow of Somoza masked the fundamental nature of the conflict. The Sandinista government, however, quickly proved more sensitive to the needs of migrant workers and peasants than to the needs of cotton growers and large cattle ranchers. Sandinista labor courts more frequently settled disputes in favor of agricultural workers than of the large growers, and when peasants moved onto uncultivated lands, the Sandinista land courts, backed by a national agrarian reform law that explicitly recognized the peasant concept of land, also settled disputes in favor of peasants more often than of large landowners. In the first few years of Sandinista rule, more than half a million acres of land were reclaimed by Nicaraguan peasants.[7]

The combined effects of land reform, labor courts sympathetic to laborers, and national programs to eradicate hunger, illiteracy, and epidemic diseases removed some of the traditional stress on the poor and made it more difficult for agricultural elites to secure a cheap and pliable labor force. The Sandinista government attempted to prevent disruption to the economy by direct subsidies to exporters,[8] but a hostile U.S. economic and military policy toward Nicaragua, combined with internal gains by peasants and workers, made it even more difficult for elites to continue with their customary way of life. U.S. import quotas on Nicaraguan sugar and beef were cut, and scarce foreign exchange was allocated first to the military and the state-owned properties, instead of being channeled to elite-owned enterprises. In increasing numbers the elites removed their support from the new government. Some formed opposition political parties within the country, and others, like Robelo, joined the armed opposition across the borders.

In summary, the attempts of the Somoza regime to repress the opposition did not have the intended effect. Instead of terrorizing people into submission, official repression emboldened them. Instead of splitting up the opposition, official terror forged closer ties between opposition groups. As the social crisis mounted, even elements of the Nicaraguan oligarchy who had benefited from Somoza's economic policies joined in efforts to overthrow the dictatorship.

The split in the elite camp made the Somoza government more brittle, and for a while it disguised the class nature of the Revolution.

The Unfolding of the Crisis in El Salvador

By the early 1970s the poor in El Salvador were the most destitute in all of Central America. Part One of this book showed how cotton and agricultural mechanization displaced people from large estates in El Salvador during the 1960s. Many of the displaced people flowed into slums of the cities, where they became a cheap labor force for the cotton, sugar, and coffee harvests. Some of those who went to San Salvador found jobs in the manufacture of goods for sale in the Central American Common Market. Those who were unwilling to give up their heritage as peasants migrated to the north and to the east. They settled on the barren stretches of northern El Salvador, or they pushed over the border into more sparsely populated Honduras.

The land base for Salvadoran peasants was reduced further in the late 1960s. Honduran ranchers disrupted the growing Honduran peasant movement by pressuring the government to expel Salvadoran peasants from Honduras, and more than a hundred thousand of them were dumped back into overpopulated El Salvador.[9] After the brief war between the two countries in 1969, the Honduran border was closed to Salvadoran migrants and manufactures. This move permanently closed off the agricultural frontier for Salvadoran peasants, and at the same time it forced layoffs in Salvadoran industry as the markets of Honduras, Nicaragua, and Costa Rica were lost.[10]

Before the world economic crisis struck, landlessness, dependence on wage income for survival, and unemployment were more severe in El Salvador than in any other Central American country. The situation was made even worse in 1972 when El Salvador received a quota to export beef to the United States, and the country's first export-packing house was approved by the USDA. In 1973 a second plant was approved, and one-third of the beef slaughtered in El Salvador that year was exported to the United States.[11] Estimates of landlessness rose from 29 percent of rural households in 1971, before El Salvador entered the beef trade, to 41 percent of rural households by 1975.[12] By 1978 the second wave of world economic crisis had hit, and beef had become El Salvador's third-most-important export, after coffee and cotton; half of the beef slaughtered in El Salvador that year was exported to the United States.[13] By 1980 estimates of landlessness in El Salvador had reached 65 percent of rural households.[14]

During the 1960s farm workers, peasants, shantytown dwellers, urban industrial workers, and teachers formed unions and pressured for better living conditions, higher wages, and land reform. During that period the camp of the poor did not engage in armed struggle but pressured for change through openings in established institutions like the church, the university, and reform-minded political parties. By the late 1960s unions were making gains through strikes, reform-oriented politicians had won mayorships and seats in the legislature, base communities were forming around the churches in the slums and in the rural villages, and issues of social justice were being raised in the universities and public schools.

As the poor were organizing for social change, the Salvadoran oligarchy was organizing for repression. In 1961 members of the oligarchy financed a media blitz portraying Alliance for Progress reforms as "communist-inspired." In the mid-1960s, at about the time the reformist politician, Napoleon Duarte, was elected mayor of San Salvador, and as expulsions of *colonos* from the large estates were reaching epidemic proportions, the paramilitary organization, ORDEN (the Democratic Nationalist Organization), was created. As pressures for social change grew, so too did ORDEN; the organization later expanded to include sixty to one hundred thousand collaborators, with informants in practically every slum and rural community in the country.[15] Attacks on union leaders, peasant organizations, and the church of the poor increased in the late 1960s and early 1970s. In 1972, the year that the beef export trade began, two avenues for social change were closed off. That year Napoleon Duarte was defrauded of a landslide victory in the presidential elections, and the military government invaded the national university and purged it of professors and administrators believed to be in the opposition.[16]

When the first wave of world economic crisis hit, the political crisis in El Salvador intensified. In addition to taking the traditional measures of arresting leaders involved in protest actions, the Salvadoran military began firing directly on mass rallies. In 1974 reports surfaced in the international press of the military forcibly removing slum dwellers from the banks of the river outside San Salvador, and in the countryside the military became more active in evictions of peasants for the expansion of cotton acreage and cattle ranches.[17] In 1974 and 1975 wholesale massacres of students and peasants began.[18]

Before the mid-1970s guerrilla actions had consisted of occasional kidnappings of members of the oligarchy and foreign businessmen, but as nonviolent procedures were met with violence from the security forces, armed guerrilla actions increased. Banks were robbed, U.S. companies were bombed, and retaliatory actions against ORDEN were stepped up. Similarly, before the mid-1970s groups of the poor were scattered and did not work closely together, but in 1974 and 1975 peasant leagues, slum-dweller organizations, trade unions, student groups, and the teachers' union began linking together into large coalitions or blocks, capable of carrying out coordinated actions to pressure for change.[19]

Even as military governments were attacking the organizations of the poor, those same governments were being pressured by the U.S. government to institute reforms. The oligarchy continued to subvert the reforms, despite appeals by some military officers that the reforms were a life insurance policy for the large landowners.[20]

A short lull in the political crisis in 1976 ended in 1977 and 1978 with the second blast of worldwide economic crisis. Inflation rates climbed to 12 percent in 1977 from the dampened rate of 7 percent in 1976. In November 1977 coffee workers went on strike for cost-of-living adjustments. After two weeks of strikes, police fired on a demonstration of coffee pickers.[21]

In 1978 and 1979 inflation rates continued to climb, and strikes and protests, death-squad assassinations, and massacres at the hands of the security forces resumed. By 1979 each popular coalition had become linked with an armed guerrilla group.[22] In 1980 Archbishop Oscar Romero was assassinated, and twenty-six people were killed and two hundred were wounded when bombs and gunfire from the National Palace disrupted the funeral. Weeks after the funeral, the popular coalitions that had formed during the first wave of crisis banded together into a united front called the FDR (Democratic Revolutionary Front), and months later the armed guerrilla organizations banded together into a parallel front called the FMLN (Farabundo Martí National Liberation Front).[23]

The course of El Salvador's civil war has taken many twists and turns as the Reagan administration has sought a military solution to the conflict. No doubt there will be important changes in the direction of the conflict before the printing of this book. Nevertheless, several geographical patterns in the war's course can be observed.

The uprising in the early 1930s was centered in the western half of the country, in four departments where 70 percent of El Salvador's coffee was raised.[24] David Browning indicates the link between the invasion of coffee estates and the earlier expropriation of these lands from peasants.[25] The earliest zones to be controlled by the FMLN in 1980 and 1981, in contrast, were in the north and east of the country, in areas along the Honduran border where the land is too poor to raise coffee. Constituting about one-fifth of the land area in the country, this block of mountainous territory was traditionally a region of extensive cattle grazing mixed with subsistence farming. The top four cattle departments in 1971 (with 44 percent of the national herd at that time) turned out to have liberated zones in 1981.[26] Taken together, the departments with large guerrilla strongholds in the north and the east of El Salvador in the 1980s had the highest rates of expulsion of *colonos* between 1961 and 1971.[27] By 1982 and 1983 the FMLN moved south and east into the coastal plain of San Vicente, Usulután, San Miguel, and La Union, where cotton expansion was most heavily concentrated in the 1950s and 1960s.

Within the Salvadoran oligarchy, the groups that have been most virulent in their obstruction of land reform have been the large cotton farmers and cattle-men from the eastern half of the country. Heading the extreme right within the oligarchy is the Hill family,[28] which has been active in FARO (Eastern Region Farmers' Front) and other organizations believed to support death squad activity. In addition to owning coffee estates, the Hills are one of the most important cotton-growing families in El Salvador; the family also has stock in two textile companies, owns a beef-packing plant, and has cattle-fattening operations.[29] In 1976, when the military government attempted agrarian reform in the cotton-growing region of eastern El Salvador, the FARO united with the ANEP (National Private Enterprise Association) to halt it.[30] These two groups are also reported to have organized the White Warriors Union and the Falange, two of El Salvador's death squads.[31]

The CIA-supported election of Duarte in 1984 successfully lured the U.S. Congress into granting the Reagan administration's requests for more aid to El Salvador. Since 1979 there has been an attempt by the U.S. military to wrest from the oligarchy its control over the Salvadoran armed forces. It remains to be seen whether the Vietnam-style pacification program being pushed by U.S. advisers—which includes aerial bombing of rebel-controlled territory and a centrally controlled land reform in other areas—will successfully quiet the peasants, or whether the death squads and other security forces with strong connections to the oligarchy will continue to disrupt the attempted reforms. According to a 1984 AID study, one-third of the sixty-three thousand applicants in the first phase of the agrarian reform program were not farming the land because they "had been threatened, evicted, or had disappeared."[32]

In summary, the social crisis in El Salvador followed a pattern similar to that of Nicaragua, in that the policy of official terror did not work in the customary manner. Instead of halting the unrest, official terror seemed to fuel it. Instead of scattering the opposition, repression united diverse opposition groups into broad coalitions.

There are several important differences between the Nicaraguan and the Salvadoran cases. For one, the Salvadoran oligarchy has displayed a much greater degree of unity than the same class in Nicaragua under Somoza. For another, the U.S. government has played a much more direct role in El Salvador attempting to control the direction of the war. Since the overthrow of

Somoza in Nicaragua in 1979, U.S. security forces have gained increasing command over the counterinsurgency program in El Salvador; elections along with centrally controlled reforms have been pushed by Washington; and the government of El Salvador has become dependent on the United States for $500 million a year in military and economic assistance. In contrast to Nicaragua, the greater unity of the oligarchy in El Salvador and the larger U.S. presence there together promise to prolong the violence in that country.

The Unfolding of the Crisis in Guatemala

From 1960 to 1972 Guatemalan inflation was mild, with consumer prices rising around 1 percent a year on the average. In 1973 world inflation blasted through the Guatemalan economy and sent consumer price inflation into the double digits, where it has remained.[33]

Beginning in 1973, Guatemala was hit by a wave of strikes, public protests, and land occupations. In June of 1973, when one thousand Guatemalan peasants organized a land occupation in Jalapa, the army was sent in and twenty to thirty peasants lost their lives in the massacre.[34] Similarly, when schoolteachers went on strike, the government arrested strike leaders. When a public protest arose over government repression of the teachers, the government attacked the protesters, injuring three hundred people and arresting sixty.[35]

Like the popular movement of El Salvador, grassroots response to government repression in Guatemala was to form large coalitions of diverse organizations. In 1973 the National Front of Popular Unity formed, drawing together participation of railway workers, trade unions, and university students. In the case of the teachers strike, public pressure was so strong on the side of the teachers that the government was forced to grant concessions.[36]

In 1974 consumer price inflation rose to 17 percent. Washington pressured for elections. What happened when Efrain Rios Montt, the reform candidate, won the Guatemalan elections in 1974 was similar to what happened when Duarte won the Salvadoran elections in 1972: the right wing within the military installed a candidate more amenable to the needs of the large landowners.[37] Protests over the fraudulent election were met with repression, and the security forces and associated death squads resumed attacks on peasant leaders, union organizers, and politicians who publicly advocated land reform or wage adjustments. On 1 May 1974 four people were killed and fifteen were injured when government forces attacked a demonstration. In June 1974 Christian Democrat politicians in the Maya Indian departments of Alta Verapáz and San Marcos were assassinated, and in October the brother of Rios

Montt was assassinated. Large numbers of people disappeared at this time, and a committee of families of those who had disappeared was formed.[38]

In late 1974 and continuing into 1975 the Guatemalan government moved to reduce the ferment by holding down price increases on certain necessities. The program included basic grain subsidies and subsidies to public transport, two items that had been singled out in public protests.[39] Under pressure from AID, a cooperative movement for a hundred thousand small farmers was begun with support from some elements in the armed forces, and an attempt was made to expand the powers of the land-reform and colonization agency. Both measures met with stiff resistance from large landowners, and in November 1975 a time bomb exploded in the agrarian reform headquarters. In December 1975 Axel Mijangos, a Christian Democrat leader who had spoken out for reforms, was assassinated.[40]

In 1976, when the rest of Central America enjoyed a brief lull in inflation and social strife, Guatemala was hit by an earthquake that killed more than 20,000 people and injured another 75,000, destroying 160 blocks of Guatemala City, and leaving 90,000 people homeless in the capital city alone.[41] Because of shortages and disruptions caused by the earthquake, consumer price inflation in Guatemala continued in the double digits even though moderation in import prices had lessened inflation elsewhere in the region. The Guatemalan government responded to the disaster much as the Somoza regime responded to the Managua earthquake in 1972. Two weeks after the quake the Guatemalan army began a counterinsurgency sweep of northern Guatemala. Especially hard hit in the rural areas was the department of Quiché, where members of Catholic Action, leaders of AID-sponsored cooperatives, and others who took responsibility in earthquake relief were targeted by the army's campaign of terror.[42] The bulk of the disaster relief was channeled through General Arana's military/paramilitary apparatus in Zacapa province; Guatemala City, where a Social Democrat reformist coalition had been elected, received little relief money despite the heavier destruction in the capital. Guatemala City officials and community leaders who were believed to side with the destitute became targets of repression by the police and paramilitary units. Only days after the media reported that a city official had suggested that the homeless squat on unoccupied private lands, the official was assassinated.[43]

Food shortages and rapidly escalating food prices triggered a series of uncoordinated strikes. Union activists were targeted by the police and the associated death squads. Tensions mounted and in March of 1976, when 152 workers at the Coca-Cola bottling plant were fired, workers responded by forming the National Committee of Trade Union Unity (CNUS) with some fifty other trade unions (CNUS). The new coalition began coordinated work stoppages all over the country. Popular support for the Coca-Cola employees forced the company to reinstate the dismissed workers, but leaders in the Coca-Cola union and the national workers' coalition became targets of police and paramilitary terror.[44] In July 1976 another coalition (National Front against Violence), composed of students, trade unionists, academics, and lawyers, formed to confront the growing repression.[45]

In addition to applying terror, the Guatemalan government once again tried to relieve some of the market pressures by placing ceiling prices on basic foodstuffs and building materials. The government imported basic grains and subsidized public transport to prevent fare increases. Government workers were provided an emergency bonus, but minimum wages were not adjusted despite intense inflationary pressures.[46]

When the second oil-price explosion hit in late 1977, conflicts mounted once more and the sides of the conflict became better defined. The army began an occupation of northern Quiché province.[47] Grassroots organizations had already established ties with one another from the first wave of economic crisis and the earthquake. The kidnapping, torture, and murder of members of these organizations forced them underground, where closer coordination was established with armed guerrilla groups. When repression against cotton workers mounted in 1977, the EGP retaliated by burning crop dusters on the cotton plantations. When union or peasant leaders were murdered, guerrilla groups would retaliate by assassinating a key police officer, an oligarch suspected of funding death squads, or a union-buster. In March 1978 eighty-five hundred public workers went on strike demanding a 50 percent wage increase,[48] and in April the Committee for Peasant Unity (CUC) formed to resist abuses by the military and large landowners. In October 1978 a week of violence was sparked when the bus companies doubled their fares, from five to ten cents. Many workers in Guatemala City were spending as much as 15 percent of their wages on bus fare before the increase. When the increase was announced bus workers went out on strike, and 60 percent of the industrial labor force, including public utility employees, later joined them with work stoppages. Six hundred people were arrested and four hundred wounded in demonstrations that included organizations of workers and slum dwellers. Union leaders disappeared, and some were found dead. The Guatemalan government pumped some $40 million of subsidies into public transportation to resume services at a lower fare.[49] At the same time, a new death squad was formed, and assassinations of reform-minded politicians, peasant leaders, and union activists continued unrestrained.

It was shown in Chapter Six how the Panzós massacre in May 1978 triggered the mass involvement of Guatemala's Indian population in the armed resistance. Northern Guatemala, which was already being developed for oil, nickel, hydroelectric power, and cattle raising, became a counterinsurgency zone. Kidnapping of peasant leaders by the army, burning of crops, raping of women, and massacring of whole villages have continued to the time of the writing of this book (1985). In January 1980, when peasants from Quiché occupied the Spanish Embassy to protest abuses by the military in northern Guatemala, security forces attacked the embassy and set it on fire, killing thirty-nine people.[50]

In February 1980 a strike supported by the CUC began on a sugar plantation. By March seventy-five thousand workers on seventy large cotton and sugar plantations had joined the strike, virtually shutting down the economy of the Pacific coastal plain. The strike was so large and so well organized that the government was forced to give in to strikers' demands. The legal minimum wage of $1.12 a day, which had been in force since 1973, was raised to $3.20 a day for all agricultural and construction workers, a step that benefited some six hundred thousand workers. To avert a general strike, the government raised the minimum industrial wage to $4.90 per day.[51]

Repression of union leaders, massacres of peasants, and attacks on demonstrations continued. After Rios Montt deposed Lucas García in a palace coup in March 1982, conditions in Guatemala City quieted, but massacres in the countryside increased. One opposition journalist claimed that Montt ordered twenty-nine massacres, killing 4,000 Guatemalans in his first two months in office. Amnesty International released a conservative estimate that in the first three months of the Rios Montt government 1,454 persons, mostly Indian peasants, were killed.[52]

Under Rios Montt, the Guatemalan military—with help from AID—began a sophisticated rural pacification program with strategic hamlets, civilian patrols, and food-for-work projects.[53] One of the food-for-work projects put gangs of Indians to work constructing roads into northern Guatemala, roads designed to increase the ability of the army to control the population of the area.

The counterinsurgency program produced predictable results: the expulsion of people from the areas affected. In 1982 the Guatemalan Bishops' Conference estimated that 1 million people had been displaced from their homes. Many sought refuge in the mountains and jungles of northern Guatemala, where they foraged for food. Others remained on the Pacific coast after harvesting crops, while others packed into the slums of Guatemala City.[54] By the end of 1982 it was estimated that ninety-one thousand people had escaped into the fifty refugee camps that ringed the counterinsurgency zones across the

Mexican border in the state of Chiapas.[55] Another seventy thousand were estimated to have relocated in the interior of Mexico.[56]

During 1983 the Rios Montt government continued clearing northern Guatemala of Indians, but a number of pressures besides the guerrilla movement began to be felt. The old guard within the military became dissatisfied with Rios Montt's attempts to halt the tradition of granting cattle ranches and lucrative business deals to high-ranking officers. Some of those who had benefited from grants during the government of Lucas García feared that their newly acquired estates would be taken away. Some of the younger, reform-minded officers who had supported Rios Montt in the first place were becoming dissatisfied with the "born-again Christian" direction of his leadership, and the Roman Catholic hierarchy was similarly displeased. A war tax from agriculture, commerce, and industry initiated under Rios Montt in late 1982 provoked the wrath of the country's business elite.[57] Most important, Rios Montt's attitudes toward land reform did not sit well with the export oligarchy. Several days after his minister of the interior responded favorably to an AID study promoting land reform on idle national lands, Rios Montt was deposed.[58] General Mejía Victores, a Roman Catholic with closer ties to the export oligarchy and the extreme right, became the new president on 8 August 1983.

Victores began his regime with a sweep of Guatemala City that was dubbed "Operation Tentacle." After ten days, thirty-five hundred people from the capital had been thrown in prison. In September 1983 AID promised Victores another $7 million to add to the 250 miles of road already constructed by food-for-work projects in the areas of conflict. A fall offensive was begun in the countryside with more bombings, massacres, and armed occupations of Indian villages.[59]

To satisfy the officer corps, Victores renewed the tradition of land grants and business deals. To please the forces of repression, a chief justice of Guatemala's Supreme Court was dismissed for upholding the arrest of a civil patrolman accused of human rights abuses. To gratify the oligarchy, export taxes were temporarily lowered, and a hard line against land reform was adopted. For the U.S. security forces, Victores openly supported Reagan administration hostilities against Nicaragua and began closer coordination with the militaries of El Salvador and Honduras. Promises of U.S. aid tripled from 1984 to 1985, although Guatemala's relationship with the International Monetary Fund (IMF) was increasingly strained because of the inability of the Victores government to cut government deficits.[60]

The methods of population control employed by the Guatemalan army are the most sophisticated in the region. To date the army has prevented the guerrilla groups from establishing areas of control within the country—as occurred in neighboring El Salvador. Nearly every adult male not fighting with the guerrillas has been drafted into the army's civil patrol system. Forty-four "strategic hamlets" have been constructed and there are plans to build another forty in areas destroyed by the war. The army-occupied zones lie squarely within Maya Indian territory. To wear traditional Indian clothes or to speak one of the native Indian dialects is to risk being branded "subversive" by the army. The destruction of traditional villages and the rebuilding of strategic ones has further threatened the survival of the Maya culture. In this way the official terror in Guatemala today resembles that of El Salvador in 1932, when Salvadoran Indians discarded their traditional dress and their native languages to avoid death at the hands of the military.

Similar to the more recent experience in El Salvador, the Guatemalan army accepted civilian elections as a way to alleviate a growing financial crisis. In December 1985, Vinicio Cerezo, a Christian Democrat and a vocal critic of the army's human rights abuses, was elected president. As the first civilian president since the late 1960s, Cerezo will have to be careful not to threaten the oligarchy or the military. It is possible that death squad attacks on middle-income urban Ladinos will be reduced and Guatemala's international image cleaned up, but chances for a halt to repression in the countryside are low. Substantial increases in military and economic aid from the United States are likely to produce results similar to those of the late 1960s, when, as was shown in an earlier chapter, a civilian facade permitted direct U.S. involvement in a counterinsurgency drive that killed thousands of Guatemalans and left the Northeast under permanent military control.

Reform and Repression in Honduras: Responses to Shocks

By the time the first wave of world economic crisis spilled into Honduras in 1973, peasant organizations and labor unions were better prepared than their counterparts elsewhere in Central America. Two decades of struggle over land, wages, and living conditions had forged alliances between Honduran labor unions and peasant leagues, and both types of organizations had developed support in national-level institutions like the church, the university, political parties, and even the army. Political sophistication among grassroots groups combined with a relatively weak oligarchy to yield a different government response when the economic shocks hit Honduras. During the first wave of crisis, the government did not attempt to crush popular groups.

In late 1972 national peasant organizations called a hunger march that precipitated the downfall of the Cruz regime, a government notorious for its support of large landowners, cattle ranchers, and businessmen. One of the first actions of the Lopez Arellano regime was to reorganize the agrarian reform agency (INA) and to issue a decree promising recovery of peasant lands. In 1973 land occupations began. Following Hurricane Fifi in September of 1974, peasants responded to the disaster by moving onto idle lands in massive numbers. In 1973 and 1974 some 190,000 acres of Honduran territory were reclaimed by 24,000 peasant households. Organized land occupations continued despite a successful coup against the reformist president in April 1975. From January 1975 to mid-1976, 3,000 peasant families claimed another 20,000 acres of land. Private titles were issued in some places, and in other places producer cooperatives were set up.[61]

At a local level large landowners continued to exercise clout through the security forces. At a national level, however, peasant leagues had a voice even under a less reformist military man at the head of the government. In three short years, from 1973 to 1976, the peasants of Honduras made the largest gains in land access anywhere in Central America from the time of the CIA overthrow of the Arbenz regime in Guatemala in 1954 until the overthrow of the Somoza regime in Nicaragua in 1979.

Union activities during the first wave of crisis were not nearly so spectacular as actions by peasant organizations. Nevertheless, the Honduran government proved more flexible in responding to wage demands than the governments of Guatemala, El Salvador, and Nicaragua. Double-digit inflation did not hit Honduras until 1974, when consumer price inflation rates rose more than 13 percent. In July of that year a teachers' strike pulled in twenty thousand participants. The government ended the strike after three weeks by agreeing to the demands of the strikers.[62] Similarly, the government raised minimum wages in 1974 in response to the rapidly escalating cost of living.[63]

By the middle of 1976 organizations of ranchers, large landowners, and businessmen had begun to unite in an effort to turn back reforms. By the end of 1976 these groups claimed that the land-reform agency was infiltrated by "Communists,"[64] and by mid-January 1977 a purge was begun among army officers sympathetic to reforms.[65] By February 1977, the Honduran military began attacks on peasant cooperatives.[66] By mid-1978 large landowners were able to oust Juan Alberto Melgar Castro, the army officer who had been in power since 1975. They replaced him with Policarpo Paz García, another army officer who was expected to take a harder line on "land invaders" and who promised to coordinate military maneuvers with Somoza's national guard.[67] Within a month after the change in government, some four hundred people who had been active in the agrarian reform movement had been jailed.[68]

In 1979, 1980, and 1981 the second wave of world inflation swept through the Honduran economy, pushing consumer price inflation into double digits once more. Land invasions, protests over escalating oil prices and bus fares, and strikes were dealt with more forcefully in this second wave than in the first. What tipped the internal balance even more toward the side of the large landowners and business elite was a massive increase in U.S. military aid to Honduras following the victory of the Sandinistas in Nicaragua in July of 1979.

To permit a sustained increase in military aid from the U.S. Congress, the Carter administration pushed for elections in Honduras. The Honduran military agreed to elections under the condition that the elected president would have no control over internal security, foreign policy, or the military.[69] The same day the elected president, Roberto Suazo Córdova, was sworn in, General Gustavo Alvarez was named as commander in chief of the armed forces. Alvarez had received training in Argentina and had served as the head of FUSEP, the Honduran security police. Through his work in FUSEP, Alvarez had established close links with landowners and businessmen of the far right, and a year after he became head of the armed forces he was named president of their lobbying group, APROH (Association for Progress in Honduras).[70]

Just as Honduras was becoming more "democratic" from the perspective of the U.S. Congress, the high command in the Honduran military was purged of officers sympathetic to peasants and wage laborers. In 1982 and 1983 Alvarez declared open hunting season on leaders of peasant leagues and labor unions. Reports of clandestine jails, death squads, and torture at the hands of the Public Security Forces (FUSEP) and the National Department of Investigation (DNI) surfaced, and the number of persons who had disappeared rose dramatically.

Peasants were hard hit by the increasing militarization of Honduras. Those who had settled on lands selected as sites for U.S. "training bases" were evicted in traditional Central American fashion.[71] Far more lasting, however, will be the impact of the strategic roads being built into the agricultural frontier areas of eastern Honduras. As was shown in Chapter Six, the agricultural frontier of eastern Honduras has been the scene of clashes between peasants and cattle ranchers since at least the mid-1960s. Taken together, roads and military operations in this zone have bolstered the side of ranchers in the struggle over untitled lands in the area.

In 1983 the presence of a small band of guerrillas was reported in the eastern half of Olancho province. Olancho, the scene of the massacre of peasants and priests at the hands of large ranchers in 1975, was declared a counterinsurgency zone in 1983. In August and September of 1983 the army claimed that it had killed twenty-six guerrillas there and had captured twenty-three more.[72] By the army's own estimates, there were only one hundred guerrillas to begin with. Nevertheless, between 30 January and 5 February 1984, five thousand troops conducted a counterinsurgency sweep of Olancho province as the final phase of the Big Pine II joint maneuvers.[73] Some two hundred members of the national association of Honduran peasants (ANACH) were reported to have been arrested in late 1983 and early 1984, and the president of ANACH accused some of the officials of INA of "supporting landowners in the repression, persecution and detention of peasants."[74]

The repression that has taken place under the democratically elected Suazo government suggests that what really matters in Honduras depends not on who holds the elected office of president of the republic but on whether the high command in the Honduran military is open to compromise with peasant and labor groups. An opening for labor appeared in late March 1984 when Alvarez was ousted as commander in chief of the armed forces. Alvarez's policy of crushing the labor leadership seemed to be working until 18 March 1984 when the head of the electrical workers' union was kidnapped.[75] The union went on strike and the Alvarez government jailed 300 strikers. On 22 March the United Federation of Honduran Workers (FUTH) staged a demonstration of 10,000 to 15,000 people in Tegucigalpa and San Pedro Sula. Within a week Alvarez was deposed.[76] On 1 May 1984, labor unions and civil rights groups called a demonstration that attracted 175,000 participants. The armed forces did not fire on the crowd or arrest the leaders. Rather, they met with a delegation of protesters to discuss grievances.[77]

With respect to the Honduran peasantry, the security forces did not appear to alter their behavior after the ouster of Alvarez. In the spring of 1984 peasants increased pressure for land reform by occupying more than fifty private properties. By June 1984 four peasants had been killed and many more wounded in evictions by security forces and death squads hired by landowners. Several hundred peasants were jailed during that same time period.[78]

In summary, the Honduran government has not been viewed by the population as a monolithic enemy. During the first wave of crisis, the upper levels of the military government showed unusual flexibility in responding to peasant pressures for land and worker demands for wage adjustments. During the second wave of crisis, however, the upper levels of the military became dominated by officers with close connections to the most reactionary landowners and businessmen in the country. The powers of the secret police and the reactionary elements within the military were reinforced when the U.S. government began the unprecedented military buildup of Honduras following the ouster of the Somoza regime in Nicaragua in 1979. If the current U.S. policy of promoting export agriculture, pumping up the military, and building strategic roads into disputed terrain continues, Honduran peasants and workers may begin to change their perception of the national government. In that case, we might expect in Honduras in the late 1980s the outcomes that followed the application of similar policies in Nicaragua, El Salvador, and Guatemala in the 1970s. As the leader of the National Union of Peasants (UNC) explained the situation, "They're forcing us to go to the mountains. We're not guerrillas, but if people keep being beaten and jailed, they're leaving us just one alternative."[79]

Government Responses to the Crisis in Costa Rica

In the late 1960s and early 1970s Costa Rica experienced mild inflation of approximately 5 percent a year, but in 1973 world inflationary pressures moved quickly through the Costa Rican economy, pushing consumer prices up 15 percent over the previous year.[80] In 1974 consumer price inflation rates surged to 30 percent, returning to approximately 17 percent in 1975. It was not until 1976 that Costa Rican inflation fell below double-digit levels.[81]

People in Costa Rica responded to the impact of the international shock wave just as people did elsewhere in Central America. Wage earners struck for cost-of-living adjustments, and peasants moved onto idle properties. Landowners called on the security forces to back up their land claims, and businessmen in general sought relief from taxes, high interest rates, and wage increases. The democratically elected government of Costa Rica responded to the first round of shocks in ways similar to those pursued by the military government of Honduras. An attempt was made to mediate the growing conflicts at a national level in ways that would avoid violent confrontations.

It was shown in Chapter Six how the rural guard in Costa Rica responded to peasant land occupations at this time just as local security forces did elsewhere in Central America: they did the bidding of the largest landholders in the area. Land occupations, evictions of peasants, and jailing of peasant leaders increased in rural Costa Rica in 1974 and 1975. Struggles in the traditional cattle-raising areas of the Pacific coastal plain intensified, and landowners there made matters worse by refusing to rent land to peasants for fear of losing it in the national agrarian reform movement.[82]

Particularly intense were the struggles in the developing cattle zone of north central Costa Rica, from the San Carlos River north of Ciudad Quesada to the Nicaraguan border, a region referred to as the Huetar Norte. Especially in 1975, violence erupted in this agricultural frontier zone. Newspaper reports that year pointed to numerous cases where ranchers claimed areas of five thousand acres or more, when they actually had legal title to only fifteen or sixteen hundred acres. When peasants occupied the idle portions of these large claims, the absentee owners would send detachments of the rural guard into the area. Peasants were jailed and their dwellings burned.[83]

During this first wave of crisis, when the local security forces were behaving in a traditional manner toward the peasants, national institutions like the agrarian reform agency (ITCO) and the national courts proved more open to peasant demands. It was in 1974 that a national court found the rancher Morice guilty of murder in the famous land-dispute case described in Chapter Six. On one occasion during this period the president of the republic revoked a local eviction order, observing that the lands in question were "state lands," not the private property of the rancher claiming them.[84] In late 1975 the national government acquired more than 40,000 acres from United Brands and began turning the land over to the peasants who had squatted on it.[85] More land disputes were brought before ITCO in 1974 than the agency had seen in any year for a decade. By March 1975, ITCO, in its fourteen-year history, had resolved in favor of peasant occupants some 118,000 acres of land previously claimed in large private holdings and another 60,000 acres of state lands.[86]

During the first wave of worldwide inflation, the Costa Rican government was more flexible than any of the other four Central American governments in granting wage adjustments and adopting measures to alleviate the rapid deterioration of living standards among the poor and middle-income groups. In April 1974, when inflation was raging at a 30 percent rate through the economy, the National Wages Council decreed an adjustment of legal minimum wages five months before the expiration date of the previously set scale. The adjustment gave greatest relief to the poorest sectors of the work force, with percentage adjustments declining at higher pay scales. The largest adjustment of all went to the nonunionized agricultural workers, who received a 41 percent increase in the daily minimum wage. The decree was far-reaching because unionized labor not covered by minimum wages used these increases in their petitions for wage adjustments. In addition to minimum-wage adjustments, the government granted an across-the-board increase of two hundred colones a month to all public-sector workers, again with the intention of guaranteeing minimum survival income for the lowest-paid workers.[87]

On the price front, the government of Costa Rica attempted to dampen increases in prices of basic foodstuffs, public transport, and electricity through a combination of price ceilings and subsidies. Furthermore, government spending on public health, education, welfare, and other social services aimed at the poor and middle-income groups surged from $55 million in 1973 to $81 million in 1974 to $114 million in 1975.[88]

Many of the government's policies designed to soothe the sting of the world crisis went against the perceived interests of large landowners, foreign investors, and exporters. On top of land reform, wage adjustments, and welfare programs came a tax on exports that increased revenues from $2.1 million in 1973 to $27 million in 1974, and then to $41 million in 1975. At the same time, the government acquired troubled firms that had previously been owned by the private sector. During the period 1973–75 the railroads, ports, and other infrastructure facilities came under the government's control, and even the untroubled petroleum-refining and -retailing business was nationalized in response to public outcries over oil-price gouging.[89]

Large landowners, multinational corporations, and exporters were understandably upset by the direction of national government policy. Like the elites in Honduras, the Costa Rican elites began to retrench in 1976, but it was not until the second wave of crisis that they were able to turn back the welfare thrust of the national government. Reinforcement for the elite position came from two international developments: the worldwide debt crisis and the alarm in international security circles over the Nicaraguan Revolution.

When the second oil-price explosion hit in late 1977 and 1978, the government of Costa Rica once more increased public health and welfare assistance programs. It covered the mounting fiscal deficits and drainage of foreign exchange just as it had between 1973 and 1975: by borrowing on international capital markets. By 1979 the per capita external debt of Costa Rica was one of the highest in all of Latin America. In an attempt to prevent political destabilization, the government maintained a fixed rate of exchange with the dollar, further worsening the drainage of foreign exchange and further enraging exporters. The average number of days' worth of foreign exchange held by the BCCR declined from 82 in 1977 to 58 in 1978 to 30 in 1979. International banks became reluctant to continue extending loans, and the government had to draw heavily on IMF credits. As early as 1978 the IMF recommended devaluation and a sweeping austerity program, but the government at that time refused to adopt the harsh measures.

Beginning in late 1979, however, one foreign exchange crisis after another forced governments to bend to policy demands of the IMF, to the delight of exporters and multinational corporations and to the displeasure of most Costa Ricans. In late 1980 the government could no longer hold up the exchange rate, and the value of the colon slid from about twelve cents (U.S.) to around two cents, where it finally stabilized in late 1982. The slide of the colon unleashed an inflation that surged to a high of 100 percent in 1982. The depreciation of the currency slashed real wages to the point where companies with access to dollars paid less for labor in Costa Rica than they paid anywhere else in Central America or the Caribbean, with the exception of Haiti.[90] The financial crisis was accompanied by attacks on portions of the government budget serving the poor and middle-income sectors. Electricity, water, and other public utility rates were doubled in mid-1982, and sales taxes were increased. All of these measures hit the poor the hardest; crime rates rose, along with reported deaths owing to malnutrition.[91] Each time cuts were made or wage freezes announced, people resisted the measures, sometimes forcing the government to compromise.[92]

In 1983 national government policy was twisted in favor of the international banking community when $655 million of the $4.1 billion external debt was renegotiated.[93] At that time the IMF, the World Bank, and a consortium of 170 international banks were able to push through a comprehensive austerity package, in return for a three-year grace period on payment of principal. Even with the stretching out of the debt, payments to banks have taken half of the country's foreign exchange earnings since 1982. Some of the measures in the austerity package include an end to price subsidies for basic foods, higher taxes, sales of government-owned enterprises to the private sector, further budget cuts, and further increases in rates charged by public utilities.[94]

Parallel to the buildup of economic attacks on wage workers and peasants was a buildup of political attacks on those groups. In August 1979, only a month after Somoza was ousted from power in neighboring Nicaragua, 7,000 banana workers struck on the Atlantic coast. The civil guard was sent in to break up the strike, and 1 person was killed and 80 were injured in clashes between strikers and police. After the violence, the national government collaborated with the fruit companies in attacking the strike organizers and weakening the union.[95] In 1980, 142 workers were arrested in a strike on the Atlantic coast, and later that year the civil guard killed a banana worker in a strike on the Pacific coast.[96] Once again in 1982 the civil guard intervened in a strike on the banana plantations, injuring 6 with gunshot wounds and arresting 20 of the strikers.[97] In 1983 President Luís Alberto Monge responded to a wave of public employee strikes by ordering the civil guard to occupy a petroleum facility to break a strike, and he threatened to do the same thing in other public employee strikes.[98]

Throughout the period from late 1979 until the present (1985), land occupations were met with the traditional response of evictions by the rural guard and the civil guard, but no longer did peasants have strong allies in the national government. In 1976 large landowners began an attack on the budget authority of ITCO, the agency in charge of settling land disputes. With the austerity measures of the early 1980s, the large landowners were successful in emasculating ITCO. In 1984 one peasant was killed and a number of others were wounded when the rural guard evicted them from a 25,000-acre corporate farm, which was reported to have only 625 acres under cultivation.[99]

The position of cattle ranchers and other large landholders has been strengthened in the countryside by international pressures to build up the Costa Rican security forces. In 1981 U.S. Ambassador to the United Nations Jeane Kirkpatrick was reported to have told Costa Rican officials that they should not expect to receive any U.S. assistance until they agreed to build an army.[100] In 1981–82 the National Police Institute and the Police College began to incorporate U.S., Panamanian, and Venezuelan advisers. At that time, military aid of $2 million a year began flowing from the United States. Additional aid came from Argentina, Taiwan, South Korea, Israel, Panama, Japan, and Spain.[101] Not only was training increased for the rural guard (3,000 men), the civil guard (5,000 men), the judicial police (OIJ—647 men), and other already established security forces, but international security agencies collaborated with the Costa Rican security forces to create a wholly new paramilitary force called OPEN (Organization for National Emergencies), begun in 1982.

The ranchers' forces have been especially strengthened in the volatile north central region. Civil guards in that region are equipped with Galil rifles and Uzi submachine guns, and a mobile guard command called the Chorotega Company has been stationed along the Nicaraguan border. A new paramilitary force with the same name as the region, the Huetar Norte Democratic Movement, has begun operations out of Ciudad Quesada on the region's southern flank. The Huetar Norte Democratic Movement is said to have around three hundred men. It is not a legal organization, but it is said to receive assistance from OPEN.[102] In addition to the rural guard, the civil guard, and the new paramilitary organization, ranchers in this area are reported to have members of the anti-Sandinista contra forces on their payrolls.[103]

The commercial development of the frontier area of northern Costa Rica, like that of northern Guatemala, will be given a boost if the oil pipeline is built. The project will bring in support infrastructure, and it will justify an even larger permanent security force presence in that area to protect the pipeline. The north central zone is also the site of a multimillion-dollar land-development project to be carried out with the aid of the governments of Israel and the United States. In August 1983 AID committed itself to a $14.2 million loan for the project.[104] The commercial value of lands in north central Costa

Rica, like those in the frontier areas of eastern Honduras, will be raised if the two strategic roads from Ciudad Quesada to the Nicaraguan border are completed.[105]

Resistance, however, has grown along with the repression. In late 1980, about the same time as the first devaluation of the colon, the United Workers' Confederation (CUT) formed. Its seventy thousand members have joined with others to fight against reductions of food subsidies, wage cuts, utility rate increases, and other austerity measures. In 1983 a national protest against hikes in electricity rates, which had risen 300 percent in two years, forced the electric company to lower the rates. In 1984 a march against foreign intervention in Central America and against the militarization of Costa Rica attracted twenty thousand protesters.

In summary, the future of democratic Costa Rica is open to question. Forces of resistance have grown, while security forces able to act above the law have been created. In 1984 the U.S. National Security Council was reported to be pushing for a quadrupling of U.S. security assistance to Costa Rica.[106] Austerity measures from the debt crisis have reduced the government's room to move in its attempts to soften the impact of the economic crisis on the poor, while multinational corporations and large exporters are being subsidized by favorable exchange rates and other incentives to boost exports and attract foreign exchange. Large landowners, foreign investors, and others on the right have attacked reformist members of the Costa Rican government, while grassroots organizations have grown distrustful of relying on the government for assistance. In short, the mediating structures that have prevented economic shocks from breaking out in violence have been systematically undermined, and official U.S. policy toward Costa Rica has furthered this process.

Summary

When the world economic crisis hit Central America in the 1970s, the five countries were exposed in the same ways. More than a decade of export-led growth had left large numbers of people landless and dependent on money wages for survival, and elites had become more dependent on the world economy for agricultural inputs and bank credit. When the crisis hit, peasants and wage workers felt similar stress throughout the five-country region, and they responded to the stress in similar ways irrespective of the country where they lived. Similarly, elites throughout the region felt threatened by the same pressures, and they responded in similar ways in all five countries. What differed from one country to the next was the way the government mediated the growing pressures between the two camps.

In Nicaragua, El Salvador, and Guatemala, national governments attempted to contain the pressures from below by terrorizing the poor. Demonstrations for higher wages were fired upon, land occupations were brutally crushed, and leaders of grassroots organizations were made to disappear. In contrast, during the first wave of crisis the governments of Honduras and Costa Rica did not side with the elites in a single-minded way, but made some concessions to the poor in land and wage disputes. By the time of the second wave of worldwide inflation, civil war had broken out in Nicaragua, El Salvador, and Guatemala, and the rich had begun to retrench in Honduras and Costa Rica.

After the overthrow of the Somoza regime in Nicaragua in 1979, the U.S. government escalated its military presence throughout the region. The increasing power of U.S. and other international security forces in shaping policy in the region has coincided with a dramatic increase in the death toll in El Salvador and Guatemala and a decline in the flexibility of the governments of Honduras and Costa Rica in responding to pressures from grassroots groups.

9. Challenge for a New U.S. Policy

In the era of Camelot, when U.S. budget deficits were small and the trade balance was in surplus, an ambitious program like the Alliance for Progress was not a huge sacrifice for the promise of stability. In an era of $200 billion federal deficits and $120 billion trade deficits, another ambitious program promising stability in Central America will have to be looked at more closely.

The Kissinger Commission Report—which has become a guide for U.S. policy—estimates that the bill for the federal government will come to $10–$12 billion from 1984 to 1990, with another $6 billion kicked in by the World Bank and other multilateral lending institutions. The actual level of spending will undoubtedly be higher. Even by the report's own admission, the cost estimates were based on the assumption that capital flight would be halted by the end of 1984, an assumption that was not met. Furthermore, the program being pursued has a large military component, which is likely to produce considerable cost overruns.

Far more serious, however, is the question of whether the policy being adopted will actually promote stability in Central America.

The perspective that guided the Kissinger Commission—and the perspective that seems to be guiding Democrats and Republicans in the Congress—is that the same mix of policies that helped produce rapid economic growth in the 1960s will create the conditions for long-run stability in the region in the 1980s and 1990s. This book shows that the most successful policies promoting economic growth in the 1960s had the long-run result of destabilizing the region. Will the results of the current policy be any different?

In the short run, more money for military aid, social reforms, investment incentives, and export promotion will serve to shore up existing regimes in Central America. At a cost of billions of dollars and thousands of lives, the program will prolong the rule of the current governments of Guatemala and El Salvador. In Honduras and Costa Rica, the program will temporarily support individuals in the military and other sections of the government who will enthusiastically embrace U.S. policy.

In the long run, results similar to those of the Alliance for Progress can be expected. More generous sugar and beef quotas, promotional efforts for new exports, and incentives for foreign investors, all recommendations of the Kissinger Commission, should generate more foreign exchange and faster economic growth; they will also intensify struggles over land. More military aid and counterinsurgency training will make evictions more effective; they will also kill civilians and create lasting hostilities. The combined effect of the military and economic programs could even produce guerrilla movements where they do not currently exist. The analysis of this book would pinpoint frontier areas like those of north central Costa Rica and eastern Honduras, where peasant settlers are coming in conflict with cattle ranchers and security forces, as places where future peasant armies might form.

On the other hand, government-controlled social reforms are less likely to absorb revolutionary pressures than similar measures that were applied in the 1960s. Grassroots organizations are far more sophisticated today than they were then, and they are less likely to be tricked by centrally controlled "reforms." Furthermore, with the most reactionary elements in the security forces being promoted by U.S. military aid and the war against "Communist subversion," the chances are slim that the poor will have any say in how social reforms are administered. If the poor were to push effectively for change through social reform agencies, the pattern that occurred in the 1970s would be repeated: large landowners and businessmen would become threatened and they would call on their traditional allies in the security forces to reverse the gains of the poor.

In summary, even if the wars in Central America were ended today, the long-run development program would produce the conditions for a resurgence of the conflict within ten or fifteen years.

To build a policy for peace in the region, an approach fundamentally different from the policies of the past will have to be taken.

Instead of attempting to crush and manipulate the grassroots movement in Central America, the U. S. government should be trying to establish a positive relationship with that movement. Viewing the popular movement as a threat to the security of the United States will continue to place the U.S. government on the side of an anachronistic oligarchy and at odds with the majority of Central Americans. Instead, the grassroots movement should be perceived as a potential ally of the United States and a creative force for a long-awaited change.

The first constructive step would be to stop funding and training the security forces that have been responsible for the attacks on grassroots organizations in the past. This step would mean reining in U.S. security elements that have been responsible for training the apparatus of official terror in the region. It would also mean withdrawing U.S. troops and advisers from Honduras and El Salvador, a proposal along the lines of the Contadora peace initiative, which calls for the parallel withdrawal from the region of Soviet, Cuban, and other foreign military personnel.

The second constructive step would be to reconsider trade and technology transfer policies toward the region. Trade with the United States and transfer of technologies developed in the United States could play a positive role in bringing about peaceful economic development in Central America, but instead of basing that policy on the desires of Central American elites and U.S. investors, the U.S. government should consult with grassroots organizations over the likely impact of the policies. If the Kissinger Commission had followed this guideline in a serious manner, it would not have made its embarrassing recommendation to expand beef quotas further. Probably the commission would also have found that sugar quotas, without adequate protections for small farmers and wage workers, might actually worsen the conditions of the majority in the areas affected, instead of improving their lot.

Consultation with grassroots organizations would restrict the freedom of movement of multinational corporations, and it would lessen the opportunities that elites have traditionally enjoyed when trade has expanded. For these groups, lower short-run profits and a reduction of control would result, but the costs to U.S. taxpayers of preserving the customary privileges of the few far exceed the total profits that could ever be extracted from the region.

A third constructive step would be to review the purpose of reforms and the way they are implemented. If reforms are designed to absorb grassroots pressures and to control those movements, they will be doomed to failure. In contrast, if grassroots organizations are allowed to participate in the design and implementation of reforms, the programs are more likely to enlist the efforts of those being affected, thereby raising the effectiveness of the programs and lowering their costs.

These three steps would require changes in the personnel hired by the U.S. government to carry out its Central America policy. The people to be recruited for the job would be those who have had experience working with the poor majority in Central America. Fortunately, there is a pool of talented North Americans capable of rising to the challenge. Some have come to understand Central America through their work in Catholic and Protestant missions in poor communities in Central America. Others have learned about Central American reality from experience in the Peace Corps, U.S.-sponsored health programs, and other U.S. government projects in poor communities. Still others have had their eyes opened to the reality of the poor majority in Central America through field research in the biological and social sciences.

Many of these potential ambassadors of peace to Central America have a deeper knowledge of the region than those currently controlling U.S. policy there, and they have been appalled by the recent direction of that policy. If a genuine effort were made to shift U.S. policy, the skills of this group could be enlisted on an official basis, and there would be no chance of Central America's slipping into the Soviet orbit.

Unfortunately, if elected officials are left alone they will come under the influence of the vested interest groups who have held Central American oligarchs in power for so long. To forge a policy that will bring peace to the region and a positive connection with the United States will require a massive effort by people in the United States. Citizens concerned about Central America will have to redouble their efforts to stay informed and to inform others of the situation as it develops. The movement that has already begun in churches, universities, and neighborhoods of North America will have to grow. Direct contacts with grassroots groups in Central America will have to be strengthened. Better coordination between Central America supporters and others working on related issues of peace and justice will have to be established. A constant vigilance over elected officials and nonelected appointees will have to be kept, and pressures will have to be applied at the national, state, and local levels.

These goals may appear unattainable under an administration that views the crisis as a result of Cuban, Soviet, and now Nicaraguan aggression. The alternative to working for a shift in policy, however, is a prolonged, costly, unwinnable war that could produce divisions within the social fabric of the United States similar to those created by the conflict in Vietnam.

Statistical Appendix

Table A-1

Cotton Production by Country, 1941–1979 (thousands of bales)

	Guatemala	El Salvador	Honduras	Nicaragua	Costa Rica	Total
1941	3	14	1	5	0	23
1942	4	4	2	8	0	18
1943	4	14	3	4	0	25
1944	2	19	2	3	0	26
1945	4	15	1	3	0	23
1946	3	11	1	4	0	19
1947	5	20	2	1	0	28
1948	5	22	3	0	0	31
1949	6	22	3	5	0	36
1950	5	30	1	21	0	57
1951	4	27	2	23	0	56
1952	11	42	2	47	1	103
1953	16	47	2	57	1	123
1954	27	57	2	105	1	192
1955	40	90	3	205	1	339
1956	44	133	4	160	1	342
1957	46	137	7	193	4	387
1958	64	165	18	219	5	471
1959	75	182	16	215	6	494
1960	68	137	7	128	5	345
1961	95	184	6	146	5	436
1962	145	259	17	255	5	681
1963	250	320	21	325	6	922
1964	300	340	—	410	—	—
1965	312	375	—	565	—	—
1966	412	235	—	505	—	—
1967	290	176	—	525	—	—
1968	350	159	—	445	—	—
1969	335	205	—	405	—	—
1970	296	212	15	314	6	842
1971	261	253	9	361	1	886
1972	373	316	11	471	1	1,172
1973	442	315	20	487	0	1,264
1974	556	345	24	670	2	1,597
1975	489	353	24	564	3	1,433
1976	455	277	14	506	1	1,254
1977	623	324	33	540	8	1,528
1978	658	369	53	565	32	1,676
1979	745	332	35	516	13	1,641

Sources: For 1941–63, Stevenson, *Cotton Production*, pp. 44, 46, 48, 50, 52. For 1963–69, Harness and Pugh, *Cotton*, p. 3. For 1970–79, SIECA, *Situación actual de algodón*, Table 6.

Table A-2
Value of Cotton Exports by Country, 1951–1978 (U.S. $ millions)

	Guatemala	El Salvador	Honduras	Nicaragua	Costa Rica	Total
1951	0	6	—	7	—	13
1952	0	2	—	3	—	4
1953	0	7	—	10	—	17
1954	2	7	—	16	—	25
1955	5	5	—	16	—	26
1956	5	20	1	34	0	60
1957	4	13	1	20	0	38
1958	6	16	2	19	0	43
1959	7	26	2	35	1	70
1960	6	16	0	15	0	38
1961	10	20	0	19	0	50
1962	15	31	2	32	0	80
1963	25	35	2	40	0	103
1964	35	37	4	46	0	122
1965	32	36	6	71	1	146
1966	42	22	6	58	2	130
1967	29	15	5	57	1	107
1968	37	13	4	60	2	115
1969	36	17	3	46	2	104
1970	25	22	1	34	0	83
1971	26	27	0	42	0	95
1972	47	37	1	64	0	150
1973	55	34	2	65	0	156
1974	95	39	3	117	0	254
1975	77	62	4	105	0	249
1976	100	56	4	121	0	282
1977	162	66	7	152	2	389
1978	145	88	16	146	10	405

Sources: For prices: 1951–73, CONAL, *Estadísticas del algodón*, Table 1 (Nicaraguan Export Prices); 1974–78; SIECA, *Situación actual de algodón*, Table 7 (Average Central America); For exports: 1951–59, Stevenson, *Cotton Production*, pp. 44, 46, 48, 50, 52; 1960–70, SIECA, *El desarrollo integrado*, Vol. 8, Tables 13–17; 1971–78, SIECA, *VII Compéndio estadístico*, Tables 125–29.

Notes: Bales weigh 480 pounds. Prices are by calendar year; exports are by crop year ending 31 July (crop year 1950–51 = calendar year 1951).

Table A-3
Value of Cotton Consumption by Country, 1951–1978 (U.S. $ millions)

	Guatemala	El Salvador	Honduras	Nicaragua	Costa Rica	Total
1951	3	3	—	1	—	—
1952	2	2	—	0	—	—
1953	2	2	—	1	—	—
1954	2	2	—	1	—	—
1955	2	2	—	1	—	—
1956	2	2	0	0	0	5
1957	2	2	0	1	0	4
1958	2	2	0	1	0	5
1959	1	2	0	1	0	4
1960	2	3	0	1	0	6
1961	2	3	0	1	0	7
1962	3	3	0	1	0	8
1963	4	4	0	1	0	9
1964	4	4	—	1	—	—
1965	3	5	—	1	—	—
1966	3	6	—	1	—	—
1967	3	6	—	2	—	—
1968	4	7	—	2	—	—
1969	4	5	—	3	—	—
1970	7	2	1	0	1	12
1971	5	3	1	1	0	10
1972	5	7	1	1	1	13
1973	7	13	2	4	1	27
1974	12	27	3	12	1	57
1975	7	−1	0	−7	0	−2
1976	6	10	2	3	2	22
1977	16	27	4	2	3	51
1978	12	18	1	18	4	53

Sources: For consumption: 1951–63, Stevenson, *Cotton Production*, pp. 44, 46, 48, 50, 52; 1964–69, Harness and Pugh, *Cotton*, pp. 8, 16, 25; 1970–78, SIECA, *Situación actual de algodón*, Table 6. For prices: 1951–73, CONAL, *Estadísticas del algodón*, Table 1 (Nicaraguan prices used for 1951–73 calculations; 1974–78, SIECA, *Situación actual de algodón*, Table 7. *Notes*: Bales weigh 480 pounds. Domestic prices were calculated from export prices, minus an estimate of loading fees (1951–60, $2.06 per bale; 1961–73, $2.59 per bale; 1974–78, $3.25 per bale). Prices are by calendar year; consumption is by crop year ending 31 July (crop year 1950– 51 = calendar year 1951).

Table A-4
Number of Cotton Farms and Average Plot Size (acres)

	Guatemala	El Salvador	Honduras	Nicaragua	Costa Rica	Total
Late 1950s						
Number	101	654	57	2,015	27	2,854
Ave. size	434	150	285	70	218	107
Mid-1960s						
Number	367	3,223	417	4,780	56	8,843
Ave. Size	690	75	85	73	140	101
Late 1970s						
Number	286	3,275	548	5,928	52	10,089
Ave. size	1,086	75	80	88	139	112

Sources: For the late 1950s: Nicaragua (1960–61), CONAL, *Estadísticas del algodón*; Table II-11; all others (1957–58), Parsons and DeTuddo, *Informe*, Table 4. For the mid-1960s: Guatemala (1965–66), Adams, *Crucifixion by Power*, Table 7-3; El Salvador (1965–66), DGECS, *El Salvador en gráficos*, San Salvador: DGECS, 1967, Table 35; Honduras (1965–66), DGECH, *Censo agropecuario, 1965–66*, p. 115; Nicaragua (1965–66), CONAL, *Estadísticas del algodón*, Table II-11; Costa Rica (1963), *Censo agropecuario, 1963*, Table 49. For the late 1970s: Costa Rica (1977–78), SEPSA, *Información básica*, pp. 3, 4; all others (Guatemala, 1978–79; El Salvador, 1977–78; Honduras, 1977–78; Nicaragua, 1977–78), SIECA, *Situación actual de algodón*, Table 4.

Table A-5
Companies Supplying Cotton Inputs

GUATEMALA
Monsanto Chemical Company (Saint Louis)
Monsanto Centroamérica (Guatemala), S.A.: est. 1965; 100% owned; mixes
insecticides

EL SALVADOR
Monsanto Chemical Company (Saint Louis)
Monsanto Centroamérica (El Salvador), S.A.: mixes insecticides
International Harvester (Chicago)
International Harvester Centroamérica, S.A. (IHCSA): est. 1965; minority
owned; assembles trucks and tractors

NICARAGUA
Monsanto Chemical Company (Saint Louis)
Monsanto Agrícola de Nicaragua, S.A.: joint venture; mixes insecticides
ADELA Investment Company (Luxembourg)
Industrias Químicas, S.A. (INQUISA): joint venture with INFONAC and
private Nicaraguans; owns 40% Hercules de Centroamérica, Eletroquímica
Pennsalt
Hercules Powder Company (Wilmington, Del.)
Hercules de Centroamérica, S.A.: est. 1967; 60% owned; produces toxaphene;
purchases chlorine from Pennwalt, turpentine from ATCHEMCO; another joint
venture among ADELA, INFONAC, local investors, and foreign companies
Atlas Chemical Industries (Wilmington, Del.)
Industrias Químicas Atlas de Centroamérica, S.A. (ATCHEMCO): 75% owned;
produces insecticides
International Ore and Fertilizer Company (subsidiary Occidental Petroleum)
(Los Angeles)
Abonos Superiores, S.A.: majority-owned joint venture; fertilizers
Olin Corporation (New York)
Fertilizantes de Nicaragua, S.A.: insecticides and fertilizers
Stauffer Chemical Company (Westport, Conn.)
Insecticidas Stauffer, S.A.: 38% owned; mixes insecticides
TENNECO (Atlanta)
Fertilizante Superior, S.A.: est. 1964; majority-owned joint venture; fertilizers
and insecticides
Van Leer (Holland)
Est. 1965; makes steel drums for packaging insecticides
CPC International
Cia. Fertilizantes Superior: 59% owned; fertilizers

Sources: Burbach and Flynn, *Agribusiness*, pp. 253–81; *NACLA Report on the Americas* 10, no.
2 (Feb. 1976): 36–38; Castillo, *Acumulación de capital*, pp. 236–68; Jonas and Tobis, *Guate-mala*, pp. 170–74.

Table A-6
The Cotton Elite of El Salvador

Family name	Bales of cotton (1972–73)	Cotton-related investments
Wright	17,327	Insecticidas de El Salvador, S.A. (INDESSA) Textilera del Pacífico Productos Agroquímicas de C.A.,S.A. RAIT, S.A.
García Prieto/ Salaverría	10,197	Textiles Tazumal Textiles del Pacífico
Dueñas	9,507	
Kriete	7,667	
Cristiani	6,057	Industrias Químicas, S.A. (IQSA) Semillas, S.A.
Hill/ Llach Hill	5,903	Textiles Tazumal Textiles del Pacífico
Guirola	5,137	Industrias Químicas, S.A. (IQSA)
Dalton	2,683	
Duke	2,607	
Homberger	2,223	Fertilizer-import business
Llach Schonenberg	2,070	
Borgonovo	1,687	Semillas, S.A.
Daglio	1,380	Industrias Químicas, S.A. (IQSA)
Nottebohm	1,380	
Avila-Meardi/ Meardi-Palomo	1,380	
Lopez-Harrison	1,073	

Source: Colindres, *Fundamentos*, Table 67.
Notes: Quintales of raw cotton were converted to bales by using the lint yield of .368 and bale weight of 480 pounds. Colindres's table does not specify raw cotton, but if the calculations were made on the assumption of cleaned cotton, these few families would have been responsible for two-thirds of the crop that year, and the Wright family would have been cultivating 28,000 acres of cotton, nearly three times the land area they own. Also, it is common practice in Salvadoran cotton statistics to measure in units of unginned cotton. These families produced a total of 78,278 bales of cotton in 1972–73, 33% of exports.

Table A-7
Number of Jobs Harvesting Cotton by Country, 1950–1981 (thousands)

	Guatemala	El Salvador	Honduras	Nicaragua	Costa Rica	Total
1950	1	8	0	6	0	15
1951	1	7	1	6	0	15
1952	3	11	1	13	0	27
1953	4	12	1	15	0	32
1954	7	15	1	28	0	51
1955	11	23	1	55	0	90
1956	12	34	1	43	0	90
1957	12	35	2	52	1	102
1958	17	42	5	59	2	125
1959	20	46	4	58	2	131
1960	18	35	2	35	2	91
1961	25	47	2	40	2	115
1962	38	66	5	69	2	179
1963	66	82	6	88	2	243
1964	79	87	—	111	—	—
1965	82	96	—	153	—	—
1966	136	61	13	137	5	352
1967	81	45	13	143	4	286
1968	89	41	12	127	4	273
1969	87	52	10	115	3	268
1970	78	54	4	85	2	222
1971	69	68	2	101	0	240
1972	98	79	3	125	0	305
1973	116	80	5	133	0	334
1974	145	94	6	183	0	428
1975	129	91	6	154	0	380
1976	119	70	4	141	0	333
1977	166	77	8	158	1	409
1978	184	91	13	177	3	468
1979	—	85	9	157	1	—
1980	—	78	10	26	—	—
1981	—	56	—	91	—	—

Sources and notes: Production figures for 1950–63, Stevenson, *Cotton Production*, pp. 44, 46, 48, 50, 52; for 1964–65, Harness and Pugh, *Cotton*, p. 3; for 1966–81, SIECA, *VII Compéndio estadístico*, Table 80. Numbers of jobs were calculated from actual harvest figures by assuming that (1) an adult male picks 75 pounds of lint a day, (2) the job is for 70 workdays, and (3) 100 percent of the crop is picked by hand. The crop year ends in the stated calendar year (e.g., 1966 = 1965–66). Production data for 1950–65 are converted from ginned bales into unginned lint using the 1970 ginning yields implicit in SIECA, *Situación actual de algodón*, Table 6.

Table A-8
U.S. Beef and Veal Imports by Country of Origin, 1957–1980 (thousands of pounds)

	Guatemala	El Salvador	Honduras	Nicaragua	Costa Rica	Total
1957	0	0	0	0	805	805
1958	0	0	409	40	2,806	3,255
1959	0	0	1,509	5,768	9,840	17,117
1960	0	0	3,391	10,127	15,335	28,853
1961	1,927	0	5,525	14,577	8,719	30,748
1962	12,268	0	9,324	15,795	8,111	45,498
1963	14,773	0	9,336	24,518	15,163	63,790
1964	11,832	0	8,572	23,566	17,662	61,632
1965	9,556	0	10,715	18,400	10,310	48,981
1966	12,903	0	13,788	24,248	12,329	63,268
1967	19,352	0	13,297	28,178	25,689	86,516
1968	22,198	0	14,614	38,025	34,163	109,000
1969	24,775	0	24,832	42,967	36,603	129,177
1970	27,574	0	26,598	49,963	41,592	145,727
1971	37,434	0	32,805	53,874	40,513	164,626
1972	38,103	7,626	37,687	60,880	50,265	194,561
1973	41,069	9,736	44,099	57,516	49,361	201,781
1974	31,360	13,275	30,105	34,120	62,063	170,923
1975	35,221	5,624	36,375	49,504	63,221	189,945
1976	35,180	11,178	46,528	54,352	69,040	216,278
1977	35,092	3,921	40,616	51,826	47,376	178,831
1978	30,587	8,723	44,637	72,299	64,585	220,831
1979	35,349	11,109	67,816	76,757	73,137	264,168
1980	19,825	5,369	57,171	46,694	47,478	176,537

Sources: For 1957–64, Gerrity, *Beef Export Trade*, p. 1. For 1965–67, Morgan, *Beef Cattle Industries*, p. 24. For 1967–80, U.S. Bureau of the Census, *U.S. General Imports*, Table 3. Washington: U.S. Government Printing Office, 1981.

Table A-9
Number of USDA-Approved Packing Plants by Country, 1956–1978

	Guatemala	El Salvador	Honduras	Nicaragua	Costa Rica	Total
1956	0	0	0	0	0	0
1957	0	0	0	1	0	1
1958	0	0	1	1	1	3
1959	0	0	1	1	1	3
1960	0	0	1	1	1	3
1961	1	0	2	1	—	—
1962	2	0	3	3	—	—
1963	2	0	3	3	—	—
1964	2	0	3	3	—	—
1965	2	0	4	3	3	12
1966	—	0	4	3	—	—
1967	—	0	5	3	—	—
1968	—	0	5	3	4	—
1969	—	0	5	3	—	—
1970	—	0	6	3	—	—
1971	—	0	7	4	—	—
1972	—	1	7	4	6	—
1973	3	2	7	4	6	22
1974	5	2	7	4	7	25
1975	—	2	7	4	—	—
1976	5	2	7	4	8	26
1977	6	2	7	5	8	28
1978	6	2	7	7	6	28

Sources: For Guatemala: Gerrity, *Beef Export Trade*, p. 8; Morgan, *Beef Cattle Industries*, p. 2. For El Salvador: Morgan, *Beef Cattle Industries*, p. 11. For Honduras: Slutzky, "La agroindustria de la carne," p. 147. For Nicaragua: de Lanuza, "La agroindustria de la carne," p. II-16. For Costa Rica: León, Barboza, and Aguilar, *Ganadería*, p. 6-11; Morgan, *Beef Cattle Industries*, p. 15.

Table A-10
Beef Exports by Country, 1960–1980 (U.S. $ thousands)

	Guatemala	El Salvador	Honduras	Nicaragua	Costa Rica	Total
1960	169	0	1,051	2,968	4,281	8,469
1961	736	0	1,518	4,043	2,781	9,078
1962	3,773	0	2,591	5,993	2,753	15,110
1963	4,363	0	2,892	8,429	5,028	20,712
1964	3,631	0	2,470	7,430	6,020	19,551
1965	4,600	100	3,200	5,800	3,300	17,000
1966	5,300	100	3,900	10,200	5,500	25,000
1967	8,000	100	4,300	12,500	8,800	33,700
1968	8,600	100	5,000	15,900	12,000	41,600
1969	12,000	0	9,000	21,000	15,200	57,200
1970	12,700	0	9,700	26,900	18,000	67,300
1971	17,400	100	12,500	28,900	20,600	79,500
1972	18,000	5,100	16,000	38,700	28,300	106,100
1973	25,100	5,000	21,900	44,700	31,600	128,300
1974	21,500	1,400	16,800	22,100	34,200	96,000
1975	17,000	2,500	18,400	27,900	32,100	97,900
1976	14,400	9,100	25,700	40,000	40,600	129,800
1977	27,900	4,000	21,700	38,600	44,100	136,300
1978	31,200	12,900	38,900	70,100	60,400	213,500
1979	41,600	14,000	61,100	95,100	81,700	293,500
1980	28,500	5,800	60,900	58,700	70,800	224,700

Sources: For 1960–64: SIECA, *El desarrollo integrado*, Vol. 8, Tables 6–12 (extraregional exports only). 1965–80: SIECA, *VII Compéndio estadístico*, Tables 124–29 (both intra- and extraregional exports; hence this source gives higher figures than the previous one).

Table A-11

Prices of Key Commodities Affecting Agricultural Elites (1972 = 100)

	Oil	Pesticide	Fertilizer	Coffee	Cotton	Beef
1970	88	68	106	100	79	79
1971	107	90	92	88	94	85
1972	100	100	100	100	100	100
1973	141	126	137	124	172	121
1974	371	136	359	161	181	111
1975	399	170	563	186	147	108
1976	419	168	257	364	215	133
1977	508	217	250	588	197	137
1978	476	217	260	398	200	173
1979	627	185	425	435	282	257
1980	1,053	222	367	386	372	269

Sources: SIECA, *VII Compéndio Estadístico*, Tables 164, 167 (input prices); IMF, *International Financial Statistics Yearbook*, 1979, 1981, Washington: IMF, 1980, 1982. (export prices).

Notes

Introduction

1. Throughout the book "Central America" refers to the five countries Guatemala, El Salvador, Honduras, Nicaragua, and Costa Rica. Panama is omitted because of its closer historical ties with Colombia and because of the Canal Zone orientation of its economy. Belize is omitted because of its cultural and political orientation as a British colony until 1981.

2. Immerman, *The CIA in Guatemala*, pp. 133–86.

3. Jonas and Tobis, *Guatemala*, p. 76. Adams, *Crucifixion by Power*, pp. 203–4. Williams, "The Central American Common Market," p. 207.

4. The costs of the Guatemala experiment were much higher than those of earlier spending programs in the region, but the outlays were justified on the grounds that they would prevent the resurgence of communism in that country. Between 1955 and 1958 Guatemala received 40 percent of all U.S. grants, aid, and loans to Central America. McCamant, *Development Assistance in Central America*, Tables 3–7.

5. SIECA, *El desarrollo integrado*, Table 5.1.

6. Black, *Triumph of the People*, pp. 58–62. Walker, *Nicaragua in Revolution*, pp. 28–29, 166–68, 185–86, 274–79.

7. Davis and Hodson, *Witnesses to Political Violence in Guatemala*, Appendix 3, pp. 47–52.

8. Kissinger et al., *Report of the National Bipartisan Commission on Central America*, pp. 52–53, 63–67.

9. Ibid., p. 41.

10. SIECA, *El desarrollo integrado*, Table 5.5.

Chapter One

1. In an earlier analysis I found that textile manufacturing was the industrial subsector most stimulated by the Central American Common Market. Out of twenty-two industrial subsectors, textile manufacturing accounted for one-fifth of the total trade expansion in manufactures owing to the Common Market, and the Guatemalan and Salvadoran mills captured 82 percent of this expanded trade. Williams, "The Central American Common Market," p. 145.

2. Here and throughout, unless otherwise indicated, money values are in U.S. dollars.

3. DGECG, *Censo agropecuario, 1964*, p. 167. Picudo literally means "pointed beak"; they were referring to some form of boll weevil.

4. Insect-control costs were estimated at 45 percent of total costs in Nicaragua in the early 1960s. Stevenson, *Cotton Production*, p. 8. For the crop year 1979–80, insecticides represented 37 percent of production costs in Guatemala, 33 percent in Honduras and Nicaragua, and 18 percent in Costa Rica. SIECA, *Situación actual de algodón*, Table 9.

5. It is impossible to use mechanical harvesters on such stands of cotton, and plants had to be bent over to enable the short Central American laborers to reach the bolls higher up. Stevenson, *Cotton Production*, p. 26.

6. Stevenson, *Cotton Production*. Harness and Pugh, *Cotton*. In Nicaragua in 1968, 59 percent of the chemical fertilizer used in the entire country was consumed by the three largest cotton-producing departments, even though those three departments had only 36 percent of the land area in cropland. Ministerio de Economia, Industria, y Comercio, *Estadísticas del desarrollo*, Table VI-I.

7. Usulután, La Paz, and San Miguel together accounted for 80 percent of the cotton harvested in El Salvador that year. DGECS, *Censo agropecuario, 1971*, Vol. 1, Table 63.

8. Ministerio de Economía, Industria, y Comercio, *Estadísticas del desarrollo*, Table VI-I.

9. Averages for the years 1969–73 are from Economics Research Service, "Statistics on Cotton," p. 112.

10. DGECS, *Censo agropecuario, 1950*, Table 10. While railroads served some portions of the coastal plain, the roads elsewhere consisted of footpaths, oxcart trails, and some stretches of beach that could be driven on at low tide. Hirsch, "Littoral Highway," in Wilson et al., *The Impact of Highway Investment*, p.90. Satterthwaite, "Campesino Agriculture," p. 7.

11. T.S.C. Consortium, *Central American Transportation Study, 1964–65* (Washington: T.S.C. Consortium, 1965), Table A III-C 4.

12. DGECN, *Censos nacionales, 1963: Agropecuario*, Table 48. Hereafter cited as *Censo agropecuario, 1963*.

13. Wilson et al., *The Impact of Highway Investment*, p. 187.

14. Ibid., pp. 143–45.

15. Adams, *Crucifixion by Power*, p. 362.

16. Estimates of the 1962–63 crop year are in Stevenson, *Cotton Production*, pp. 7, 17, 30.

17. Harness and Pugh, *Cotton*, pp. 6, 13, 23.

18. SIECA, *Situación actual de algodón*, Table 9.

19. Stevenson, *Cotton Production*, p. 29. Harness and Pugh, *Cotton*, p. 23.

20. In Guatemala cotton provided 12 percent of export earnings during the period 1969–78 but absorbed 37 percent of agricultural credit. In El Salvador cotton provided 9 percent of the foreign exchange but absorbed 28 percent of agricultural credit. In

Nicaragua cotton provided 25 percent of the country's export earnings but absorbed 65 percent of agricultural credit. SIECA, *Situación actual de algodón*, Table 10. SIECA, *VII Compéndio estadístico*, Tables 125, 126, 128.

21. For details of the coup see Immerman, *The CIA in Guatemala*.

22. Adams, *Crucifixion by Power*, p. 358.

23. Ibid., pp. 361, 374.

24. Harness and Pugh, *Cotton*, p. 13.

25. CONAL, *Estadísticas del algodón*, Table X-65.

26. Stevenson, *Cotton Production*, p. 39.

27. Reynaldo Santos y Victor Alonso, "Informe sobre el crédito agrícola en Honduras," in AID, *Compilación de los estudios básicos del diagnóstico del sector agrícola* (Tegucigalpa: AID, 1978), Annex Table 5.

28. Stevenson, *Cotton Production*, pp. 41, 42.

29. This proportion rose to 5 percent in 1977 and 1978. SIECA, *Situación actual de algodón*, p. 18.

Chapter Two

1. SIECA, *Situacíon actual de algodón*, Tables 11–14.

2. DGECN, *Censo agropecuario, 1963*, Table 31.

3. DGECH, *Censo agropecuario, 1965–66*, p. 115.

4. DGECS, *Censo agropecuario, 1961*, Table 38.

5. Nuñez, *El Somocismo y El Modelo Capitalista Agroexportador* (Managua: UNAN, 1981), p. 57.

6. DGECN, *Censo agropecuario, 1963*, Table 31.

7. DGECS, *Censo agropecuario, 1961*, Table 38.

8. DGECG, *Censo agropecuario, 1964*, Table 49.

9. DGECS, *Censo agropecuario, 1961*, Table 38.

10. DGECN, *Censo agropecuario, 1963*, Table 31.

11. DGECCR, *Censo agropecuario, 1963*, Table 49.

12. DGECG, *Censo agropecuario, 1964*, Table 49.

13. DGECS, *Censo agropecuario, 1961*, Table 38.

14. DGECN, *Censo agropecuario, 1963*, Table 31.

15. DGECCR, *Censo agropecuario, 1963*, Table 50.

16. Satterthwaite notes that the Wright family (Hacienda La Carrera), the Guirola family (Hacienda La Cangrejera), and several other very large growers were planting on their family haciendas in the 1950s. Satterthwaite, "Campesino Agriculture," p. 134.

17. The number of bales constituting the crop was estimated under the assumptions that the reported harvest was for unginned cotton (a commonplace in Salvadoran cotton statistics), the lint yield from raw cotton was 36.8 percent (the average for 1970–71),

and bales were of 480 pounds (to correspond to my other calculations). A list of over sixty important families and their business activities is given in Colindres, *Fundamentos económicos de la burguesía salvadoreña*, Table 67.

18. Stevenson, *Cotton Production*, p. 26.

19. Cited in Adams, *Crucifixion by Power*, p. 366.

20. See annex in Nuñez, *El Somocismo*, pp. 129–42.

21. Hirsch, "Littoral Highway," in Wilson et al., *Impact of Highway Investment*, p. 100.

22. Satterthwaite, "Campesino Agriculture," pp. 136–37.

23. Biderman, "Class Structure," p. 102.

24. Wilson, "Additional Cases," in Wilson et al., *Impact on Highway Investment*, p. 147.

25. Belli, "Inquiry," p. 48. See also Hirsch, "Littoral Highway," p. 100; and Biderman, "Class Structure," p. 85.

26. Adams, *Crucifixion by Power*, p. 356.

27. DGECH, *Censo agropecuario, 1952*, Table 12. DGECN, *Censo agropecuario, 1962–63*, Table 2.

28. DGECG, *Censo agropecuario, 1963*, Table 5-1.

29. DGECS, *Censo agropecuario, 1971*, Table 20.

30. Satterthwaite, "Campesino Agriculture," p. 224.

31. White, "Adult Education Program," p. 832. A USDA cotton report from the mid-1960s attributes the escalation of Honduran rental rates from $12 per acre in 1960–61 to $17 per acre in 1962–63 up to $20 per acre in 1963–64 to the vigorous competition from Salvadoran growers for Honduran cotton lands. Stevenson, *Cotton Production*, p. 39.

32. In 1966–67, 80 percent of the rented acreage was paying Nicaraguan landlords over $16 per acre in 1966–67, where only 58 percent of the rental land was paying that much in 1969–70. Stevenson, *Cotton Production*, p. 31.

33. By 1972–73 rentals of cotton land in Nicaragua had surpassed the peak years of the mid-1960s: 81 percent of the land area rented was once more paying over $16, and the very best cotton land (9 percent of that rented) was renting for more than $33 per acre. Ibid., p. 31.

34. By the late 1970s common rental rates in Central America stood at around $70 per acre in the big three cotton producers, $35 per acre in Honduras, and $57 per acre in Costa Rica. SIECA, *Situacíon actual de algodón*, Table 9. Honduran rental rates have been low historically, but after the war between El Salvador and Honduras in 1969, Salvadoran renters were pushed out of the rental market in Honduras, a partial contribution to the large differential in rental rates experienced in the 1970s.

35. Stevenson, *Cotton Production*, p. 11. Harness and Pugh, *Cotton*, p. 24. Nuñez, *El Somocismo*, p. 46.

36. In the early 1960s ginning fees ranged from $12.50 per bale in El Salvador to $15.65 per bale in Honduras, and they climbed several dollars during the late 1960s. Stevenson, *Cotton Production*, pp. 10, 20, 31.

37. Potential losses from fire could be insured against.

38. Guatemala (21), El Salvador (13), Honduras (1), Nicaragua (22), and Costa Rica (3).

39. CONAL, *Estadísticas del algodón*, Table VIII-51.

40. Adams, *Crucifixion by Power*, p. 362.

41. Stevenson, *Cotton Production*, p. 40.

42. Wheelock, *Imperialismo y dictadura*, p. 199.

43. Stevenson, *Cotton Production*, p. 34.

44. Stevenson noted the existence of these houses in the early 1960s in El Salvador but said they were declining in importance. Ibid., p. 20.

45. Ibid., p. 40.

46. Ibid., p. 11.

47. List from CONAL, published in Nuñez, *El Somocismo*, Table 17.

48. In 1962–63 the growers in the sample spent on the average $23.52 per acre for insecticides (not including the cost of application) and $8.30 an acre for fertilizer. By 1964–65 insecticide expenditures per cultivated acre had risen to $33.10, and fertilizer expenditures had risen to $12.59. Data from the surveys are reproduced in CONAL, *Estadísticas del algodón*, Table IV-29. Price data are from Belli, "Inquiry," Table III-16. (Note that 7.03 córdobas = $1; 1.73 acres = 1 *manzana*.)

49. By 1971–72 sales of insecticides to Nicaraguan growers reached $10.4 million and fertilizer sales reached $3.5 million. Cost estimates for 1971–75 were taken from ICAITI, *Consecuencias*, Tables 90–94. Insecticide expenditures are assumed to be 80 percent of the category *insecticidas + aplicaciones*, a figure arrived at from cost estimates averaged for Nicaragua and Honduras in 1978–79. Cost estimates for 1978–79 were taken from SIECA, *Situación actual de algodón*, Table 9. (Note that 2.47 acres = 1 hectare.)

50. The estimates for Nicaragua show that cotton-grower spending on fertilizers expanded from $5.8 million in 1972–73 to $15.7 million in 1978–79.

51. The other advantages of mixing locally were cheap Central American labor and the ability to change mixes depending on the local conditions.

52. Belli, "Inquiry," p. 40.

53. Exxon has petrochemical operations in Guatemala and El Salvador, and the Royal Dutch Petroleum Company has Shell Chemical dealerships in Guatemala, El Salvador, and Nicaragua. Shell operates a petrochemical dealership in Costa Rica as well.

54. The Banco de América (BANAMER) was formed in 1952 with participation from Wells Fargo Bank and the First National Bank of Boston. In 1953 the Banco Nicaraguense (BANIC) was formed with stock participation of Chase Manhattan Bank, Morgan Guaranty, and Multibank and Trust. In the early 1950s the Banco Calley-Dagnall was formed out of a prosperous coffee-processing and export house with participation from the First National Bank of Philadelphia. Wheelock, *Imperialismo y dictadura*, pp. 142–48, 199–200. Castillo, *Acumulación de capital*, p. 254.

55. In the sense that the cotton boom created a wage-labor force, it was part of the

more general changes that stimulated the demand for wage goods like clothing and processed foods.

56. Information on foreign investments comes from Castillo, *Acumulación de capital*, Appendix C, pp. 236–68; and from Jonas and Tobis, *Guatemala*, pp. 170–74.

57. Biderman, "Class Structure," p. 101.

58. The list of financial groups and their holdings is in Wheelock, *Imperialismo y dictadura*, pp. 199–201. Names of export houses and a list of cotton growers are in Nuñez, *El Somocismo*, pp. 47, 129–41.

59. Most of the information on these members of the cotton elite came from a list of twenty elite families published in Jonas and Tobis, *Guatemala*, pp. 216–51.

60. Colindres, *Fundamentos*, p. 55.

61. Seafood-export firms appear prominently in the portfolios of the cotton elite, perhaps because of their other investments near the coast.

62. The three big-grower board members were Juan T. Wright, Hans Homberger, and Ricardo Avila-Meardi. The list is in Colindres, *Fundamentos*, p. 150.

63. These storms occurred especially in the Nicaraguan cotton growing districts of León and Chinandega. Biderman, "Class Structure," p. 105.

64. The two USDA studies prepared during the 1960s reported that only rarely was a cover crop used by growers in the region, and Parsons points out that growers objected when the government of Guatemala passed a law in 1963 requiring that land planted for four consecutive years in cotton must be rested for two years with leguminous cover. Parsons, "Cotton and Cattle," p. 153.

65. Adams, *Crucifixion by Power*, p. 379.

66. Sean Swezey, "Transformation of Cotton Pest Management," *Nicaraguan Perspectives*, p. 2.

67. ICAITI, *Consecuencias*, Table 52. In 1974–75, 67 percent (by weight) of the insecticide applied was still of the chlorinated variety, with the remaining 33 percent of the organophosphate variety. Ibid., Table 54.

68. Some of this reduction was due to conscious government efforts to open up the coastal plain to migrants from the healthier highlands by killing off the anopheles mosquitos with DDT; but the spraying of insecticides on the fields probably made a more important contribution over time.

69. Experiments in Guatemala and El Salvador in the early 1970s showed that anopheles mosquitoes were increasingly resistant to DDT in the cotton-growing *municipios* of those two countries. In El Salvador the incidence of malaria among the population of the cotton zone increased from 35 per 1000 to 65 per 1000 between 1972 and 1974 despite increases in cotton acreage and the increasing use of insecticides applied per acre over the same period. ICAITI, *Consecuencias*, pp. 139–40. Governments responded just as growers did: by shifting the mix and increasing the doses applied. The malaria-control agencies began a partial shift from DDT to the more costly OMS-33 (Propuxur, Baygon) in the early 1970s.

70. ICAITI, *Consecuencias*, Table 7.

71. In Escuintla, where half of Guatemala's cotton is grown and where one-fifth of

Guatemala's cattle herd grazes, the 34 samples of milk taken contained on the average 5.2 parts of DDT per million, and the 126 samples taken of the fat from beef cattle contained 5.27 parts of DDT per million; roughly similar levels of contamination were found in the other two important cotton departments, Retalhuleu and Suchitepequez. Smaller samples from milk and beef fat in non-cotton-growing departments contained much lower levels of DDT. Ibid., Table 8.

72. Ibid., Tables 27, 28.

73. Ibid., Table 65.

74. Swezey, "Transformation of Cotton Pest Management," p. 3.

Chapter Three

1. As Chapter Two demonstrated, the peasants' perception of the Pacific lowlands as an unhealthy place had a basis in fact. Malaria remains a health problem there, especially in swampy areas near the coast.

2. Some of the Central American agricultural censuses have data at the very detailed *municipio* level. Whenever possible, comparisons are made at this level of detail; otherwise, departmental data are used. To give an idea of the geographical specificity of the *departamento* and the *municipio*: Guatemala, with a land area of 42,040 square miles, is divided into 22 departments and 178 *municipios*; El Salvador's 8,061 square miles are divided into 14 departments and 260 *municipios*; Honduras's 43,280 square miles are divided into 18 departments and 281 *municipios*; Nicaragua's land area of 54,342 square miles is divided into 16 departments and 125 *municipios*; Costa Rica's 19,575 square miles are divided into 7 *provincias* and 68 *cantones*.

3. Stevenson, *Cotton Production*, p. 25.

4. DGEG, *Censo agropecuario, 1950*, Vol. 1, Table 16. DGECG, *Censo agropecuario, 1963*, Vol. 2, Table 7-2.

5. The 1950–51 census records that in El Salvador's eight most important cotton-producing *municipios* 17 percent of the land area covered by the census was still in forests, 26 percent was in cropland, and 49 percent was in pasture. By 1970–71 only 6 percent of the land area surveyed was still in forests; pastures had been reduced to 36 percent of the area; and cropland covered 48 percent of the area, with over half of the cropland devoted to cotton. DGECS, *Censo agropecuario, 1950–51*, Table 7. DGECS, *Censo agropecuario, 1970–71*, Vol. 1, Table 3.

6. Satterthwaite, "Campesino Agriculture," p. 12.

7. In 1965–66 the top five cotton-producing *municipios* of Honduras (82 percent of cotton acreage that year) had 17 percent of the country's census area in forests, 49 percent in pasture, and 23 percent in cropland. Forty percent of the cropland in this zone of Honduras was in cotton that year. DGECH, *Censo agropecuario, 1965–66*, Table 11.

8. The top five cotton-producing *municipios* of Nicaragua in 1963–64 (representing 64 percent of the cotton acreage) had 23 percent of the census area still in forest, 41

percent in pasture, and 27 percent in cropland, cotton taking 78 percent of the cropland in those counties. El Viejo in the north still had 39 percent of the land area surveyed in forest cover. DGECN,*Censo agropecuario, 1963*, Tables 4, 8.

9. The three most important cotton-producing departments of Guatemala, where forest reserves were plentiful before the boom, experienced some of the highest population growth rates in the country between the population census of 1950 and that of 1964. A similar pattern of inmigration occurred in the northernmost department of Chinandega, Nicaragua, where forest reserves were plentiful. In other portions of the coastal plain where deforestation came in advance of cotton, mild to strong population expulsions occurred when cotton was introduced. This was what happened in coastal El Salvador and the coastal department of León, Nicaragua. CSUCA, *Estructura demográfica*, Tables 1–14.

10. This is a conservative estimate of the difference in yields between the coastal plains and the highlands because the severe drought in 1947 hit the coastal plains harder than the highland departments. DGECN, *Anuario estadístico, 1947* (Managua: DGECN, 1948), p. 373.

11. Blandón, "Land Tenure in Nicaragua," p. 87.

12. DGECN, *Anuario estadístico, 1959* (Managua: DGECN, 1960).

13. DGECN, *Censo agropecuario, 1963*.

14. During the sixteen-year period from 1947 to 1963, cropland increased fivefold in El Viejo, while corn acreage was cut in half. DGECN, *Anuario estadístico, 1947*. DGECN, *Censo agropecuario, 1963*.

15. DGECS, *Censo agropecuario, 1950–51*, Tables 10, 20. DGECS, *Censo agropecuario, 1970–71*, Tables 12, 13, 20.

16. One *municipio*, Champérico, achieved three times the national average yield per acre for corn in 1950. DGEG, *Censo agropecuario, 1950*.

17. DGECG, *Censo agropecuario, 1963–64*, Vol. 2, Tables 10, 11–2. DCEGG, *Censo agropecuario, 1950–51*, Vol. 1, Table 20.

18. "Ejido" literally means "common, public land." It differs from "communal" holdings in the sense that ejidal lands are attached to the governments of *municipios*, which distribute the lands among the residents in return for a fee called a cañon. "Communal" lands usually refer to those attached to an Indian village.

19. Taylor, "Agricultural Settlement," pp. 79–80.

20. The traditional peasant forms of tenure included in the census are illegal squatting, usufruct rights by permission, payments of rent in kind (by share of the crop or by performance of a service), and ejidal access rights. DGECN, *Censo agropecuario, 1963–64*, Tables 4, 8.

21. White, "Adult Education Program," pp. 816–33. I will deal with the peasant movement and land reclamations (invasions) in Part Two.

22. The best lands during the peak of the cotton boom could be rented to cotton growers for forty-six dollars an acre. Satterthwaite, "Campesino Agriculture," pp. 224–26.

23. For Guatemala's eight most important cotton-producing *municipios*, the number

of *colonos* increased from 784 in 1950 to 1,704 in 1963. DGEG, *Censo agropecuario, 1950*, Vol. 1, Table 12. DGECG, *Censo agropecuario, 1963–64*, Table 5-2. In the cotton departments of Usulután, La Paz, and San Miguel in coastal El Salvador, the number of *colonos* nearly doubled from 6,448 in 1950 to 11,871 in 1961. DGECS, *Censo agropecuario, 1961*, p. xvii.

24. Machine-picked cotton is inferior in quality to hand-picked cotton, and the plants grow so tall and bushy in Central America that picking by machine is difficult.

25. According to the 1970–71 census, the top eight cotton *municipios* of El Salvador had nearly one-third of all the tractors in the country. Sixty-three percent of the tractors in these counties were owned by private contractors. DGECS, *Censo agropecuario, 1970–71*, Vol. 1, Table 63.

26. In the three most important cotton-producing departments of El Salvador, the number of *colono* parcels dropped from 11,871 to 2,141 between 1961 and 1971. The land area worked by *colonos* in those three departments collapsed from 25,189 acres to 2,880 acres over the same ten-year period. Ibid., Tables 2, 3.

27. The evictions hit hardest in the cotton-growing regions of Guatemala, where, in contrast to the situation in the coffee-growing regions, once peasants were displaced most of them were not rehired as part-time day laborers. Bataillón and Lebot, "Migración interna," p. 53.

28. For a fuller account of the patterns of permanent migration see CSUCA, *Estructura demográfica*; and the series of articles that appeared in the 1970s in *Estudios Sociales Centroamericanos*.

29. The Nicaraguan Cotton Commission estimates on the basis of an average of seventy days per seasonal worker, and Schmid's sample of Guatemalan cotton workers in 1965–66 showed an average of seventy-four days of harvest work that season. Nuñez, *El Somocismo y el Modelo Capitalista Agroexportador* (Managua: UNAN, 1981), p. 52. Schmid, "Role of Migratory Labor," p. 25.

30. Schmid estimates that for Guatemala in 1965–66, the average that could be picked by a normal adult male was between seventy and eighty pounds per day. Schmid, "Role of Migratory Labor," p. 25. This figure is in line with what I found in Honduras and Nicaragua in 1982, though people stress the wide range between individuals and the considerable decline after the fields have been picked once. The actual numbers of people who have directly relied on cotton-harvest wages for survival is a multiple of the numbers in the chart, because many people work on a noncontract basis for only a few weeks at the peak of the cotton season, but they depend on this source of money income nevertheless. Furthermore, the work force is composed not just of able-bodied adult males but of women and children as well. Sometimes it is reported that women can outpick men, but women's productivity is severely limited when they have to carry their infants into the fields, as they often must. Children, on the average, can pick only one-half to two-thirds of the cotton of a normal adult male. Depending on the particular conditions in the labor market, women and children have ranged between one-tenth and one-third of the picking force in the cotton harvest, so that the numbers in the chart are a low estimate for the numbers of people who actually work in the cotton harvest.

31. The Nicaraguan Cotton Commission estimated the number of seasonal workers in the 1973–74 harvest as 202,295. This figure is higher than my estimate because the CONAL estimate includes women and children in the count. Nuñez, *El Somocismo*, p. 53.

32. The cottonfields begin within a few miles of the city of Escuintla, the thriving hub of the Guatemalan coastal plain, and the slums of San Salvador are only fifteen miles from the cottonfields of San Pedro Masahuat, so that workers are able to leave before dawn and return to the capital after dusk. The second- and fifth-largest cities of Nicaragua, León and Chinandega, are located in the heart of the cotton belt, and by 1963 a string of a dozen or so lesser towns, each with a population exceeding a thousand, had formed along the major roadways of Nicaragua's cotton district. DGECN, *Censo de población, 1963* (Managua: DGECN, 1965), Table F. Even on the outskirts of Managua, toward the airport, there is a minor cotton zone where people are recruited from the slums during picking time.

33. For an analysis of labor flows using statistics on economically active population in agriculture, see the chapter on seasonal migration in CSUCA, *Estructura demográfica*, pp. 345–60.

34. Schmid estimates that in 1965–66 between 118,000 and 150,000 pickers migrated to the coastal plain for Guatemala's cotton harvest. Guatemalan coffee farms absorbed between 167,000 and 237,000 seasonal migrants that year, and sugar imported 17,500 to 21,000. Schmid's dissertation estimates are given in CEPAL, FAO, OIT, *Tenencia de la tierra*, p. 120. A source published in 1962 placed the total of Nicaragua's temporary migrants for the major export crops at between 63,000 and 120,000 and estimated that by 1970 the number had swollen to 200,000. Nuñez, *El Somocismo*, p. 70.

35. The squalid conditions of the seasonal migrants on the cotton plantations are described in Bataillón and Lebot, "Migración interna," pp. 66–67. Schmid found the living conditions of seasonal workers on cotton plantations to be worse than those on either coffee or sugar estates. Schmid, "Role of Migratory Labor," p. 38.

36. These estimates include seasonal migrants for coffee, cotton, and sugar. Bataillón and Lebot, "Migración interna," p. 51.

37. Biderman, "Class Structure," p. 108.

38. CEPAL, FAO, OIT, *Tenencia de la tierra*, p. 119.

39. This zone of El Salvador, which for years provided the coast with an abundant supply of harvest labor, became a stronghold of support for the FMLN in the late 1970s. Today (1985) this area is being subjected to aerial bombardment, and traditional migratory patterns have been seriously disrupted. CSUCA, *Estructura demográfica*, p. 352.

40. The most successful contractors were able to recruit many thousands of workers. CEPAL, FAO, OIT, *Tenencia de la tierra*, p. 121. There are also indications of considerable seasonal movement from the poorer, drier parts of the Nicaraguan coastal plain (especially from the department of Rivas) to the cotton fields farther north, and

some seasonal workers travel to the Pacific coast from as far away as the frontier areas of Zelaya on the Atlantic side. CSUCA, *Estructura demográfica*, p. 356.

41. In the late 1970s northwest Guatemala became a stronghold of guerrilla resistance, and the Guatemalan government declared it a counterinsurgency zone. Today (1985), the army occupation of this area and the war that continues to be fought there have seriously disrupted traditional migratory patterns.

42. Another 12 percent of the seasonal migrants in 1966 came from the peripheral areas of adjacent San Marcos. Baillón and Lebot, "Migración interna," p. 51.

43. The remainder of the seasonal migrant workers, one-fourth of the sample, did not receive advances or obligate themselves to long-term contracts but worked on a short-term basis. These *voluntarios* were in a position to move from one plantation to another seeking out the best work conditions and wages; their situation permitted them to exact higher wages than contract workers and to avoid the 10 percent merchant fee to the contractor. By one report *voluntarios* received 25 percent more per pound picked than *cuadrilleros*. Ibid., p. 65.

44. Ibid., pp. 55–67. Schmid, "Role of Migratory Labor," pp. 15–18.

45. In the 1965–66 season some ten persons were reported to have died from cotton poisoning in Guatemala, and fifteen hundred more were treated; this is acute cotton poisoning and does not include chronic or long-term complications from exposure to smaller, more regular doses. Schmid, "Role of Migratory Labor," p. 20.

46. Ibid.

47. Contractors from some of the slightly better-off highland villages reportedly refused to recruit for cotton. One study claimed that the cotton contractors tended to be newcomers in the business and faced stiff competition from other contractors in recruiting workers; the coffee and sugar contractors were better established and had more regular marketing channels between plantations and the peasant areas.

48. In the late 1960s some thirty thousand Guatemalan Indians from the Department of San Marcos were said to migrate over the Mexican border at harvest time to pick coffee and cotton in the Soconusco, Mexico's portion of the Pacific export belt. Guatemalans living near El Salvador participate in El Salvador's coffee harvest, and some Hondurans used to migrate to El Salvador and Nicaragua for the harvest; Nicaraguans on the border of Honduras (before the border war broke out) picked cotton in Choluteca, Honduras.

49. Baillón and Lebot, "Migración interna," pp. 51, 57.

50. Carías, Slutzky, et al., *La guerra inútil*, p. 50.

51. From 1964 to 1970 cotton prices declined from $122 for a 480-pound bale to $112 a bale.

52. With the disruptions of civil war in the early 1980s, cotton growers in Guatemala turned cottonfields into pasture at an alarming rate. One reason was the disruption of the traditional supply of labor caused by the strife in northern Huehuetenango and Quiché.

53. These prices are for raw sugar delivered in New York, calculated from FAO,

Yearbook, 1970, 1974 (Rome: Food and Agriculture Organization of the United Nations, 1971, 1975).

54. The estimate includes only Guatemala, El Salvador, Honduras, and Nicaragua. The strongest surge occurred in Honduras and Nicaragua, which together accounted for 110,000 acres of the increase. Foreign Agricultural Service, *Sugar.*

55. In Guatemala sugar and coffee are frequently grown on the same estates, with coffee cultivated at higher altitudes and sugar at lower. Nine of Guatemala's thirteen sugar mills are located in the upper piedmont portion of the Pacific strip, not falling within easy access of the cotton lands; the other four are more accessible to the cotton country in Escuintla, and so some switching from cotton to sugar was possible there.

56. Farms that enter into contracts with the sugar mills are confusingly called *colonos* in Nicaragua and Honduras.

57. The data on Nicaraguan sugar were taken from Banco Central de Nicaragua sources and compiled by the able staff members of INIES, who were kind enough to give me a copy of their sugar statistics. INIES, "Pautas para el estudio de los subsistemas azucareros en America Central y el Caribe," mimeo, Managua, June 1982.

58. DGECH, *Censo agropecuario, 1965–66,* Table 16.

59. In the autumn of 1982 the newer mill, La Grecia (jointly owned with the government) had 7,000 acres of its own planted in sugar in Marcovia and had contracts on another 8,500 acres owned independently. The smaller mill, Los Mangos, had a total of 7,000 acres, including its contracts on independently held lands.

60. He said that harvest wages are very high, much more than the 180 lempiras a month ($90) made by "un cowboy." For 1982–83 the total wage bill of the complex was expected to come to 22 million lempiras ($11 million). The wages of upper-level management, engineers, and agronomists must have been included in this figure because the average wage comes to about $22 per day, assuming a 280-day work year for permanent workers and a 100-day work year for seasonal workers. Personal interview with Licenciado Bonilla Mazier, Ingenio La Grecia, Municipio de Marcovia, Choluteca, Honduras, Oct. 1982. Licenciado Bonilla was employed by the other sugar mill up the road before Azucarera Central, S.A., built La Grecia.

61. Harness and Pugh, *Cotton,* p. 5. Approximately one-third of the acreage in hybrid corn in the cotton departments of La Paz and San Miguel in El Salvador in 1971 was on holdings larger than 125 acres, and in Usulután the portion was 17 percent. DGECS, *Censo agropecuario, 1971,* Vol. 2, Table 8.

62. Ruíz Granadino, "Modernización agrícola en El Salvador," p. 94 (translation mine).

63. Bank financing of corn increased by 23,000 acres, and rice increased by 19,000 acres over the two-year period. As acreage planted in cotton declined, the cotton departments of León and Chinandega witnessed an increase of 12,000 acres of corn and 3,800 acres of irrigated rice.

64. For a good article on this process in El Salvador, where the reduction of people to pure wage laborers is most complete, see Toye Helena Brewer, "Women in El Salva-

dor," in Stanford Central America Action Network, *Revolution in Central America*, pp. 400–407.

65. The same depersonalization process was hitting coffee and sugar, but studies have shown that in cotton the tendency was more extreme and pure. Cotton plantations have been shown to be much less likely to hand out food rations to supplement wages than coffee or sugar plantations. Also, as noted previously, the seasonal workers' quarters tend to be the worst in cotton, and cotton plantations, unlike coffee and sugar estates, almost never have health clinics or doctors available for the seasonal work force. Schmid, "Role of Migratory Labor," pp. 18–34. Bataillón and Lebot, "Migración interna," pp. 55–57.

Chapter Four

1. United Nations, *Yearbook*, 1980 (New York: United Nations, 1981), p. 14.

2. Kissinger et al., *Report of the National Bipartisan Commission on Central America*, p. 55.

3. For good descriptions of breed characteristics see the three USDA studies on the beef cattle industry of Central America: Gerrity, *Beef Export Trade*, 1965; Rourk, *Beef Cattle Industries*, 1969; and Morgan, *Beef Cattle Industries*, 1973. For the best analysis of beef technology in Costa Rica see León, Barboza, and Aguilar, *Ganadería*, 1981.

4. Reported in León, Barboza, and Aguilar, *Ganadería*, p. 2-19.

5. The remedy for this second drawback was to set fire to the fields when the dry season hit. With some justification it was believed that the firing would destroy the weeds in their seeding phase and that an annual burning helped control ticks, torsalo worms, and snakes. The ashes were also thought to rejuvenate the soil. However, an FAO ecologist reporting on pasture management in Nicaragua in 1959 claimed that yearly burning encouraged the formation of unpalatable tuffets of grass; he recommended mowing three years in a row and burning only one out of four. B. W. Taylor, "Ecological Land Classification in Nicaragua: Land Potential of the León-Chinandega" (Rome: FAO mimeo, Oct. 1959), p. 85. When burning was used as a means of controlling weeds, the herds had greater difficulty finding forage during the most critical time of the year, so that on the Pacific coastal plain the weight loss per animal averaged sixty-six pounds during a normal dry season. León, Barboza, and Aguilar, *Ganadería*, p. 4-34.

6. Taylor, "Ecological Land Classification," p. 85.

7. John Thompson, "Production, Marketing and Consumption of Cattle in El Salvador," *The Professional Geographer* 8/5 (Sept. 1961), p. 19.

8. Ibid.

9. Ibid.

10. León, Barboza, and Aguilar, *Ganadería*, p. 2-15 (translation mine).

11. Van Meir, *Mercado ganadero en centroamérica*, p. 46 (translation mine).

12. León, Barboza, and Aguilar, *Ganadería*, p. 2-15 (translation mine).

13. Van Meir, *Mercado ganadero en centroamérica*, p. 46 (translation mine).

14. Thompson, "Cattle in El Salvador," p. 20.

15. Ibid.

16. Ibid.

17. Van Meir, *Mercado ganadero en centroamérica*, p. 47 (translation mine).

18. Ibid., p. 49.

19. Thompson, "Cattle in El Salvador," pp. 19–20.

20. Ibid., p. 19.

21. This was 92 percent higher than the rate for the European Economic Community, where consumption per capita was 49 pounds, also high by world standards. The average Canadian consumed around 78 pounds of beef and veal in 1961. See Table A.3 in Simpson and Farris, *World's Beef Business*, p. 284.

22. Labor costs were a greater disadvantage for U.S. meat packers than for cattlemen.

23. The aftosa quarantine has been so effective that cooked and processed meat, which is not subject to import quotas, has amounted to only 15 percent of all U.S. beef imports. Shane, *Hoofprints*, p. 97.

24. Simpson and Farris, *World's Beef Business*, p. 243.

25. Shane, *Hoofprints*, p. 103.

26. Simpson and Farris, *World's Beef Business*, p. 229.

27. However, road development in Central America was uneven. With the second largest land area in the region, Honduras had the least-developed road network, as Table 4-4 reveals. As late as 1969 a USDA report complained that the truck and rail system were both "in need of expansion and modernization. Many [cattle] are driven overland, which is extemely inefficient in that the cattle, none too fat at the beginning of the drive, lose considerable weight enroute." Rourk, *Beef Cattle Industries*, p. 7.

28. By 1973 the total lent by the World Bank for transportation in the region had reached $161 million, about 27 percent of the bank's total lending to the region. IBRD, *The World Bank Group*, p. 101. During its first fifteen years of operations (1960–74), the IADB lent $140 million to the five governments of Central America and $37 million to the CABEI for transportation and communications development. IADB, *Inter-American Development Bank*, pp. 10–80. By the end of 1971 the CABEI had authorized the lending of $119 million for highways, a sum representing 93 percent of its "integration" fund and 42 percent of its total authorizations since it began in 1962. SIECA, *El desarrollo integrado*, Vol. 9, Table 8. The bulk of the CABEI funds, in turn, came from AID and IADB loans earmarked for highway development. Between 1962 and 1972 half of the CABEI's external financing came directly from AID. Around 20 percent came from the IADB, and the remainder came from other U.S. government agencies, foreign government agencies, and loans from private interna-

tional banks. The five governments of Central America were also required to put up capital subscriptions. DeWitt, *The Inter-American Development Bank and . . . Costa Rica*, p. 57.

29. In its first two decades of development lending, the World Bank spent $154 million on livestock development in Central America and the Caribbean, 56 percent of its total direct commitments to agriculture. Figures for the 1948–71 period are in IBRD, *World Bank Operations*, pp. 74–75. A study of the IADB in Costa Rica concludes that "of the total contribution to the agricultural sector, the vast majority of funds have been channeled into livestock development projects and rural credit—with the credit provided for the cattle industry." DeWitt, *The Inter-American Development Bank and . . . Costa Rica*, p. 104.

30. In 1970 cattle raising received 22 percent of government agricultural loans in Guatemala, 43 percent in Honduras, 39 percent in Nicaragua, and 37 percent in Costa Rica. In 1970 cattle raising attracted 21 percent of private agricultural lending in Guatemala, 21 percent in El Salvador, 43 percent in Honduras, and 39 percent in Nicaragua. SIECA, *El desarrollo integrado*, Vol. 9, Tables 39–50.

31. SIECA, *Situación actual de la carne bovina*, Table 10.

32. In the first half decade of the export boom (1959–63) the average imports of breeding cattle from the United States were 749 per year. As the boom picked up and herd-improvement loans expanded during the period 1964–72, the average annual imports of breeding animals nearly doubled, to 1,384.

33. Morgan, *Beef Cattle Industries*, p. 26.

34. One study in Costa Rica claimed that adult mortality rates were reduced from 13 percent to 2 percent, and calf mortality rates were reduced from 50–60 percent to 5–10 percent, merely by the crossing of Zebu with the native criollo. Reported in León, Barboza, and Aguilar, *Ganadería*, p. 4-39. In Costa Rica modern ranching practices anticipated the export boom. Half the national herd was already crossbred criollo and Zebu by the time of the 1955 census, but by 1963, 83 percent of the herd had Zebu blood, and by the early 1970s, after fifteen years of export-led growth, 94 percent of the national herd was Zebu crossed with criollo. Ibid., p. 4-11. The rest of Central America has lagged behind Costa Rica in introducing the beefier bloodlines, but the direction of genetic evolution has been the same in the other countries.

35. By the mid-1970s "animal medicine" was the third largest imported agricultural input for Costa Rica, after "pesticide" and "fertilizer." SEPSA, *Información básica*, p. 109.

36. The main grasses introduced have been Jaragua, Pará, Guinea, and, most recently, African Star.

37. The area of fertilized pasture in Costa Rica in 1955 is estimated at only 5,434 acres, most of that in dairy zones. By 1973 the area in fertilized pastures had increased to an estimated 101,311 acres, most of that in beef-producing zones. León, Barboza, and Aguilar, *Ganadería*, p. 4-22.

38. The use of herbicides as a means of controlling weeds was not noticeable before

the mid-1960s in Costa Rica, but by 1974 some use of herbicides was reported in a sample of larger-than-average farms, ranging from 25 percent of the sample in the Pacific north to 79 percent of the sample in the wetter north region. Ibid., p. 4-24.

39. In 1955 rotational grazing was rare in Costa Rica, but by the 1970s more than half of the fattening operations reported rotation at least once every four weeks. Ibid., p. 4-42.

40. Costa Rican statistics show that from the mid-1940s to the mid-1970s, the average age at slaughter for steers dropped from around 5 years to only 3 ½ years. Weight gain in the final fattening stage increased from 19 pounds a month in the 1940s to 29 pounds a month in the 1970s. Even though the average steer was a year and a half younger at slaughter, the average weight at slaughter increased from 940 pounds in the 1940s to 998 pounds in the 1970s. The yield of meat per liveweight increased from 51–54 percent in the mid-1940s to 55–57 percent in the 1970s. Ibid., p. 4-34. The rate of technical change in the other Central American countries must have been more pronounced, because they were several decades behind Costa Rica in cattle technology when the beef-export boom hit.

Chapter Five

1. Simpson and Farris, *World's Beef Business*, p. 247.

2. As was shown in the previous chapter, the trade restraint is not a strict quota but a "voluntary export restraint" whereby a quota is triggered if exports from the country exceed 110 percent of the negotiated levels.

3. Prices to ranchers are quoted in liveweight, whereas export prices are quoted in boneless weights. Larger cattle have more beef per pound liveweight, and ranchers are paid more per pound for larger animals. To calculate the boneless beef equivalent from liveweight, it was assumed that an animal weighing between 600 and 700 pounds would dress out (carcass weight—bone in) at 48 percent of liveweight, a 700–800 pound animal at 50 percent, an 800–900 pound animal at 52 percent, a 900–1,000 pounder at 54 percent, and animals in excess of 1,000 pounds at 56 percent. The conversion of carcass weight to boneless was assumed to be 69 percent, or 145 percent from boneless to carcass. Prices for 1968 were taken from Rourk, *Beef Cattle Industries*, and conversion factors were calculated from information in Rourk's study, other USDA reports, and León, Barboza, and Aguilar, *Ganadería*.

4. When the Nicaraguan revolution hit in the late 1970s, ranchers engaged in capital flight by driving their herds over the border into Costa Rica, where foreign exchange could be obtained.

5. Burbach and Flynn, *Agribusiness*, p. 256.

6. Holden, "The Hamburger Connection," p. 18.

7. Slutzky, "La agroindustria de la carne," p. 147.

8. Castillo, *Acumulación de capital*, p. 249.

9. Wheelock, *Imperialismo y dictadura*, p. 172.

10. Somoza installed his cousin Noel Pallais as head of INFONAC, the government development bank. Millett, *Guardians*, p.232. According to a 1974 Central Bank of Nicaragua report, 66 percent of all the loans to the category "refrigeration" were from INFONAC and the Banco Nacional de Nicaragua, two recipients of international beef-development loans. Latinoconsult, *Mercadeo de ganado y carne*, Table 2.11.

11. Colindres, *Fundamentos*, Table 67.

12. ADELA is listed in some sources as "North American" capital, but it is incorporated in Luxembourg with offices in Washington, D.C., Lima, and Zurich; most of its investments are in Latin America.

13. IADB, *Inter-American Development Bank*, p. 79.

14. Shane, *Hoofprints*, p. 78.

15. Castillo, *Acumulación de capital*, p. 249.

16. Juvenal Angel, *Directory of American Firms Operating in Foreign Countries*, Vol. 2, 8th ed. (New York: Simon and Schuster, 1975).

17. The export percentages differed from country to country. In 1978 exports accounted for 52 percent of Guatemala's beef production, 50 percent of El Salvador's, 79 percent of Honduras's, 78 percent of Nicaragua's, and 74 percent of Costa Rica's. SIECA, *Situación actual de la carne bovina*, Tables 1, 4, 8.

18. Estimates for Nicaragua indicate that the export houses increased their share of domestic sales from 9 percent in 1960 to 37 percent in 1973. Banco Central de Nicaragua, *Situación y perspectivas*, Table 10.

19. In Costa Rica during the 1960s, cattle slaughtered for export weighed 180 pounds more on the average than cattle for the domestic market. In Costa Rica during the 1970s, 38 percent of all the animals slaughtered were cows, but 72 percent of the animals for domestic consumption were cows. León, Barboza, and Aguilar, *Ganadería*, Table 3-5. A similar pattern was found in other countries. Gerrity, *Beef Export Trade*, p. 9. De Lanuza, "La agroindustria de la carne," pp. III-23, II-15. When excessive pesticide levels, parasites, or other foreign matter are found in the meat, shipments are turned back. Where this condemned meat ends up depends on effective health standards practiced in the individual countries. When asked about practices in this regard, the executive giving the tour of a packing plant in Costa Rica swore that such meat would have to be discarded under Costa Rican law, whereas the manager of a Honduran export plant claimed that the meat was not necessarily inedible just because it did not pass USDA standards; he admitted that it was sometimes sold domestically.

20. Gerrity, *Beef Export Trade*, Tables 2–5. SIECA, *Situación actual de la carne bovina*, Table 8. Beef-consumption estimates do not include figures for livers, kidneys, tripe, hearts, and other organs that are not exported. Domestic beef shortages were relieved by increased domestic sales of organs.

21. In Costa Rica, for example, more than half of the cattle fattened for slaughter in 1963 were on farms exceeding 1,724 acres. Solís, "La ganadería de carne," pp. 224–81.

22. In Costa Rica the export premium for live cattle has ranged from as low as 17 percent to as high as 41 percent over the period 1955–74. León, Barboza, and Aguilar, *Ganadería*, p. 3-14.

23. The same Salvadoran businessmen who own Mataderos de El Salvador also own a modern fattening operation called Centro Ganadero de Desarrollo. The Somoza family owned modern ranches with improved pasture management that supplied its family-owned packinghouses.

24. Agrodinamica Holding Company owns two large fattening operations in Honduras, Ranchos de Choluteca and Repastadora de Oriente, operations that supply finished beef to its two packing plants. Slutzky, "La agroindustria de la carne," p. 178.

25. Castillo, *Acumulación de capital*, p. 249.

26. Colindres, *Fundamentos*, Table 67.

27. *Moody's Industrial Manual*, 1983, p. 3312. CSUCA, *El universo bananero*, p. 37. D. Slutzky and E. Alonso, *Empresas transnacionales y agricultura: el caso del enclave bananero en Honduras* (Tegucigalpa: Editorial Universitaria, 1980), Table 4.

28. Angel, *Directory of American Firms*, 1975.

29. Holden, "The Hamburger Connection," p. 18.

30. White, "Adult Education Program," p. 829. Taylor, *Agricultural Settlement*, p. 56.

31. In Guatemala 27 percent of the cattle were on farms smaller than eighteen acres in 1950, but by 1963 small farmers' holdings had collapsed to 16 percent of the national herd. DGEG, *Censo agropecuario, 1950*. DGECG, *Censo agropecuario, 1963*. In Honduras 31 percent of the cattle were on farms smaller than twenty-five acres in 1952, but by 1974 small farms had only 18 percent of the national herd. DGECH, *Censos agropecuarios, 1952, 1974*. In Costa Rica farms of fewer than twenty-five acres had 9 percent of the cattle in 1950, but by 1973 small farms had only 5 percent of the national herd. DGECCR, *Censos agropecuarios, 1950, 1973*.

32. A USDA report of the early 1960s accurately reflects the sentiment: "At the present time the Banco de Guatemala has under study a program to promote all phases of livestock development in the Pacific zone through financial and technical assistance to the medium and large-sized ranches that are judged to be more adaptable to new methods and to have the managerial and financial capacity to undertake the program." Rourk, *Beef Cattle Industries*, p. 5.

33. From 1975 to 1980 "medicines for animals" ranked third in imported inputs for the agricultural sector of Costa Rica, following "pesticides" and "fertilizers." SEPSA, *Información básica*, Table 71.

34. Angel, *Directory of American Firms*, 1975.

35. Castillo, *Acumulación de capital*, Appendix C, pp. 236–68. Burbach and Flynn, *Agribusiness*, pp. 253–81. *Moody's Industrial Manual*, 1982. United Brands owned John Morrell Meat Company.

36. Shane, *Hoofprints*, p. 79.

37. R. J. Reynolds Industries, *1982 Annual Report*.

Chapter Six

1. On the average, the number of acres of pasture per head rose from 1.8 in the early 1950s, when small operators were more prevalent, to 2.2 in the early 1960s as the cattle became more concentrated in large, extensive holdings. By the early 1970s, however, modernization in pasture management on the large holdings allowed for an improvement in herd densities to around 2 acres per head on the average, although the densities varied from one zone to the next and from one country to the next. Figures on herd sizes in the 1950s were taken from agricultural censuses. Herd sizes from 1965 through 1979 were taken from SIECA, *VII compendio estadístico*, Table 88.

2. DGEG, *Censo agropecuario, 1950*, DGECG, *Censo agropecuario, 1964*.

3. DGECH, *Censos agropecuarios, 1952, 1964–65, 1974*.

4. DGECCR, *Censos agropecuarios, 1950, 1963, 1973*.

5. Sáenz, *Deforestación*, pp. 26, 30. Thrupp , "Deforestation . . . and Cattle Expansion," p. 30.

6. SEPSA, *Ganadería*, pp. 9–11. Parsons, "Forest to Pasture," p. 124.

7. Peter White and James Blair, "Tropical Rain Forests: Nature's Dwindling Treasures," *National Geographic* 163 (Jan. 1983): 10.

8. Thrupp, "Deforestation . . . and Cattle Expansion," p. 38.

9. Boyer, "Agrarian Capitalism . . . in Southern Honduras," p. 94.

10. Browning cites it as the dominant method in nineteenth-century El Salvador for turning forest into coffee plantations. Browning, *El Salvador*, p. 158. Satterthwaite cites it as the most common method of converting forest into cottonfields during El Salvador's cotton boom in the 1950s and 1960s. Satterthwaite, "Campesino Agriculture," pp. 9–10, 53, 83. Adams reports that before the beef export era, it was the method traditionally used by haciendas on the Pacific side of Nicaragua to clear more land for cattle. Adams, *Cultural Surveys of Panama, Nicaragua, Guatemala, El Salvador, Honduras* (Washington: World Health Organization, 1957), p. 169.

11. White, "Adult Education Program," p. 832.

12. In the Pacific banana zone of Costa Rica near Quepos, about ten thousand acres of land that had been abandoned by the company reverted to secondary forest growth. The company, seeking alternative income from the land, allowed "one year leases to small, subsistence, slash-and-burn farmers. . . . After a couple of years the company converted most of this area into pastures for a large scale ranching operation." Pierre Stouse, "Effective Agricultural Development of Former Banana Lands: The West Coast of Costa Rica," *Revista Geográfica* 66 (June 1967), p. 157. In the early 1970s, in a remote, frontier area of Costa Rica, it was reported that some of the large properties allowed peasants to remain on the land without paying any rent at all for periods of one to three years, after which time they were required to seed into pasture the land they had cleared. Spielmann, "La expansión ganadera," p. 66. In eastern Guatemala in the mid-1960s, Wood noted, "land on the large estates of the region is made suitable for grazing by the efforts of short-term tenants, who clear the trees and bush from plots they are allocated but which they are required to leave after a year or two, their last responsi-

bility being to plant grass in the plots for the landlord's cattle." Wood, "Crop/Livestock Relationship," p. 98. A report by an AID consultant in the 1960s compared the costs of mechanized and hand clearing and concluded: "It now appears that hand clearing and hand farming around the stumps until they rot out—the traditional Guatemalan method—turns out to be the superior alternative." Hildebrand, "Guatemalan Colonization," pp. 48–49.

13. See the bibliographical outline on swidden cycles in Conklin, "The Study of Shifting Cultivation,"pp. 27–61, for the types of conditions that allow for secondary forest growth.

14. Parsons, "Forest to Pasture," pp. 126–31.

15. See the January 1983 issue of *National Geographic* for a description of the biological diversity of tropical forests and the delicate ecological balance on which that diversity rests.

16. Parsons, "Forest to Pasture," pp. 126–28. Thrupp, "Deforestation . . . and Cattle Expansion," pp. 45–47. Tosi and Voertmann, "Some Environmental Factors," pp. 189–205.

17. Of course, there was always the risk that rich mineral deposits might be discovered in peripheral areas, as in the case of northern Guatemala.

18. The conservative estimates (for Central American farms exceeding eighty-six acres) were 68 man days per acre per year for coffee, 30 for cotton, 38 for sugar, and 5 for cattle. SIECA, *El desarrollo integrado*, Vol. 5, Table 30, p. 74. The more extreme estimates (taken from samples in the province of Guanacaste, Costa Rica) were 63 man days per acre per year for coffee, 49 for cotton, 31 for sugar, and 2 for cattle. Lungo Ucles, "Políticas del estado," p. 49.

19. This series of studies was published in the journal *Estudios Sociales Centroamericanos*, mainly between 1974 and 1976. Updated versions of some of the articles were compiled and edited by CSUCA and published by EDUCA under the titles *Estructura agraria, dinámica de población, y desarrollo capitalista en centroamérica*, (1978) and *Estructura demográfica y migraciones internas en centroamérica* (1978).

20. *Ganadero* means "cattleman."

21. The time was three years according to the 1872 agrarian law in Honduras, five years according to the 1917 agrarian law in Nicaragua, and ten years according to the 1841 law in Costa Rica.

22. Settlement clauses have provided a source of revenue for the government titling agency, and they have been used less as a method of peasant protection than as a way to carve more territory into private property.

23.This is an altered form of an earlier peasant practice by which lands were assigned to members of the community according to their ability to make use of them. The modern ejidal form places a "title" to the land in the name of the municipal government, which, in turn, assigns the land to peasants who pay a nominal yearly fee called a *cañon*.

24. In his study of southern Honduras, White found that "many of the large landowners have title to a small piece of land but have extended the boundaries of their holdings

out over adjacent national lands." White, "Adult Education Program," p. 820. In the municipality of Langue, Honduras, Durham found that a local rancher whose wife had inherited a portion of land with legal title illegally extended the acreage by enclosing some 5,000 acres of national lands. Newspaper coverage tells of the same pattern in other sections of Costa Rica. A ranch with 1,500 legally titled acres in a frontier area of north central Costa Rica was reported in 1975 to be claiming 5,000 acres. *La Libertad*, 22 Mar. 1975. Another case was reported where only 1,800 of 5,000 claimed acres were legally titled. Ibid., 12 Apr. 1975. On one 47,000-acre ranch, the president of the republic intervened to stop a local eviction order on the grounds that the peasants were being evicted from "state lands." Ibid., 22 Mar. 1975.

25. Sometimes a rancher will offer to pay peasants a small sum for having cleared the area of trees. If the peasants accept the payment, they are acknowledging the rancher's right to the area. If they refuse to accept the payment, the rancher will remind them that they have no legal title to the land and that they cannot afford to hire a lawyer and a surveyor to acquire a legal title. If the peasants still do not budge, the escalation of conflict begins.

26. In these cases it is rarely known until a careful title search has been conducted which lands have long-standing titles and which are state lands, and even then it may be difficult to tell. Two things are clear in these cases, however: the peasants who have been working the land have a strong conviction that it is rightfully theirs, and the ranchers, local police, and local governments have an equally strong conviction that what is being done is, as White put it, "important for the development of the region." White, "Adult Education Program," p. 831.

27. This is a tactic used throughout Central America. For a vivid description of how it was applied by the fruit company in northern Honduras, see Posas, *Conflictos agrarios*, p. 39.

28. In the case studied by Durham, the fences were cut three times.

29. Durham reports that the landowner in Langue hired fifty armed guards to patrol the perimeter and had forty members of "Los Baldíos," the land-defense committee, put in jail. Durham, *Scarcity and Survival*, p. 156.

30. In Namasigue, Honduras, White found that some of the leaders of the small-farmer-defense committee knew the municipal documents well because they had held posts in the municipal government registering titles; the peasants were convinced that the land had been the property of the village and that because the village claim had never been legally alienated, the rancher's claim was invalid. White, "Adult Education Program," p. 831. Durham reports that one of the first actions of "Los Baldíos" was to get a sympathetic local lawyer to assist in a title search.

31. White found that in one community in southern Honduras where peasant resistance had been strong, after the homes had been burned the head of the rural police had the peasants who resisted "strung up in trees in the patio of their house, beaten, and left to hang until someone dared to come back and cut them down." White, "Adult Education Program," p. 831.

32. In 1959 the federation of students at the national university in Tegucigalpa,

Honduras, helped peasants of the south coast pressure the government to rule in their favor on lands that had been taken into cattle ranching in Monjarás, Choluteca; Posas argues this was a very important ingredient in the success of the action. Posas, *Conflictos agrarios*, pp. 28–35. In Costa Rica peasants who had been evicted from an expanding cattle ranch sought refuge in the recreation center at the national university, which became the launching pad for a national protest. Ibid., 12 Apr. 1975.

33. For early twentieth-century struggles on the coastal plain of Costa Rica see Gudmundson, "Las luchas agrarias." For a penetrating comparison of post–World War II struggles with earlier conflicts see Edelman, *Consolidación de las Haciendas*.

34. White, "Adult Education Program," p. 832.

35. What is surprising is that even in cases like Somoza's Nicaragua, where there was abundant evidence that the national authorities represented the local ranchers, peasants held onto the belief that their appeals would be heard. In October of 1982 in Managua, an agricultural technician for a protestant relief organization told me that in 1974—after the Managua earthquake and the well-known atrocities committed by the guard at that time—a high officer in the national guard laid claim to a large area of land in Boaco. The officer wanted the land for a cattle ranch. The peasants of the area formed a committee, collected oral testimony from the old-timers in the community who knew the traditional claims to land in the area, and appealed to none other than Anastasio Somoza Debayle for justice to be done.

36. White, "Adult Education Program," p. 833.

37. Seligson, *Peasants*, p. 109. From reading the minutes of the Guanacaste Ranchers' Association, Marc Edelman found that the ranchers on several occasions attempted to secure a legal pardon for Morice, even though Morice escaped justice by leaving the country. After the Sandinista Revolution, Morice moved back to Costa Rica and is now reported to be supporting contra forces from his ranches there.

38. Posas, "Política estatál," pp. 83–84. Posas has a full account of the period during which the government was open to peasant demands and of its aftermath.

39. Barahona Riera, *Reforma agraria*, p. 275.

40. Posas, "Política estatál," p. 80.

41. *Latin America*, 20 June 1975.

42. Lernoux, *Cry of the People*, pp. 109–13.

43. Ibid., p. 113.

44. DGECH, *Censo agropecuario, 1974*.

45. The Olancho beef herd expanded by 60 percent from approximately 122,000 head in 1965–66 to 196,000 head in 1974. Over that decade Olancho moved from third-place cattle producer to second-place, just behind Choluteca's 197,000 head. DGCEH, *Censos agropecuarios, 1965–66, 1974*.

46. Not by pure chance does the acronym (FENAGH) resemble that of the already existing peasant federation, FENACH.

47. Parsons, *Agrarian Reform*, p. 17.

48. Durham, *Scarcity and Survival*, p. ·165.

49. Parsons, *Agrarian Reform*, p. 18.

50. Ibid. Posas, "Política estatál," p. 81.

51. Posas, "Política estatál," pp. 80–84.

52. From an examination of INA reports, the decree and its application look more like a desperate attempt by the government to contain the land occupations and direct them in an orderly way, putting lands into INA-controlled *asentamientos* instead of allowing the movement to be directed by the more radical peasant groups.

53. The 1962 law had defined one head per two hectares as adequate for good bottomland, but the new law stipulated two head of cattle per hectare. Posas, "Política estatál," p. 90.

54. *Latin America*, 23 May 1975, 30 May 1975.

55. Black, *Triumph of the People*, p. 81.

56. Ibid.

57. Ibid., p. 84.

58. The category "occupied without title" does not include ejidal rights, usufruct rights, or other peasant forms of tenure that were legally recognized. DGECN, *Censo agropecuario, 1963*, Table 2.

59. The 1952 census counted Matagalpa in third place with 126,000 head of cattle. By 1963 the herd had grown to 178,000 head.

60. DGECN, *Censo agropecuario, 1963*. MIDINRA, *Diagnóstico*, Vol. 11, Table 15.

61. According to the survey the whole department of Matagalpa was hit by the titling process. By 1976 only 2.5 percent of the area surveyed in the whole department was occupied without legal rights. MIDINRA, *Diagnóstico*, Vol. 11, Table 13.

62. Taylor, *Agricultural Settlement*, p. 28.

63. Black, *Triumph of the People*, p. 53.

64. The road to Waslala was probably a mule path for transporting coffee. The path runs through a low zone where coffee could not be cultivated, hence corn was grown there, by people who probably supplemented their income by working the coffee harvest higher up.

65. Black, *Triumph of the People*, p. 53.

66. MIDINRA, *Diagnóstico*, Vol. 11, Table 13.

67. By the mid-1970s half of Guatemala's beef, two-thirds of the coffee, three-fourths of the sugar, and all of the cotton were grown on the Pacific strip. A recent attempt to quantify violence in Guatemala estimates that outside the capital city, the Pacific coastal departments registered the highest incidence during the decade 1966–76. Aguilera, Romero, et al., *Dialéctica del terror*, p. 155. The estimation procedure consisted of defining six indicators of violence and measuring reports of these acts as they were observed in the three national newspapers, *Prensa Libre*, *Gráfico*, and *Impacto*. The categories were assassinations, attempted assassinations, kidnappings, cadavers found, terrorist attacks, and arms caches. "Cadavers found" are almost exclusively the work of the military or death squads, whereas arms caches are the work of

militant worker and peasant organizations. The other categories involve both groups. The estimation procedure contains a downward bias for peripheral areas, where reports are less likely to reach the newspapers.

68. Corn shows an increase for Izabál, probably owing to the settling of forested areas to the north of Lake Izabál by Kekchí Indians. Disaggregated figures are not available to separate these two very different zones in the department of Izabál.

69. Louisa Frank, "Resistance," in Jonas and Tobis, *Guatemala*, p. 182.

70. The heaviest death tolls from La Mano Blanca and Nueva Organización Anti-communista during this period were in the towns of Teculután, Morales, Río Hondo, Chiquimula, and Zacapa. Howard Sharckman, "The Vietnamization of Guatemala," in Jonas and Tobis, *Guatemala*, p. 202. All of these are towns or departmental capitals located along the main highway or along the improved road that goes into the department of Chiquimula. These towns held many of the bitter victims of cattle evictions.

71. Arana now holds vast acreages in Guatemala, including ranches in Zacapa and Izabál, a sugar estate on the Pacific coast, and other properties.

72. *Latin America*, 9 Apr. 1976.

73. Arthur Schmidt, "Report on a Visit to Refugee Camps in Honduras," mimeo (Philadelphia: American Friends Service Committee, June 1982), p. 20.

74. This amounted to less than 1 percent of the paved road grid of the country. Per land area, these departments were consistently among the lowest in all-weather roads as well. T.S.C. Consortium, *Central American Transportation Study, 1964–65* (Washington: T.S.C. Consortium, 1965), calculated from Table A IV-B 1.

75. Wood, "Crop/Livestock Relationship," p. 101.

76. Gerrity, *Beef Export Trade*, p. 7.

77. Part of this increase was undoubtedly in the already developed part of Izabál. This data source does not have a more disaggregated breakdown, so we are not able to distinguish between the peripheral zone of Izabál and its highly developed portion south of the lake.

78. Thomas Maloney, "El impacto de la franja," pp. 91–106.

79. EXMIBAL is a joint venture among International Nickel Company (50 percent—Canadian based), Hanna Mining Company (20 percent—U.S. based), and the Guatemalan government (30 percent), with loans from the World Bank, the U.S. Export-Import Bank, the Central American Bank for Economic Integration, and a consortium of private banks headed by Chase Manhattan. The history of this concession, which stretches back to the mid-1950s after the coup against Arbenz and the liberalization of the mining code, is neatly documented in Fred Goff, "EXMIBAL," in Jonas and Tobis, *Guatemala*, pp. 151–66.

80. Nancy Peckenham, "Guatemala: Peasants Lose Out in Scramble for Oil Wealth," *Multinational Monitor* 2/5 (May 1981), pp. 9–11.

81. The first loan was provided by the CABEI ($7.8 million), the second by the World Bank in 1975 ($145 million), and a third by the IADB in 1976 ($105 million). More than $100 million in additional financing has been lent to the Guatemalan government by private international banks. Black, "Garrison Guatemala," p. 10.

82. The Chulac complex is expected to cost $600 million. Maloney, "El impacto de la franja," p. 96.

83. Nickel processing is very energy intensive.

84. Black, "Garrison Guatemala," p. 11.

85. One of the estates is a 25,000-acre spread near Sebol, Alta Verapáz. Lucas purchased the rights to the titled portion of this estate from one of the old coffee families of Alta Verapáz in 1975, before it was announced that two major roads, the Transversal Highway and the Coban-Petén road, were to be constructed across this land.

86. The western highland departments of Totonicapán, Sololá, Sacatepequez, and Chimaltenango, where some of the centers of marketing and craft production of the Indian economy are located, registered the lowest on the violence scale of Aguilera, Romero, et al., and the departments with zones lying in the periphery of this network, Huehuetenango, El Quiché, Alta Verapáz, and Petén, registered very low on the scale. Aguilera, Romero, et al., *Dialéctica del terror*, pp. 158–59.

87. Ibid., p. 153. *Latin America*, 13 June 1975. Mario Payeras, "The Tiger of Ixcán," in Gettleman, Fried, et al., *Guatemala in Rebellion*, pp. 264–69.

88. Smith's "core" communities, where the major marketing and petty commodity production of the Indian system are located, participated in seasonal plantation work but at a much lower rate, typically exporting fewer than 10 percent of their adult males seasonally. Carol Smith, "Beyond Dependency Theory," *American Ethnologist* 5 (1978): 574–617.

89. Davis and Hodson, *Witnesses to Political Violence in Guatemala*, p. 47.

90. When asked how the people in the settlement cooperative responded when they heard of Father Woods's death, the nun who reported the story said, "They went to the mountains with the guerrillas."

91. Most of the accounts in English are derived from the sources reprinted in Aguilera, Romero, et al., *Dialéctica del terror*, pp. 193–205.

92. *La Hora*, 30 May 1978, in ibid., p. 193 (translation mine).

93. Ibid., p. 204.

94. "The Massacre of Panzos," *Green Revolution* 37/5 (Winter 1981): 19.

95. One of the routes the coffee trade took went from the German-owned fincas in the highlands along the Cahabón to Lake Izabál and from there to Europe. The corn producers settling the lower altitudes and other lands where coffee could not be profitably cultivated probably earned seasonal money incomes picking coffee higher up.

96. Aguilera, Romero, et al., *Dialéctica del terror*, p. 198.

97. By 1963 there was already a dirt road along this path; it was classified as "all weather" but of the slowest category, according to the 1964 transportation study. T.S.C. Consortium, *Transportation Study*, p. 154. By 1966 plans had been drawn up for a major road there. Martin Klein, "The Atlantic Highway in Guatemala," in Wilson et al., *The Impact of Highway Investment*, p. 82.

98. FIASA (Industrial and Agricultural Finance Company) was set up in the late

1960s with seed money of $5 miilion from AID and with starting capital subscriptions from a consortium of major multinational corporations and holding companies, including ADELA and LAAD, which were shown to be large investors in the beef boom. FIASA also sold initial stock to Guatemalan oligarchy families. See David Tobis, "FIASA," in Jonas and Tobis, *Guatemala*, pp. 143–50.

99. Aguilera, Romero, et al., *Dialéctica del terror*, pp. 194, 201.

100. One usually finds partial denials, inconsistent positions taken by different government bodies, and all sorts of chicanery, but rarely does one find absolute rejection of a peasant appeal.

101. Aguilera, Romero, et al., *Dialéctica del terror*, p. 198.

102. The ranchers were Flavio Monzón (Rancho San Vicente and Tinajas), Enrique Edwin Bics (Rancho Polochíc), Manuel Moco Sanchez (Rancho Sachoc), Joaquin Gonzalez (Rancho La Soledad), and several others. "The Massacre of Panzós," p. 19. Some of the villages (mentioned in various reports) from which the peasants came have place names identical to the ranches: San Vicente, Cahaboncito, La Soledad, Sachoc, and Panzós. The Tinajas is a river that feeds into the Polochíc.

103. *La Nación*, 31 May 1978. Aguilera, Romero, et al., *Dialéctica del terror*, p. 195.

Chapter Seven

1. OAS, *América en cifras, 1977* (Washington: OAS, 1978), Table 351-52.

2. In Guatemala real wages of workers covered by social security (this figure includes coffee workers) declined 6.8 percent between 1974 and 1975, and even with some recovery of real wages during the coffee-price recovery of 1976 and 1977, by 1980 the real wage stood at 70 percent of what it had been in 1970. In El Salvador the real wage of coffee workers declined 12 percent between 1973 and 1974. In Costa Rica the real wage in agriculture dropped 6.7 percent over the same period. Ibid., Table 351-21. United Nations, *Economic Survey of Latin America, 1977, 1980* (New York: United Nations, 1978, 1981).

Chapter Eight

1. UN estimates from *Latin America*, 9 Feb. 1973.

2. Michael Dodson and T. S. Montgomery, "The Churches in the Nicaraguan Revolution," in Walker, *Nicaragua in Revolution*, p. 165.

3. *Latin America*, 25 Jan. 1974.

4. Black, *Triumph of the People*, p. 92.

5. Ibid., pp. 58–62.

6. *Latin America*, 12 July 1974.

7. Of the 2,000 Somoza dynasty properties, peasants were able to take the 300 least

profitable farms as privately titled small holdings. The rest remained in state farms or producer cooperatives. By 1982, 94 more properties had been expropriated, adding another 400,000 acres to the total area subject to the reform. Collins et al., *What Difference Could a Revolution Make?* pp. 66, 96.

8. *Latin America Weekly Report*, 17 Dec. 1982.

9. At the time of the 1969 war between the two countries, the Honduran land-reform agency estimated 219,619 undocumented Salvadorans living in Honduras. Carías, Slutzky, et al., *La guerra inútil*, p. 294. Durham, *Scarcity and Survival*, Chapter 6.

10. Williams, "The Central American Common Market," Chapter 6.

11. SIECA, *Situación actual de la carne bovina*, Table 8.

12. Burke, "El sistema de plantación," p. 476. The estimate was made by subtracting the number of agricultural units (agricultural census) from the number of rural households (population census). Some rural families operate more than one agricultural unit, so that these estimates of landlessness are downward-biased.

13. SIECA, *Situación actual de la carne bovina*, Table 8.

14. Simon and Stephens, *El Salvador Land Reform*, p. 38.

15. Harald Jung, "Class Struggle and Civil War in El Salvador," in Gettleman, Lacefield, et al., *El Salvador*, p. 76.

16. *Latin America*, 13 Oct. 1972.

17. Ibid., 9 Aug. 1974.

18. Ibid., 5 Jan. 1975, 8 Aug. 1975, 22 Aug. 1975.

19. Armstrong and Shenk, *El Salvador*, p. 75.

20. *Latin America*, 10 Oct. 1975, 5 Nov. 1976.

21. A week after the incident the government raised the minimum wage covering harvest workers by 10 percent. *Latin America Economic Report*, 4 Nov. 1977. United Nations, *Economic Survey of Latin America*, 1977 (New York: United Nations, 1978), p. 228.

22. American Civil Liberties Union and Americas Watch, *Report on Human Rights in El Salvador* (New York: Random House, 1982), p. 10.

23. Armstrong and Shenk, *El Salvador*, pp. 149–55. Gettleman, Lacefield, et al., *El Salvador*, p. 63.

24. DGECS, *Censo agropecuario, 1950*, Table 26.

25. Browning, *El Salvador*, pp. 156, 191.

26. These departments were San Miguel, La Union, Chalatenango, and Morazán. DGECS, *Censo agropecuario, 1971*.

27. The only exception among the nine departments with guerrilla strongholds was Cuscatlán, which had the smallest number of *colonos* to begin with. Ibid., Vol. 1, p. xxix.

28. Jung, "Class Struggle," p. 84.

29. In 1972–73 the Hills had the fifth-largest cotton harvest in El Salvador. Colindres, *Fundamentos*, Table 67.

30. American Civil Liberties Union and Americas Watch, *Report on Human Rights*, p. 11.

31. Jung, "Class Struggle," p. 81.

32. *Latin America Weekly Report*, 2 Mar. 1984.

33. The exception was in 1978, when consumer price inflation briefly dipped down to 8 percent. OAS, *Statistical Bulletin* (Washington: OAS, Jan.–June 1982).

34. *Latin America*, 1 June 1973.

35. Ibid., 3 Aug. 1973.

36. The government settled the six-months' teachers' strike with a 25 percent wage increase and a release of political prisoners arrested in the protests surrounding the strike.

37. *Latin America*, 10 May 1974.

38. The committee estimated that between 1970 and the end of 1973, fifteen thousand people disappeared in Guatemala, and there was evidence of security-force involvement in 75 percent of the cases. Ibid., 16 May 1975.

39. United Nations, *Economic Survey of Latin America*, 1975, p. 230.

40. *Latin America*, 24 Jan. 1975, 21 Nov. 1975, 26 Dec. 1975.

41. Ibid., 9 Apr. 1976.

42. Davis and Hodson, *Witnesses to Political Violence in Guatemala*.

43. *Latin America*, 9 Apr. 1976.

44. CIDAMO, "The Worker's Movement in Guatemala," *NACLA Report on the Americas*, 14, no. 1 (Jan.–Feb. 1980): 28–33.

45. *Latin America*, 23 July 1976.

46. United Nations, *Economic Survey of Latin America*, 1977, p. 251.

47. Davis and Hodson, *Witnesses to Political Violence in Guatemala*, p. 47.

48. *Latin America Weekly Report*, 3 Mar. 1978.

49. Ibid., 13 Oct. 1978.

50. Davis and Hodson, *Witnesses to Political Violence in Guatemala*, p. 49.

51. United Nations, *Economic Survey of Latin America*, 1980, p. 300. Concerned Guatemala Scholars, *Guatemala: Dare to Struggle Dare to Win* (Brooklyn, N.Y.: Concerned Guatemala Scholars, 1982), p. 34.

52. Beverly Treumann, "A Righteous General, a Frightened People," *Christianity and Crisis*, 4 October 1982, p. 278.

53. Peckenham, *Guatemala*, p. 19.

54. Ibid., p. 16.

55. Coordinadora de Ayuda a Refugiados Guatemaltecos, "Zonas de Refugiados Guatemaltecos en Mexico," mimeo (Mexico City: Coordinadora de Ayuda a Refugiados Guatemaltecos, Dec. 1982).

56. Alan Riding, "Guatemalan Refugees Flood Mexico," *New York Times*, 18 Aug. 1982.

57. *Latin America Weekly Report*, 24 Dec. 1982.

58. Peckenham, *Guatemala*, p. 26. For the response of large landowners to the AID study see *Latin America Weekly Report*, 4 Mar. 1983.

59. Peckenham, *Guatemala*, p. 28.

60. *Latin America Weekly Report*, 1 June 1984.

61. With few exceptions, the producer cooperatives were a way for the government and multinational corporations to exercise control over the peasant movement by controlling both credit and the regulations regarding purchase of inputs and sale of outputs. See Posas, *El movimiento campesino hondureño*.

62. *Latin America Report*, 2 Aug. 1974.

63. United Nations, *Economic Survey of Latin America*, 1977, p. 296.

64. *Latin America Report*, 3 Dec. 1976.

65. *Latin America Political Report*, 21 Jan. 1977.

66. Ibid., 4 Mar. 1977.

67. *Latin America Report*, 11 Aug. 1978.

68. *Latin America Political Report*, 1 Sept. 1978.

69. *Latin America Weekly Report*, 11 May 1984.

70. *Honduras Update*, July 1984, p. 2.

71. See the article on the history of peasant evictions at the Trujillo training center in *Latin America Weekly Report*, 20 July 1984. In July 1984, ninety-two peasant families were told to move to make way for the expansion of the Aguacate base near the Nicaraguan border. Ibid., 27 July 1984.

72. *Honduras Update*, Nov./Dec. 1983, p. 8.

73. Ibid., Mar. 1984, p. 8.

74. Ibid., Feb. 1984, p. 8.

75. In 1982 the same leader was kidnapped and tortured by DNI and later released.

76. The ouster of Alvarez, who did the bidding of the Reagan administration in the regional war, was not due merely to labor strife. Alvarez had invoked the distrust of some of the high command because of his agreement with the United States to train Salvadoran troops in Honduras. Many officers in the Honduran military forces fought in the war with El Salvador in 1969. These officers view the Salvadoran military as a threat second to the threat from Nicaragua and will not be willing to train the Salvadoran enemy or to move Salvadoran refugee camps inland, away from the border, unless the border areas taken by El Salvador in 1969 are returned to Honduras. Nor did all the officers in the Honduran military support Alvarez's plans to invade Nicaragua. *Latin America Weekly Report*, 6 July 1984.

77. *Honduras Update*, June 1984, p. 8.

78. *Latin America Weekly Report*, 29 June 1984. *Honduras Update*, June 1984, p. 8.

79. *Latin America Weekly Report*, 29 June 1984.

80. SIECA, *VII Compéndio estadístico*, Table 300. OAS, *Statistical Bulletin*, Jan.–June 1982.

81. OAS, *Statistical Bulletin*, Jan.–June 1982.

82. *La Libertad*, 1 Feb. 1975, 15 Feb. 1975.

83. Ibid., 15 Mar. 1975, 22 Mar. 1975, 15 Apr. 1975.

84. Ibid., 22 Mar. 1975.

85. Ibid., 18 Oct. 75.

86. Barahona Riera, *Reforma agraria*, pp. 119, 275. ITCO issued titles to peasants for a total of 2.3 million acres over this fourteen-year period, although only a small

portion of the total was hotly disputed land; in the majority of the cases the land was "donated" or relinquished without protest to ITCO.

87. United Nations, *Economic Survey of Latin America*, 1974, p. 136.

88. SIECA, *VII Compéndio estadístico*, Table 276.

89. *Latin America*, 12 Sept. 1975.

90. Edelman and Hutchcroft, "Costa Rica: Resisting Austerity."

91. *Latin America Regional Report: Mexico and Central America*, 4 June 1982.

92. Rivera Urrutía, *El fondo monetario internacional*.

93. *Latin America Weekly Report*, 20 July 1984.

94. Edelman and Hutchcroft, "Costa Rica: Resisting Austerity," pp. 37–40.

95. *Latin America Weekly Report*, 24 Aug. 1979.

96. Ibid., 18 Jan. 1980, 14 Aug. 1980.

97. *Latin America Regional Report: Mexico and Central America*, 29 Oct. 1982.

98. Edelman and Hutchcroft, "Costa Rica: Resisting Austerity," p. 39.

99. *Latin America Regional Report: Mexico and Central America*, 4 May 1984.

100. Ibid., 9 July 1982.

101. Edelman and Hutchcroft, "Costa Rica: Modernizing the Non-Army," p. 9.

102. *Latin America Regional Report: Mexico and Central America*, 8 June 1984.

103. *Latin America Weekly Report*, 13 May 1983.

104. Edelman and Hutchcroft, "Modernizing the Non-Army," p. 11.

105. Until 1984 the building of the strategic roads through the Huetar Norte was postponed because of an uproar in Costa Rica over having the U.S. Army finance the project and send a thousand combat engineers to complete it. Ibid.

106. Ibid., p. 10.

Bibliography

This selected list of articles, books, pamphlets, and documentary sources is organized according to geographical area, beginning with the Central American region as a whole and then proceeding to each of the separate countries from north to south. Periodicals and other reference materials have separate listings.

Central America

Barry, Tom, Beth Wood, and Deb Preusch. *Dollars and Dictators*. Albuquerque, N. Mex.: The Resource Center, 1982.

Berryman, Phillip. *Inside Central America: The Essential Facts Past and Present on El Salvador, Nicaragua, Honduras, Guatemala, and Costa Rica*. New York: Pantheon Books, 1985.

———. *What's Wrong in Central America and What to Do about It*. Philadelphia: American Friends Service Committee, 1983.

Castillo Rivas, Donald. *Acumulación de capital y empresas transnacionales en Centroamérica*. Mexico City: Siglo XXI, 1980.

CEPAL, FAO, and OIT. *Tenencia de la tierra y desarrollo rural en Centroamérica*. San José: EDUCA, 1980.

CSUCA. *Estructura agraria, dinámica de población, y desarrollo capitalista en Centroamérica*. San José: EDUCA, 1978.

———. *Estructura demográfica y migraciones internas en Centroamérica*. San José: EDUCA, 1978.

———. *El universo bananero en Centroamérica*. San José: EDUCA, 1977.

Equipo de Investigación de Ciencias Sociales del CSUCA. "Regiones agrícolas en Centroamérica: Una aproximación socio-económica." *Estudios Sociales Centroamericanos* 17 (May–Aug. 1977): 95–109.

Foreign Agricultural Service. *Sugar: World Supply and Distribution 1954/55–1973/74*. Statistical Bulletin no. 562. Washington, D.C.: USDA, Oct. 1976.

Gerrity, Martin. *The Beef Export Trade of Central America*. Washington, D.C.: USDA, Nov. 1965.

Harness, Vernon, and Robert Pugh. *Cotton in Central America*. FAS-M154. Washington, D.C.: USDA, Aug. 1970.

Holden, Robert. "The Hamburger Connection." *Multinational Monitor* 2, no. 10 (Oct. 1981): 17–18.

ICAITI. *Estudio de las consecuencias ambientales y económicas del uso de plaguici-*

das en la producción de algodón de Centroamérica. Guatemala City: ICAITI, 1977.

Kissinger, Henry, et al. *Report of the National Bipartisan Commission on Central America.* Washington, D.C.: U.S. Government Printing Office, 1984.

LaFeber, Walter. *Inevitable Revolutions: The United States in Central America.* New York: W. W. Norton & Co., 1983.

Leogrande, William. "Through the Looking Glass: The Kissinger Report on Central America." *World Policy Journal,* 1, no. 2 (Winter 1984): 251–84.

McCamant, John. *Development Assistance in Central America.* New York: Praeger Publishers, 1968.

Molina Chocano, Guillermo. *Centroamérica: La crisis del viejo orden.* Tegucigalpa: Editorial Guaymuras, 1981.

————. "Crisis capitalista, inflación, y papel económico del estado en Centroamérica." *Revista Centroamericana de Economía* 4 (Jan.–Apr. 1981): 57–94.

Morgan, Q. Martin. *The Beef Cattle Industries of Central America and Panama.* FAS-M208. Washington, D.C.: USDA, July 1973.

Parker, Franklin. *The Central American Republics.* London: Royal Institute of International Affairs, 1964.

Parsons, F. Stewart and Angelo DeTuddo. *Informe sobre los aspectos agrícolas, técnicos, y económicos de la producción de algodón en Centroamérica.* Rome: FAO, 1959.

Parsons, James. "Cotton and Cattle in the Pacific Lowlands of Central America." *Journal of Inter-American Affairs* 7, no. 1 (Jan. 1965): 149–59.

————. "Forest to Pasture: Development or Destruction?" *Revista de Biología Tropical* 24, supp. 1 (June 1976): 121–38.

Peace Alternatives for the Caribbean and Central America. *Changing Course: Blueprint for Peace in Central America and the Caribbean.* Washington, D.C.: Institute for Policy Studies, 1984.

Richard, Pablo, and Guillermo Melendez, eds. *La iglesia de los pobres en América Central.* San José: Departamento Ecuménico de Investigaciones, 1982.

Rourk, J. Phillip. *The Beef Cattle Industries of Central America and Panama.* FAS-M208. Washington, D.C.: USDA, June 1969.

Roux, Bernard. "Expansión del capitalismo y desarrollo de subdesarrollo: La integración de América Central en el mercado mundial de la carne vacuno." *Estudios Sociales Centroamericanos* 19 (Jan.–Apr. 1978): 9–33.

SIECA. *El desarrollo integrado de Centroamérica en la presente década.* Buenos Aires: INTAL/BID, 1973.

————. *Estadísticas macroeconómicas de Centroamérica, 1970–79.* Guatemala City: SIECA, 1980.

————. *VII compéndio estadístico Centroamericano.* Guatemala City: SIECA, 1981.

————. *Situación actual y perspectivas del algodón y la semilla de algodón.* Guatemala City: SIECA, 1980.

———. *Situación actual y perspectivas de la carne bovina en Centroamérica*. Guatemala City: SIECA, 1980.

Stanford Central America Action Network, ed. *Revolution in Central America*. Boulder, Colo.: Westview Press, 1983.

Stevenson, Joseph. *Cotton Production in Central America*. Washington, D.C.: USDA, 1964.

Torres Rivas, Edelberto. *Crisis del poder en Centroamérica*. San José: EDUCA, 1981.

Van Meir, Lawrence. *Informe final sobre el mercado ganadero y de productos ganaderos en Centroamérica*. Rome: FAO, 1959.

Williams, Robert. "The Central American Common Market: Unequal Benefits and Uneven Development." Ph.D. dissertation, Stanford University, 1978.

Wilson, George, et al. *The Impact of Highway Investment on Development*. Washington, D.C.: Brookings Institution, 1966.

Woodward, Ralph. *Central America: A Nation Divided*. New York: Oxford University Press, 1976.

Wynia, Gary. *Politics and Planners: Economic Development Policy in Central America*. Madison: University of Wisconsin Press, 1972.

Guatemala

Adams, Richard. *Crucifixion by Power: Essays on Guatemalan National Social Structure, 1944–46*. Austin: University of Texas Press, 1970.

Aguilera Peralta, Gabriel, Jorge Romero Imery, et al. *Dialéctica del terror en Guatemala*. San José: EDUCA, 1981.

Bataillón, Claude, and Ivan Lebot. "Migración interna y empleo agrícola temporal en Guatemala." *Estudios Sociales Centroamericanos* 13 (Jan.–Apr. 1976): 35–67.

Black, George. "Garrison Guatemala." *NACLA Report on the Americas* 16, no. 1 (Jan.–Feb. 1983): 2–35.

Davis, Shelton, and Julie Hodson. *Witnesses to Political Violence in Guatemala: The Suppression of a Rural Development Movement*. Boston: Oxfam America, 1982.

DGECG. *Censo agropecuario, 1964*. Guatemala City: DGECG, 1966.

DGEG. *Censo agropecuario, 1950*. Guatemala City: DGEG, 1954.

Gettleman, Marvin, Jonathan Fried, et al. *Guatemala in Rebellion*. New York: Grove Press, 1983.

Hildebrand, John. "Guatemalan Colonization Projects: Institution Building and Resource Allocation." *Inter-American Economic Affairs* 19, no. 4 (Spring 1966): 41–51.

IBRD. *The Economic Development of Guatemala*. Washington, D.C.: IBRD, 1951.

ICAITI. *Comercialización de ganado bovino y de carne en Guatemala*. Guatemala City: ICAITI, 1974.

Immerman, Richard H. *The CIA in Guatemala: The Foreign Policy of Intervention*.

Austin: University of Texas Press, 1982.

Jonas, Susanne, and David Tobis, eds. *Guatemala*. New York: NACLA, 1974.

Maloney, Thomas. "El impacto del esquema de desarrollo de la franja transversal del norte sobre los Maya-Kekchí en Guatemala." *Estudios Sociales Centroamericanos* 29 (May–Aug. 1981): 91–106.

National Lawyers Guild and La Raza Legal Alliance. *Guatemala: Repression and Resistance*. San Francisco: National Lawyers Guild, 1980.

Orellana, René, Virginia Pineda de Grácias, and Andrés Opazo Bernales. "Migraciones internas y estructura agraria: El caso de Guatemala." *Estudios Sociales Centroamericanos* 12 (Sept.–Dec. 1975): 41–91.

Peckenham, Nancy. *Guatemala, 1983*. Philadelphia: American Friends Service Committee, 1983.

Schmid, Lester. *The Productivity of Agricultural Labor in the Export Crops of Guatemala*. RP#48. Madison: Land Tenure Center, 1968.

———. *The Role of Migratory Labor in the Economic Development of Guatemala*. RP#22. Madison: Land Tenure Center, 1967.

Smith, Carol. "Does a Commodity Economy Enrich the Few While Ruining the Masses? Differentiation among Petty Commodity Producers in Guatemala." *Journal of Peasant Studies* 11, no. 3 (Apr. 1984): 60–95.

———. "Local History in a Global Context: Social and Economic Transitions in Western Guatemala." *Comparative Studies in Society and History* 26, no. 2 (Apr. 1984): 193–228.

Wood, Harold. "The Crop/Livestock Relationship in Guatemala, Central America." *Revista Geográfica* 66 (June 1967): 95–103.

El Salvador

American Civil Liberties Union and Americas Watch. *Report on Human Rights in El Salvador*. New York: Random House, 1982.

Anderson, Thomas. *Matanza: El Salvador's Communist Revolt of 1932*. Lincoln: University of Nebraska Press, 1971.

Armstrong, Robert, and Janet Shenk. *El Salvador: The Face of Revolution*. Boston: South End Press, 1982.

Baloyra, Enrique. *El Salvador in Transition*. Chapel Hill: University of North Carolina Press, 1982.

Bourgois, Philippe. "Rural El Salvador: An Eyewitness Account." *Monthly Review* 34, no. 1 (May 1982): 14–30.

Browning, David. *El Salvador: Landscape and Society*. Oxford: Oxford University Press, Clarendon Press, 1971.

Burke, Melvin. "El sistema de plantación y la proletarización del trabajo agrícola en El Salvador." *Estudios Centro Americanos* 31 (Sept.–Oct. 1976): 473–86.

Colindres, Eduardo. *Fundamentos económicos de la burguesía Salvadoreña*. San Salvador: UCA, 1977.

_____. "La tenencia de la tierra en El Salvador," *Estudios Centro Americanos* 31 (Sept.–Oct. 1976): 463–72.

DGECS. *Primer censo agropecuario, 1950*. San Salvador: DGECS, 1954.

_____. *Segundo censo agropecuario, 1961*. San Salvador: DGECS, 1967.

_____. *Tercer censo agropecuario, 1971*. San Salvador: DGECS, 1974.

Durham, William. *Scarcity and Survival in Central America: The Ecological Origins of the Soccer War*. Stanford, Calif.: Stanford University Press, 1979.

Gettleman, Marvin, Patrick Lacefield, et al. *El Salvador: Central America in the New Cold War*. New York: Grove Press, 1981.

Ménjivar, Rafael. *Formación y lucha del proletariado industrial salvadoreño*. San Salvador: UCA, 1979.

Ruíz Granadino, Santiago. "Modernización agrícola en El Salvador." *Estudios Sociales Centroamericanos* 22 (Jan.–Apr. 1979): 71–95.

Satterthwaite, Ridgway. "Campesino Agriculture and Hacienda Modernization in Coastal El Salvador, 1949–1969." Ph.D. dissertation, University of Wisconsin, 1971.

Simon, Laurence, and James Stephens. *El Salvador Land Reform, 1980–81*. Boston: Oxfam America, 1981.

Wheaton, Philip. *Agrarian Reform in El Salvador: A Program of Rural Pacification*. Washington, D.C.: Ecumenical Program for Interamerican Communication and Action Task Force, 1980.

White, Alistair. *El Salvador*. New York: Praeger Publishers, 1973.

Honduras

Boyer, Jefferson. "Peasant and Proletarian Praxis in Southern Honduras." Mimeo of paper prepared for 80th meeting of the American Anthropology Association, Los Angeles, Dec. 1981.

_____. "Simple Commodity Production, Agrarian Capitalism, and Economic Rationality in Southern Honduras." Ph.D. dissertation, University of North Carolina—Chapel Hill, 1982.

Carías, Marco Virgilio, Daniel Slutzky, et al. *La guerra inútil: Análisis socioeconómico del conflicto entre Honduras y El Salvador*. San José: EDUCA, 1971.

Del Cid, Rafael. "Las clases sociales y su dinámica en el agro hondureño." *Estudios Sociales Centroamericanos* 18 (Sept.–Dec. 1977): 119–55.

_____. *Formas de organización productiva en el agro hondureño: La economía campesina y las empresas capitalistas*. San José: CSUCA, 1982.

DGECH. *Primer censo agropecuario, 1952*. Tegucigalpa: DGECH, 1954.

————. *Segundo censo agropecuario, 1965–66.* Tegucigalpa: DGECH, 1968.

————. *Tercer censo agropecuario, 1974.* Tegucigalpa: DGECH, 1978.

Honduran Institute of Rural Development (IHDER). *La tenencia de la tierra en Honduras.* Tegucigalpa: Talleres "El Arte," 1981.

Kincaid, Douglas. *Movilización campesina y cambio social: Enfoques alternativos y el caso de Honduras.* San José: V Congreso Centroamericano de Sociología, Nov. 1982.

Meza, Victor. *Antología del movimiento obrereo hondureño.* Tegucigalpa: Editorial Universitaria, 1981.

————. *Política y sociedad en Honduras.* Tegucigalpa: Editorial Guaymuras, 1981.

Molina Chocano, Guillermo. *Estado liberal y desarrollo capitalista en Honduras.* Tegucigalpa: Editorial Universitaria, 1982.

————. "Población, estructura productiva, y migraciones internas en Honduras (1950–1960)." *Estudios Sociales Centroamericanos* 12 (Sept.–Dec. 1975): 9–39.

Parsons, Kenneth. *Agrarian Reform in Southern Honduras.* RP#67. Madison: Land Tenure Center, 1976.

Posas, Mario. *Conflictos agrarios y organización campesina.* Tegucigalpa: Universidad Nacional Autónoma de Honduras, 1981.

————. *El movimiento campesino hondureño.* Tegucigalpa: Editorial Guaymuras, 1981.

————. "Política estatál y estructura agraria en Honduras (1950–1978)." *Estudios Sociales Centroamericanos* 24 (Sept.–Dec. 1979): 37–116.

Salomón, Leticia. *Militarismo y reformismo en Honduras.* Tegucigalpa: Editorial Guaymuras, 1982.

Slutzky, Daniel. "La agroindustria de la carne en Honduras." *Estudios Sociales Centroamericanos* 22 (Jan.–Apr. 1979): 101–205.

White, Robert. "The Adult Education Program of Acción Cultural Popular Hondureña: An Evaluation of the Rural Development Potential of the Radio School Movement in Honduras." Mimeo. St. Louis University Department of Anthropology, St. Louis, Mo., 1972.

Nicaragua

Banco Central de Nicaragua. *Situación y perspectivas mundial y nacional de la carne de res.* Managua: División Agropecuario del Banco Central de Nicaragua, 1974.

Belli, Pedro. "An Inquiry concerning the Growth of Cotton Farming in Nicaragua." Ph.D. dissertation, University of California—Berkeley, 1968.

Biderman, Jaime. "Class Structure, the State and Capitalist Development in Nicaraguan Agriculture." Ph.D. dissertation, University of California—Berkeley, 1982.

Black, George. *Triumph of the People: The Sandinista Revolution in Nicaragua.* London: Zed Press, 1981.

Blandón, Alfonso. "Land Tenure in Nicaragua." Master's thesis, University of Florida, 1962.

CIERA. *Tres años de reforma agraria.* Managua: CIERA, 1982.

Collins, Joseph, with Frances Moore Lappé, Nick Allen, and Paul Rice. *What Difference Could a Revolution Make? Food and Farming in the New Nicaragua.* San Francisco: Food-First, 1985.

CONAL. *Estadísticas del algodón en Nicaragua, 1950–1972.* Managua: CONAL, 1973.

de Lanuza, Maria. "La agroindustria de la carne: Caso de Nicaragua." Mimeo. Managua: CIERA, 1980.

DGECN. *Censos nacionales, 1963: Agropecuario.* Managua: DGECN, 1966.

Finley, Robert. "Analysis of Livestock Farms in Nicaragua: A Detailed Study of Costs and Returns." Mimeo. Columbia, University of Missouri, 1974.

Latinoconsult. *Mercadeo de ganado y carne bovina en Nicaragua.* Managua: Banco Central de Nicaragua, 1975.

MIDINRA. *Diagnóstico socio-económico del sector agropecuario.* Managua: CIERA, 1980.

Millett, Richard. *Guardians of the Dynasty: A History of the US-Created Guardia Nacional de Nicaragua and the Somoza Family.* Maryknoll, N.Y.: Orbis Books, 1977.

Ministerio de Economía, Industria, y Comercio. *Estadísticas del desarrollo agropecuario de Nicaragua, 1965–68.* Managua: Ministerio de Economía, Industria, y Comercio, 1969.

Real Espinales, Blas. "Dinámica de población y estructura agraria en Nicaragua." *Estudios Sociales Centroamericanos* 9 (Sept.–Dec. 1974): 165–206.

Rosset, Peter, and David Vandermeer, eds. *The Nicaraguan Reader: Documents of a Revolution under Fire.* New York: Grove Press, 1983.

Taylor, James. *Agricultural Settlement and Development in Eastern Nicaragua.* RP#33. Madison: Land Tenure Center, 1969.

Walker, Thomas, ed. *Nicaragua in Revolution.* New York: Praeger Publishers, 1982.

Warnken, Philip, et al. *An Analysis of Agricultural Production in Nicaragua.* Washington, D.C.: AID, 1974.

Wheelock Román, Jaime. *Imperialismo y dictadura: Crisis de una formación social.* Mexico City: Siglo XXI, 1975.

Costa Rica

Barahona Riera, Francisco. *Reforma agraria y poder político.* San José: Editorial Universidad de Costa Rica, 1980.

Buarque de Hollanda, Teodoro, and Carlos Raabe Cercone. "Costa Rica: migración rural-rural y estructura agraria en el periodo 1950–1963." *Estudios Sociales Centroamericanos* 11 (May–Aug. 1975): 9–55.

DeWitt, Peter. *The Inter-American Development Bank and Political Influence with Special Reference to Costa Rica.* New York: Praeger Publishers, 1977.

DGECCR. *Censo agropecuario, 1950.* San José: Instituto Geográfico, 1953.

————. *Censo agropecuario, 1963.* San José: DGECCR, 1965.

————. *Censo agropecuario, 1973.* San José: DGECCR, 1974.

Edelman, Marc. *Apuntes sobre la consolidación de las haciendas en Guanacaste.* Avance de Investigación No. 44. San José: Instituto de Investigaciones Sociales, 1981.

Edelman, Marc, and Jayne Hutchcroft. "Costa Rica: Modernizing the Non-Army." *NACLA Report on the Americas* 17, no. 2 (Mar.–Apr. 1984): 9–11.

————. "Costa Rica: Resisting Austerity." *NACLA Report on the Americas* 17, no. 1 (Jan.–Feb. 1984): 9–11.

Gudmundson, Lowell. "Las luchas agrarias del Guanacaste (1900–1920)." *Estudios Sociales Centroamericanos* 32 (May–Aug. 1982): 75–96.

León, Jorge, Carlos Barboza, and Justo Aguilar. *Desarrollo tecnológico en la ganadería de carne.* San José: CONOCIT, 1981.

Lungo Uncles, Mario. "Las Políticas del estado y la inversión de capital en Guanacaste." Ph.D. dissertation, University of Costa Rica, 1975.

Rivera Urrutía, Eugenio. *El fondo monetario internacional y Costa Rica, 1978–1982.* San José: Departamento Ecumenico de Investigaciones, 1982.

Sáenz Moroto, Alberto. *Erosión, deforestación, y control de inundaciones en Costa Rica.* San José: Editorial de la Universidad de Costa Rica, 1981.

Seligson, Mitchell. *Peasants of Costa Rica and the Development of Agrarian Capitalism.* Madison: University of Wisconsin Press, 1980.

SEPSA. *Características de la ganadería de carne y lineamientos de política.* San José: SEPSA, 1980.

————. *Información básica del sector agropecuario y de recursos naturales renovables de Costa Rica.* San José: Ministerio de Agricultura y Ganadería, 1982.

Solís, Manuel. "La ganadería de carne en Costa Rica." Master's thesis, University of Costa Rica, 1981.

Spielman, Hans. "La expansión ganadera en Costa Rica." *Revista Geográfica* 77 (Dec. 1972): 57–84.

Thrupp, Lori Ann. "Deforestation, Agricultural Development, and Cattle Expansion in Costa Rica." Undergraduate honors thesis, Stanford University, 1980.

Tosi, Joseph, and R. Voertmann. "Some Environmental Factors in the Economic Development of the Tropics." *Economic Geography* 40, no. 3 (July 1964): 189–205.

Vega Carballo, José Luís. *Orden y progreso: La formación del estado nacional en Costa Rica.* San José: Instituto Centroamericano de Administración Pública, 1981.

Other Works

Burbach, Roger, and Patricia Flynn. *Agribusiness in the Americas*. New York: Monthly Review/NACLA, 1980.

Conklin, Harold. "The Study of Shifting Cultivation." *Current Anthropology* 2, no. 1 (Feb. 1961): 27–61.

Dell, Sidney. *The Inter-American Development Bank*. New York: Praeger Publishers, 1972.

Economic Research Service. *Statistics on Cotton and Related Data, 1920–1973*. Statistical Bulletin no. 535. Washington, D.C.: USDA, Oct. 1974.

IADB. *Inter-American Development Bank: Fifteen Years of Activities, 1960–1974*. Washington, D.C.: IADB, 1975.

IBRD. *The World Bank Group in the Americas*. Washington, D.C.: IBRD, 1974.

———. *World Bank Operations*. Baltimore: Johns Hopkins University Press, 1972.

Lernoux, Penny. *Cry of the People: United States Involvement in the Rise of Fascism, Torture, and Murder, and the Persecution of the Catholic Church in Latin America*. Garden City, N.Y.: Doubleday Publishing Co., 1980.

Shane, Douglas. *Hoofprints on the Forest: An Inquiry into the Beef Cattle Industry in the Tropical Forest Areas of Latin America*. Washington, D.C.: Department of State, Mar. 1980.

Simpson, James, and Donald Farris. *The World's Beef Business*. Ames: Iowa State University Press, 1982.

USDA. *Foreign Meat Inspection Act, 1976*. Washington, D.C.: USDA, 1977.

Magazines and Periodicals

Estudios Centro Americanos (San Salvador)

Estudios Sociales Centroamericanos (San José)

Guatemala! (Berkeley, Calif.)

Honduras Update (Cambridge, Mass.)

Latin America (London)

Latin America Commodities Report (London)

Latin America Economic Report (London)

Latin America Political Report (London)

Latin America Regional Report: Mexico and Central America (London)

Latin America Weekly Report (London)

La Libertad (San José)

La Nación (San José)

NACLA Report on the Americas (New York)

News from Guatemala (Toronto)

New York Times

El Nuevo Diario (Managua)
La Prensa (Managua)
UnoMásUno (Mexico City)
Wall Street Journal
Washington Post

Index